NUMEROLOGY
The Complete Guide

VOLUME TWO

NUMEROLOGY
The Complete Guide

VOLUME TWO

ADVANCED
PERSONALITY
ANALYSIS
AND
READING THE PAST,
PRESENT AND FUTURE

Matthew Oliver Goodwin

NEWCASTLE PUBLISHING COMPANY, INC. • NORTH HOLLYWOOD, CALIFORNIA • 1981

A NEWCASTLE BOOK
First printing October 1981
8 9 10
Printed in the United States of America

Design: Riley K. Smith
Typography: Freedmen's Organization
Printed by Delta Lithograph • Van Nuys, CA

TO ARLENE

ACKNOWLEDGMENTS

I would like to acknowledge the many people who helped.

Thanks—
>
> to the special friend (who prefers to remain anonymous) who first introduced me to numerology,
>
> to Naomi Weisman, who shared her insights,
>
> to Dana Holliday, who contributed her unique awarenesses,
>
> to Kelley Jeane Younger, for helping to make this project a reality and for consulting on the book,
>
> to Anne Brenden Monkarsh, for her gracious special help,
>
> to Pam Cisneros, who typed so much of the mountain of manuscript,
>
> to Judy Yerman, whose contribution when needed was so important,
>
> to Mary Leipziger, who contributed the back-cover photograph (and the pastries to help my occasionally lagging spirit).

Thanks to those whose encouragement for my special project was so meaningful:
>
> Ida Goodwin, Jean Brill, Miriam Miller, Harvey Yerman, Elliot Brill, Susan Brill, Bill Brill, Helen Brill, Antonino Bruno, Lenore Goldman, Bernie Weisman, Audrey Simmons, Neil Perlmutter, Boris Marks, Julian Hanberg, Gerta Farber.

And, of course, thanks to Josh Goodwin for his support, to Lisa Goodwin for her encouragement from around the world, to Adam Chess for his concern—and especially to Arlene Goodwin who was always there to listen, discuss and lend loving sustenance.

Los Angeles, 1981

CONTENTS

PART IV:
CHARACTER DELINEATION—
ADVANCED TECHNIQUES

INTRODUCTION
TO ADVANCED DELINEATION

In Parts II and III in Volume 1, we defined, weighted and analyzed the elements and modifiers in order to clarify the essential nature of the pieces making up a delineation.

Here in Part IV, our point of view shifts. We are going to enlarge the context so that our readings become more subtle and complex interweavings of energies than can possibly be devised by following any steps by rote. We want to move from the memorization of information and procedure, so important as a beginning step, to a broader understanding of the energies which vitalize or inhibit the individual.

In succeeding chapters, we will

> expand our awareness of the symbolism of numbers;
>
> expand our ability to interpret individual characteristics;
>
> investigate the energies derived from names other than the birth name;
>
> develop a framework for an advanced reading;
>
> and finally, proceed, step by step, through a complete delineation.

CHAPTER 22

ADVANCED SYMBOLISM
OF NUMBERS

Back in Chapter 2, we presented keywords for each of the numbers and indicated that the keywords actually represented only the positive potential of a particular number. Each number, we said, could be thought of as a continuum of energies with the keywords as a desirable focus. In the chapters that followed, we explored many of the positive and negative energies along the continuums. This is a good time to consolidate and expand our understanding of these continuums.

The eleven numbers—1 through 9, 11 and 22—describe all the types of potential energy available. Within the eleven continuums, then, are all the possible awarenesses, experiences and characteristics.

In Chapter 2, for the sake of simplicity, we described a continuum with positive potential at one end and negative potential at the other. Visualize the continuum instead having positive energy at the center and negative energy at the two ends. Here's a diagram of a typical continuum:

A typical continuum

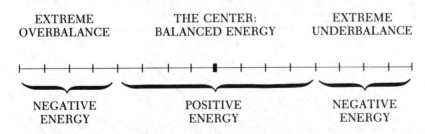

EXTREME OVERBALANCE	THE CENTER: BALANCED ENERGY	EXTREME UNDERBALANCE
NEGATIVE ENERGY	POSITIVE ENERGY	NEGATIVE ENERGY

The center of each continuum represents the balanced energy of the number, the positive potential.

At the left extreme of the continuum is the negative potential described by an overbalance of the energy, an overbalance caused by (1) the presence of too much of a given energy (for example, with repeated core elements), or (2) an individual's exclusive use of an energy without the offsetting use of other available energies (a free-wheeling individual with a 5 Life Path, for instance, who chooses not to use the balance provided by a 4 Soul Urge).

At the right extreme is the negative potential described by an underbalance of the energy, an underbalance due to (1) the lack of an energy or the relatively limited amount of an energy (a core with a 22 Life Path, 8 Expression, 1 Soul Urge and 2 Birthday; so little 2 energy in contrast with the powerful 22, 8 and 1 energies may produce a 2 negative potential of ill-manneredness or lack of tact), or (2) an individual's avoidance of the use of the energy (a subject choosing to concentrate on his 6 Expression and bypass his 1 Soul Urge, for instance, may emphasize the 1 negative extreme of resignation or submissiveness).

A look at the 1 continuum

A diagram of the continuum with 1 energy might look like this:

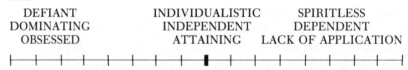

DEFIANT	INDIVIDUALISTIC	SPIRITLESS
DOMINATING	INDEPENDENT	DEPENDENT
OBSESSED	ATTAINING	LACK OF APPLICATION

Or we might think of the 1 energy as these three continuums added together:

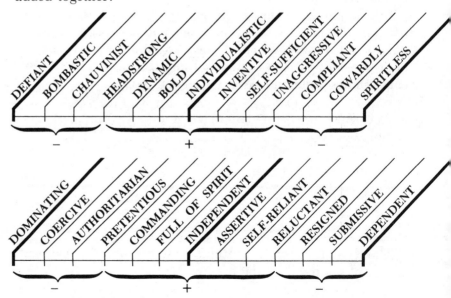

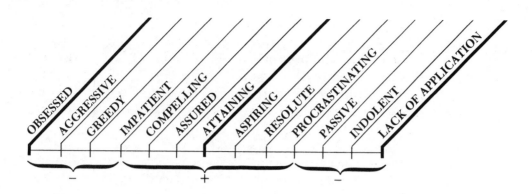

The three keywords describing the 1 energy have been expanded to almost forty characteristics. We could, of course, draw similar diagrams for all the numbers.

Chart 13: The Numbers— Advanced Symbolism

If you turn to CHART 13: THE NUMBERS—ADVANCED SYMBOLISM on page 682, you'll find a list of words and phrases for each number describing the balanced, overbalanced and under-balanced potentials. The three keywords for the 1 energy, for example, have been enlarged to a list of over *120* potentials.

The lists, incomplete at best, are purposely arranged alphabetically rather than by continuum. The emphasis on Chart 13 is not on the continuums which are, of course, arbitrary constructs, but rather on the broad sweep of the energies with which we're dealing. Keep the continuums in mind, though, as you explore the infinity of subtle nuances in people's behavior.

Start thinking in terms of the subtleties of the continuums rather than just the keywords. Observe the next person, for example, with strong 5 energy. Is she unconventional, contrary, dissident, deviant, mannerist or bizarre? Is she spontaneous, emancipated, unchecked or licentious? Is she curious, snoopy, meddling or officious? (And what about the subtleties when there's two or three divergent energies present?)

As you proceed with your own advanced delineations, you'll increase your ability to distinguish and describe the multitudinous shades of differences. Awareness of these nuances will add considerable depth to your readings.

CHAPTER 23

ADVANCED ANALYSIS OF CHARACTERISTICS

A character delineation is a portrayal of the total of an individual's energies. The energies are usually depicted as groups of traits so that the delineation is, in fact, a description of a series of characteristics which define the subject. The success of our advanced delineations will depend on our conversance with the traits and their modifications.

We should be able to answer these questions about each characteristic:

> How is each characteristic derived?
> What is the probability of the presence of each characteristic in the subject?
> How is a characteristic modified by the other energies present?

In this chapter, we'll discuss each of these questions. Just as the last chapter was intended to expand your awareness of the numbers from the simple keywords to the broad continuums, this chapter proposes to broaden your understanding and use of the traits in a reading.

HOW IS EACH CHARACTERISTIC DERIVED?

The characteristics can only be derived from

> the continuums of the core elements
> the continuums of the modifiers

How each characteristic is derived

In practice, the characteristics discussed in a delineation are based on a study of the charts along with your experience—as well as an expansion of this information based on your knowledge of the involved continuums.

Within the eleven continuums, there are a few characteristics that appear only once. The "differentness" of the 7 and the "background contribution" of the 2, for instance, are qualities that seem unrelated to other numbers. Most of the traits, though, have matching characteristics in several of the continuums.

Let's examine a broad trait—I could just call it "affection," but I'd prefer to expand it to "giving friendship, showing affection, expressing love." I'd view these as ever-deepening manifestations of a single trait. When I encounter a balanced 6 potential, for example, I would expect that the subject would be fully expressing the different shadings of this characteristic. I'd expect most of the friendship, affection and love to be devoted to family and close friends. The balanced 6 is likely to be a loving, passionate spouse, a devoted parent and a warm, affectionate friend.

The balanced 2 has a similar quality, but with some difference in its expression. Like the 6 potential, the 2 energy is devoted to people close to the subject. But there's a qualitative difference—although the affection and love of the 2 are given as tenderly as the 6, they're given less emotionally, less passionately. There's a shyness, a timidity, a holding back that's part of the basic nature of the 2—it reduces the forward thrust of *all* the 2 energy. So the love and affection of the 2 is less intense, less dramatic, less overtly displayed than the 6. The 6, in its purest form, represents the height of romantic love; the pure 2 is the essence of filial love.

The balanced 9 feels just as strongly as the 6—sometimes far more intensely—but the 9 expresses more impersonally. The 9 love of mankind may know no bounds, the 9 concern for the brotherhood of man may be the focus of a lifelong dedication. But, though the 6 and 9 loves are passionate, the 6 love is aimed directly at a few intimates, the 9 radiates its aura to the world. The 6 is the passion of the young lover, the 9 the passion of the zealous teacher. Both are beautiful but very different.

The pure 3 expresses the sharing of friendship. Here, the emphasis is on camaraderie, enjoying good times together—a relation of far less intensity than even the quiet love of the 2. The balanced 5 expresses friendship in a manner similar to the 3 but with the heightened excitement of youthful enthusiasm. And the balanced 11 expresses an abstract love, impersonal like the 9, but less passionate, too, far more concerned with dreams and fantasies than the everyday realities.

Six of the eleven continuums describe this trait of "giving friendship, showing affection, expressing love." In each, the trait can be seen as part of the general class. And, in each, the expression of the characteristic is markedly different. In the delineations in Parts II and III, Volume 1, we carefully separated the energies and their traits by modifier number. In our advanced delineations, we're opening the way to far more subtlety by our understanding of the related characteristics. Think about self-centeredness, business ability, emotional expression, freedom, rigidity, to name but a few traits repeated in several continuums, and become familiar with their different manifestations.

When a subject has several strong continuums (that is, elements and strong modifiers) with related traits, the description of the characteristics will be more meaningful when the description expresses the several continuums combined. Cultivate an awareness of the related traits. For instance, learn to express "giving friendship, showing affection, expressing love" as expressed by combined 6·9 energy; be able to contrast that potential with the 2·6 or 2·9 potential; or visualize the energy expressed by the heaviness of the 9·11 or the lightness of 3·5 potential.

WHAT IS THE PROBABILITY OF THE PRESENCE OF EACH CHARACTERISTIC IN THE SUBJECT?

The probability of each characteristic

With experience, you'll distinguish the specific traits which are almost always expressed when certain continuums are present. With a 5 continuum, for instance, we would usually find an enthusiastic subject; 6 almost always produces a giving individual; 7 describes a person whom we'd expect to be at least a little different.

Often, though, the presence of a specific characteristic is not that clear. If Barry has strong 2 energy, is he sensitive or oversensitive, is he friendly or shy (or possibly both), is he cooperative or apathetic? In a numerology reading, we determine the probability of a characteristic simply by how many elements and strong modifiers express that particular quality. (A strong modifier would be a Karmic Debt, a Karmic Lesson, an Intensity Point, a strongly divergent Prime Intensifier, repeated sub-elements, or a Challenge.)

If Emily had only one element or strong modifier attesting to her stubbornness, the best we could say is that Emily is "apt to" be stubborn. If Emily had a strong 4, I'd expect, from my experience, that I'd be right about her stubbornness about seventy-five percent of the time. In any event, although the odds would be in my favor, there would still be many subjects with one element or strong modifier who would *not* display this particular characteristic.

Now, if Emily had two elements or strong modifiers describing her stubbornness, I would consider it "most likely" that she's stubborn. If Emily had 4 energy and 7 energy, I'd expect I'd be correct at least ninety percent of the time. If, instead, Emily had 4 energy and 1 energy, I'd probably be right only about eighty percent of the time. Although the specific energy source is of importance, it's the *repetition* of the characteristic which substantially increases the *probability* of its presence.

If Emily had three elements or strong modifiers dealing with stubbornness, there would be hardly a question of the existence of that characteristic. When there are three or more sources, it doesn't matter, in the case of stubbornness, if it's 1, 4 or 7 energy—the multiple source usually confirms the presence of the trait. Even if there are five or six sources, though, you'll still never find one hundred percent verification. You're bound to run into an occasional subject who *won't* manifest a particular quality, no matter the odds. (I've learned to be content with the *general* success of my delineations. With experience and practice, about eighty to ninety percent of the subject matter of readings should ring true—perfection, I'm sorry to say, is unattainable.)

Don't make the mistake of assuming that the multiple repetition of a trait necessarily intensifies that trait—that just isn't so! If Arthur has a 1 Expression, a 7 Birthday and two 4's Intensity Point, I would say Arthur undoubtedly has a stubborn streak. The "undoubtedly" derives from the three sources, but there is no indication of the intensity of the stubbornness. If Agatha has a 1 Expression and seven 1's Intensity Point, I would expect that she's most likely an extremely stubborn person. I would use "most likely" because there are only two sources; I use "extremely stubborn" because of the strong divergence of the Intensity Point.

How a characteristic is modified

HOW IS A CHARACTERISTIC MODIFIED BY THE OTHER ENERGIES PRESENT?

In the delineations in Parts II and III, Volume 1, we used CHART 6: THE ASPECTS to distinguish whether energies usually combined harmoniously or discordantly. In our advanced work, we're looking at *individual* traits rather than the entire group of traits making up an energy. We have to determine whether the other energies present—the elements and modifiers—affect each specific trait in a harmonious or discordant manner. Let's look at some examples:

Here's Arthur with a 4 Life Path
                8 Expression
                1 Soul Urge
           22/4 Birthday

With a 4 Life Path, Arthur would tend to be realistic and practical. We know that the 8 Expression energy is also realistic and practical, often with an eye for commercial values. The 1 Soul Urge, too, is generally practical, although the self-centered direction of the 1 may tend to distort Arthur's realistic approach. The 22 Birthday is eminently practical, with a sense of worldwide vision. The 4 lower level of the Birthday, along with the 4 Life Path, may tend to be so realistic and practical as to disbalance the view by omitting the possibility of any fanciful factors.

The 4 and 8 energies make up seventy percent of Arthur's core energy. The 1 and 22/4 energies would, therefore, have relatively minor impact.

If we think of "realistic and practical" as a characteristic derived from Arthur's 4 Life Path, that characteristic, modified by the other core energies, might read like this:

> Arthur tends to benefit by his ability to be quite realistic and practical, often with an eye to commercial values. Occasionally, his practicality doesn't allow for the input of any fanciful views of value or, at times, his own needs may distort his practical approach.

Jacqueline has a 4 Life Path, too, along with
           11/2 Expression
                7 Soul Urge
                5 Birthday

For Arthur, the other core elements had energy similar to the practicality of his 4 Life Path. For Jacqueline, the other elements have little, if anything, to do with realism or practicality. The 11 Expression, as a matter of fact, is dreamy and idealistic, often surprisingly impractical, with difficulty separating fantasy and reality. The 2 level of the Expression is usually more aware of reality than the 11, but with little special concern with practicality. The 7 Soul Urge tends to live in dreams and fantasies, with little realistic grounding. The 5 Birthday, with its carefree imagination, doesn't particularly stress reality, either.

The 4 energy accounts for the forty percent of the core energy concerned with practicality. Fifty percent of the energy, the 11 Expression and the 7 Soul Urge, tend to the impractical while ten percent of the energy, the 5 Birthday, is relatively neutral.

Jacqueline's practicality, then, is considerably different than Arthur's:

> Although there's a part of Jacqueline that is realistic and practical, there's another whole side that tends to dreams and fantasy. Jacqueline may be the sort of person who is sometimes practical, sometimes impractical (*using parts of her energy alternately*) or, she may tend to combine her practical view with her dreamy approach so that her manner tends to be relatively unrealistic (*using these two energies simultaneously*). Jacqueline, by the use of her free-will, will determine which approach is more comfortable for her.

From my experience, I would feel fairly certain that Jacqueline would be using these discordant energies simultaneously. I know, too, the unreality that often accompanies both the 11 and the 7 energies. I would expect Jacqueline to be a relatively dreamy unrealistic person with occasional flashes of practicality.

In this portion of the chapter, I'm demonstrating the approach to the modification of the traits. In this aside, I'm showing how particular experience—mine, in this case—is added to the general approach and further alters the description of the characteristic.

Ina, too, has a 4 Life Path. In her case, it's accompanied by
2 Expression
1 Soul Urge
9 Birthday

Here's the same 4 characteristic of being realistic and practical. Similar to Arthur's example is the 1 Soul Urge, adding its own practicality occasionally overridden by the strong personal needs. The 2 Expression is neither harmonious nor discordant with this characteristic. It doesn't stress the practical or impractical—it neither adds to nor subtracts from this trait. The 9 Birthday isn't much involved, either.

With sixty percent of the energy (4 Life Path and 1 Soul Urge) firmly directed to practicality and the other forty percent (2 Expression and 9 Birthday) neutral, the description might read like this:

> Ina tends to benefit by her ability to be quite realistic and practical, only occasionally distorting her approach because of her strong personal needs.

Ina's description is not too different than Arthur's. For Arthur, though, his practicality, being involved with a hundred percent of his core energy, would tend to affect many of his other characteristics, while Ina's practicality, with a much smaller percent of her core energy, would have considerably less effect on her other traits.

When a characteristic appears several times, we usually get a more complete description than if it appears only once. In the examples so far, we've dealt only with the core elements. Though they have both positive and negative potential, the elements rarely indicate extreme positive energy, and only when there are repeated number elements or a Karmic Debt do they describe extreme negative energy. In the following example, with both elements *and* strong modifiers, we see how the description reflects the extremes added by the modifiers.

We'll look at Maggie and her emotions.

When a characteristic appears several times in the elements and modifiers

Maggie has a 6 Life Path
            5 Expression
            7 Soul Urge
        20/2 Birthday
    three 8's Intensity Point
      six 9's Intensity Point

With Maggie's 6 Life Path, we know, from CHART 2: THE LIFE PATH, that she is likely to be emotional. From my own experience, I know that 6 energy almost always represents extremely deep feelings, often clearly expressed.

Maggie's 5 Expression gives little indication of her emotional bent.

Her 7 Soul Urge, from CHART 4: THE SOUL URGE, indicates that her emotions may be very strong, although most of them may be repressed, too. The 7 energy, in my experience, is virtually always related to the deepest of emotions, but the 7 is usually relatively inarticulate, sometimes only partially aware of these feelings. These repressed emotions of the 7, particularly if supported by some other source, may be a significant part of the individual's structure.

Her 20/2 Birthday (CHART 5: THE BIRTHDAY) confirms her sensitive emotional nature.

Maggie's strongly divergent three 8's Intensity Point involves her emotions. CHART 8: THE INTENSITY TABLE indicates that Maggie approaches business affairs without being carried away with feelings and probably suppresses a good deal of feelings in areas other than business as well.

And there's still Maggie's strongly divergent six 9's Intensity Point. From CHART 8: THE INTENSITY TABLE again, I would expect Maggie to be very emotional but with her feelings suppressed or expressed in poorly balanced ways.

Our complete description must be consistent with the individual descriptions above as well as consistent within itself.

> Maggie is undoubtedly emotional (*three elements and two strong modifiers*), most likely, she's extremely emotional (*7 Soul Urge and very divergent six 9's Intensity Point*). She most likely suppresses a good deal of her feelings most of the time or expresses them in poorly balanced ways. (*The 7 Soul Urge and two Intensity Points indicate the suppression. Because the six 9's Intensity Point is so divergent, I'd expect Maggie to be so emotional that she couldn't possibly repress all her feelings—therefore the use of "most of the time."*) She can usually approach business affairs, though, without being carried away by her feelings. (*"Usually" is used instead of "likely to" because, again, the strength of those six 9's would mean such strong emotions that they'll probably push through some of the time.*)

I use phrases like "at times," "sometimes," "on occasion" when there are, as there often are, differing views of the same characteristic. Rarely does someone act consistently all the time. These and similar phrases acknowledge that state of affairs.

In Chapter 26, we will complete a delineation using the principles outlined here. We will list the traits, determine their probabilities, discuss their modifications. The points covered in this chapter are very much the essence of the advanced delineation.

CHAPTER 24

ADVANCED ENERGY MODIFICATION: USING NAMES OTHER THAN THE BIRTHNAME

If a woman is born Jane Mary Doe, that name, along with her birthdate, will, of course, describe her basic potential. If she usually uses the name Jane Doe, or signs her checks Jane M. Doe, or is called Jill Doe by her close friends, each of these names will indicate an energy somewhat different than the basic energy. If she marries and becomes Jane Smith or Jane M. Smith or Jill Smith, each of these married names will also describe a somewhat different potential.

We know that the basic potential is subject to some modification, dependent on a person's free will and environment. In addition, the use of names other than the birthname describe changes in the basic energy available. Any name is simply a symbolic representation of the traits a person presents when using that name.

Yes, you *can* change the energy available to you by changing your name. But some energies different than your basic energies are easier to use than others. And there are limits to just how much of that basic energy can be changed.

About half of the basic potential is derived from the Life Path and Birthday. Since there is no way to change the date of birth from which these elements are derived, approximately fifty percent of the basic energy can't be changed at all. Perhaps half of the remaining fifty percent of the energy can be modified with a strong name change. In other words, only a maximum of a quarter of the basic energy is changeable at all.

Many times, though, the change of twenty-five percent of the basic energy will be strong enough to induce the *beginning* of major changes in the expressed characteristics. When we discuss Becky Balfour later in this chapter, you'll see an example of this change.

The eight-step comparison of the new name with the birthname

The qualitative change in the basic energy and the strength of that change can be determined by comparing a new name to the birthname. The energy added by the new name must always be viewed *relative* to the birthname, not as some separate added potential. Many areas of the chart are involved in the eight-step comparison:

STEP 1

COMPARE THE BIRTH CORE (BIRTHNAME AND BIRTHDATE) TO THE NEW CORE (NEW NAME AND BIRTHDATE).

A. What characteristics are added, emphasized or deemphasized with the new core?
B. Are there repeated elements in the core?
    Are there the same or different repeated elements in both cores?
    Are there repeated elements in the birth core which are deleted in the new core?
    Are there repeated elements in the new core which are not found in the birth core?
C. Are there master numbers in the core?
    Is there the same or different master number(s) in both cores?
    Is there a master number(s) in the birth core which is deleted in the new core?
    Is there a master number(s) in the new core which is not found in the birth core?
D. Is there a substantial difference in the harmony (or discord) of the birth core and the new core?
E. Is there a substantial difference in the effectiveness (or ineffectiveness) of the birth core and the new core?

STEP 2

COMPARE THE KARMIC DEBTS.

Are there Karmic Debts in either name which are not present in the other name?

STEP 3

COMPARE THE INTENSITY TABLES.

A. Are there Karmic Lessons, Modified Karmic Lessons or significantly divergent negative Intensity Points in the birthname which are "made up" in the new name, that is, replaced by average or strongly divergent positive Intensity
Points?

B. Are there any strongly divergent positive Intensity Points in
the new name replacing average Intensity Points in the
birthname?

STEP 4

COMPARE THE SUB-ELEMENTS.

A. Is there a sub-element with the same number as a core element in either name which isn't present in the other name?

B. Are there repeated sub-elements in either name which
aren't present in the other name?

STEP 5

COMPARE THE MATURITY NUMBER TO BOTH NAMES.

If the subject is younger than thirty-five, omit this step.

Is there more or less energy related to the Maturity Number
sub-lesson available with the new name? The Maturity
Number, derived from the birthname and birthdate, doesn't
change when a new name is used.

STEP 6

COMPARE THE TEMPERAMENTS.

Are there strong or average components in either name which
are weak components in the other name?

STEP 7

COMPARE THE FIRST LETTERS AND FIRST VOWELS.

Are there significant differences in the approach between the
birthname and the new name?

STEP 8

COMPARE THE GROWTH NUMBER TO BOTH NAMES.

Is there more or less energy available to help expand the development with the new name? The Growth Number, derived
from the birthname, doesn't change when a new name is used.

How new names change basic energy

The use of different names can change the basic energy in several ways:

1. A portion of the basic energy may be emphasized.
2. A portion of the basic energy may be converted to more usable energy.
3. A portion of the basic energy may be converted to less usable energy.
4. Some new energy may be introduced.
5. A combination of several of the above.

When you first begin comparing new names to birthnames, it may look like you're almost always dealing with the case where new energy is being introduced. Strictly speaking, if the new Expression and Soul Urge have different numbers than the basic core elements or the strong basic modifiers, new energy *is* being added. But the characteristics of that new energy are often a secondary effect. The primary effect is usually the *modification of the basic energy* due to the introduction of the new Expression and Soul Urge.

I think you'll see this primary and secondary effect more clearly after you've studied the examples in this chapter. Just remember that the basic energy is an inherent part of each individual and is, therefore, comparatively easy to assimilate, develop and use; new energy is somewhat foreign and requires a good deal more time and effort to be useful.

We're going to analyze the new names of four fictitious subjects. We'll study the first subject in step-by-step detail. In the other three examples, we'll just summarize the comparisons and the results.

Example 1: Portion of basic energy emphasized

In our detailed example, we'll study *a subject who has a portion of his basic energy emphasized by his new name.* The fictitious individual, Norman Eddy Parker, was born September 21, 1940. For the last few years, he's been using the name Norman Claude Parker. To compare the two names, we'll prepare a complete calculation sheet for the birthname (Figure 24-1 on page 401) and a partial calculation sheet containing only the information required for comparing of the new name (Figure 24-2 on page 402):

Norman Eddy Parker has a complex basic energy. He is likely to be active in the business world (*8 Life Path*) although his idealistic, spiritual, cooperative ways (*11/2 Expression*) may not mesh well with

September   21,   1940

$$9 \quad + 3 + \; 5 \quad = \quad 17 \; = \; \boxed{8}$$

$$9 - 3 = 6$$
$$5 - 3 = 2$$
$$6 - 2 = 4 \text{ CHALLENGE}$$

$$\frac{7}{6 \quad 1} \; + \; \frac{(12)\, 3}{5 \quad 7} \; + \; \frac{6}{1 \quad 5} \quad = \quad \boxed{16/7}$$

NORMAN   EDDY   PARKER

$$\frac{5 \quad 9\,4 \quad 5}{(23)\; 5} \; + \; \frac{4\,4}{8} \; + \; \frac{7 \quad 9\,2 \quad 9}{(27)\; 9} \; = \; 22 \text{ SECRET SELF}$$

$$\frac{5\,6\,9\,4\,1\,5}{(30)\; 3} \; + \; \frac{5\,4\,4\,7}{(20)\; 2} \; + \; \frac{7\,1\,9\,2\,5\,9}{(33)\; 6} \; = \; \boxed{11/2}$$

two 1's
one 2
no 3 ←
three 4's
four 5's
one 6
two 7's
no 8 ←
three 9's

PHYSICAL	MEDDE	5–Strong
MENTAL	NANPA	5–Strong
EMOTIONAL	ORRR	4–Strong
INTUITIVE	YK	2–Average

MATURITY NUMBER = 8 + 11 = 19 = 1

Figure 24–1
Calculation Sheet:
Norman Eddy Parker

his executive or administrative potential (*8 Life Path*). His verbal abilities, his creativity and his sociability (*21/3 Birthday*) will probably be of use in both his business and idealistic ventures, but his introspective nature, his "differentness," his self-centered tendency (*7 Soul Urge, 16/7 Karmic Debt*) and his nervous tension (*11/2 Expression*) are likely to prove handicaps.

$$\frac{7}{6 \quad 1} \; + \; \frac{9}{13 \; 5} \; + \; \frac{6}{1 \quad 5} \; = \; \boxed{22/4}$$

NORMAN CLAUDE PARKER

$$\frac{5\,6\,9\,4\,1\,5 \quad 3\,3\,1\,3\,4\,5 \quad 7\,1\,9\,2\,5\,9}{(30) \; 3 \quad + \quad (19) \; 1 \quad + \quad (33) \; 6} \; = \; 10 \; = \; \boxed{1}$$

three 1's
one 2
three 3's
two 4's
four 5's
one 6
one 7
no 8←
three 9's

PHYSICAL	MDEE	4–Average
MENTAL	NANLAPA	7–Strong
EMOTIONAL	ORRR	4–Average
INTUITIVE	CUK	3–Average

Figure 24–2
Calculation Sheet:
Norman Claude Parker

What kind of changes are reflected when he changes his name to Norman Claude Parker? We will study the changes here, point by point. As in Chapter 21, the delineation (here the delineation of the changes) is shown indented. The eight steps are listed along with explanations of the derivation of the portions of the delineation.

STEP 1

COMPARE THE BIRTH CORE TO THE NEW CORE.

The 22/4 and 1 energies of the new name go better with the 8 Life Path than the 11/2 and 7 energies of the birthname.

> With his new name, Norman Eddy's diffused energy coalesces into Norman Claude's more focused energy devoted to the potential for leadership in the business world.

When using the new name, there's a diminished emphasis on the 11/2 Expression of the birthname. When a portion of the core is emphasized, the other portion is diminished.

With this portion of his basic energy emphasized, I would expect a diminished emphasis on the divergent idealistic and spiritual energy.

The new 1 Expression and 1 Expression/1 sub-element (along with the 8 Life Path) emphasize some negative traits.

He's likely to appear somewhat more self-centered and stubborn.

Norman Eddy Parker has an average effectiveness of 9, while Norman Claude Parker has an average effectiveness of 17. The new name is extremely ineffective. See the calculation of the effectiveness below.

Although the new name produces a more harmonious blend of energies, it also produces a far more ineffective blend. Although Norman will feel more focused, he'll probably be frustrated with his inability to easily accomplish what he would like.

Calculating the effectiveness of the birthname and the new name

We can compare the effectiveness of the birthname and the new name by adding the differences between the Life Path, Expression and Soul Urge of both names and comparing the totals. The subtractions follow the rules outlined in Chapter 7 on page 51.

If two elements have the same number, this is a very ineffective combination. When this occurs, call the effectiveness of that combination equal to 10.

When a master number is present, as in this case, two totals are obtained, one using the master number and the second using the reduced number. The two totals are then averaged.

Norman Eddy Parker:

11 Expression	− 8 Life Path	=	2	8 Life Path	− 2 Expression	= 6
8 Life Path	− 7 Soul Urge	=	1	8 Life Path	− 7 Soul Urge	= 1
11 Expression	− 7 Soul Urge	=	3	7 Soul Urge	− 2 Expression	= 5
			6			12

Average effectiveness $= \dfrac{6 + 12}{2} = \dfrac{18}{2} = 9$

Norman Claude Parker:

8 Life Path – 1 Expression = 7	8 Life Path – 1 Expression = 7
22 Soul Urge – 8 Life Path = 3	8 Life Path – 4 Soul Urge = 4
22 Soul Urge – 1 Expression = 10	4 Soul Urge – 1 Expression = 3
20	14

$$\text{Average effectiveness} = \frac{20 + 14}{2} = \frac{34}{2} = 17$$

The lower the effectiveness number, the more effective the combination. In this case, Norman Eddy Parker is almost twice as effective as Norman Claude Parker.

STEP 2

COMPARE THE KARMIC DEBTS.

The 16/7 Karmic Debt of the birthname does not appear in the new name.

> Norman is likely to appear less "different" and less introspective.

STEP 3

COMPARE THE INTENSITY TABLES.

In comparing the Intensity Tables, we inspect the birthname Intensity Table and find all the Karmic Lessons, Modified Karmic Lessons and significant negative Intensity Points, i.e. Intensity Points likely to present obstacles. We then check the new name Intensity Table to see if any of these problem areas have been "made up." If so, this is a significant change to be described.

For Norman, the 3 Modified Karmic Lesson of the birthname has been "made up" by the three 3's Intensity Point of the new name.

> He'll find it a little easier to express his feelings, and he'll tend to be a bit more comfortable in social situations.

The 8 Modified Karmic Lesson of the birthname is not "made up" by the new name and needs no comment.

Since most individuals usually find it easier to operate with the birthname Intensity Table, we assume that Norman will usually work on that level, and only look to the new Intensity Table to alleviate problem areas. However, if there's a significant positive Intensity Point in the new Table replacing an average birthname Intensity Point, the subject may choose to use that new energy and this should be duly noted.

Norman has no significant positive Intensity Points on his new Intensity Table.

STEP 4

COMPARE THE SUB-ELEMENTS.

The 7 Soul Urge/7 sub-element of the birthname doesn't appear in the new name. The 7·7 negative potential would tend to be lessened with the new name.

The 7·7 potential is similar to the 16/7 effect already covered in Step 2.

The 1 Expression/1 sub-element of the new name doesn't appear in the birthname, but it's already described in Step 1.

STEP 5

COMPARE THE MATURITY NUMBER TO BOTH NAMES.

Since Norman is past his mid-thirties, this step is followed. Note that Norman's 1 Maturity Number does not change when he changes his name.

The 1 Expression of the new name increases the energy available for the new sub-lesson.

> Norman is likely to make increased progress in the direction of independence.

STEP 6

COMPARE THE TEMPERAMENTS.

There aren't any significant differences here. Only rarely is the Temperament an important factor in a name change—usually when all or most of the name changes.

STEP 7

COMPARE THE FIRST LETTERS AND FIRST VOWELS.

Since the first name Norman is the same, there's no change here.

STEP 8

COMPARE THE GROWTH NUMBER TO BOTH NAMES.

The Growth Number is 3. The 3 Modified Karmic Lesson of

the birthname has been replaced by the 3 Intensity Point of the new name.

> He's likely to feel somewhat more optimistic and creative and, because of this, be able to expand and develop more readily.

In Norman's example, the primary effect of the new name is the emphasis on the 8 Life Path energy and related de-emphasis on the 11/2 and 16/7 energy; the secondary effect is the addition of new 1 and 22/4 energy. If this was a real life situation, Norman would probably feel the change as an upsurge in his inherent business abilities—rather than an addition of new leadership and organizational abilities.

Example 2:
Portion of
basic energy
converted to
more usable
energy

Becky Balfour, our second fictitious subject, was born on January 3, 1962 with an extremely difficult basic energy. An early marriage, at eighteen, changed her name to Becky Blake. Becky is a good example of *a subject who has converted a portion of the basic energy to more usable energy by changing her name.*

Here are Becky's calculation sheets (Figure 24-3 on page 407 and Figure 24-4 on page 408). Note the effectiveness calculation in the lower left-hand corner of both sheets. The effectiveness calculation for Becky Balfour shows how two elements with the same number are handled.

> Becky Balfour has an extremely discordant basic energy. She will probably feel limited and frustrated, is likely to be rigid and stubborn, may be obsessed with system and order. She's likely to find her opportunities most limiting (*all from the 4 Life Path/4 Expression/4 Soul Urge and the 13/4 Karmic Debt*). Although she has some feeling and sensitivity, a creative imagination and a sociable nature, these traits (*3 Birthday, 2 Intensity Point and 3 Intensity Point*) are probably not fully used because of her rigidity (*the 4·4·4 and the 13/4 Karmic Debt*), her lack of confidence (*one 1 denotes a significant 1 Intensity Point*), her fears and insecurities (*one 5 denotes a significant 5 Intensity Point*) and her lack of awareness of others' feelings (*one 9 denotes a significant 9 Intensity Point*).

We'll study the change when Becky uses her married name:

January 3,   1962
    1   + 3 + 9   =   (13/4)

        3 – 1 = 2
        9 – 3 = 6
        6 – 2 = 4 CHALLENGE

$\dfrac{(12)\ 3}{5\quad 7}\ +\ \dfrac{(10)\ 1}{1\quad 6\,3}\ =\ (4)$

BECKY   BALFOUR

$\dfrac{2\quad 3\,2}{7}\ +\ \dfrac{2\quad 3\,6\quad 9}{(20)\ 2}\ =\ 9\ \text{SECRET SELF}$

$\dfrac{2\,5\,3\,2\,7}{(19)\ 1}\ +\ \dfrac{2\,1\,3\,6\,6\,3\,9}{(30)\ 3}\ =\ (4)$

one 1
three 2's
three 3's
   no 4   ←
one 5
two 6's
one 7
   no 8   ←
one 9

PHYSICAL	E	1–Weak
MENTAL	AL	2–Average
EMOTIONAL	BBOR	4–Strong
INTUITIVE	CKYFU	5–Strong

MATURITY NUMBER = 4 + 4 = 8

EFFECTIVENESS:

(4) – (4) = 10
(4) – (4) = 10
(4) – (4) = 10
                    ―――
                    30

Figure 24–3
Calculation Sheet:
Becky Balfour

$$\frac{(12)\ 3}{5\quad 7} + \frac{6}{1\quad 5} = (9)$$

BECKY   BLAKE

$$\frac{2\,5\,3\,2\,7}{(19)\ 1} + \frac{2\,3\,1\,2\,5}{(13)\ 4} = (5)$$

one 1
four 2's
two 3's
no 4 ←
two 5's
no 6 ←
one 7
no 8 ←
no 9 ←

PHYSICAL	EE	2–Average
MENTAL	LA	2–Average
EMOTIONAL	BB	2–Average
INTUITIVE	CKYK	4–Strong

EFFECTIVENESS:

$$(5) - (4) = 1$$
$$(9) - (4) = 5$$
$$(9) - (5) = \frac{4}{10}$$

Figure 24–4
Calculation Sheet:
Becky Blake

STEP 1

COMPARE THE BIRTH CORE TO THE NEW CORE.

The 5 Expression of the new name replaces the 4 Expression of the birthname.

The 9 Soul Urge of the new name replaces the 4 Soul Urge of the birthname.

The 4·4·4 of the birthname doesn't appear in the new name, making the new name more harmonious.

The new name (effectiveness = 10) is more effective than the birthname (effectiveness = 30).

STEP 2

COMPARE THE KARMIC DEBTS.

No change.

STEP 3

COMPARE THE INTENSITY TABLES.

The new name has four 2's, an Intensity Point with a significant divergence compared to the three 2's Intensity Point of the birthname.

STEPS 4 THROUGH 8

No significant changes.

> With her married name, Becky is likely to feel somewhat less limited and less rigid (*omission of the 4·4·4*). She'll be more capable at systematizing and managing, displaying her practical and responsible side as well as her capability at bringing plans to a concrete form (*positive 4 energy*). In the past, she had these skills but seemed to run into blockages which prevented her from using these capabilities as well as she would have liked. With her married name, the impediments seem to be of a much lesser nature (*omission of the 4·4·4·*).
>
> She'll probably be more adaptable and more enthusiastic (*5 Expression replaces the 4 Expression*) and is likely to show more concern for her fellow man (*9 Soul Urge replaces the 4 Soul Urge*). She may find more opportunities to put her abilities to work and can derive more satisfaction out of life. (*Increased harmony and effectiveness are found with the new name.*) Although Becky will still have to work on her feelings of subservience and fear of others, she is likely to show increased sensitivity and considerateness. (*Four 2's replace the three 2's.*)

I've chosen to present Becky's name change as an example, not an uncommon one, of converting restricted energy to usable energy, rather than as an example of adding new energy. It's true that, with her married name, Becky receives the addition of 5 and 9 energies. But while Becky now has new potential to learn to use, she has also, to some extent, freed up her basic 4 energy. (The 13/4 Karmic Debt is still there, but the elimination of the 4·4·4 is a significant step in removing the impediments to the use of the 4 potential.) It's always easier to use inherent energy, in this case Becky's 4 energy, than the newly introduced energy.

You may wonder how much difference that new name will make. After all, Becky can only change about a quarter of her basic energy at most. Will that really be enough to matter? Think of Becky's basic chart as analogous to a giant traffic jam where no one can move. Becky's married name opens a small path so that a thin trickle of cars can move slowly out of the jam. By judicious use of her free will, Becky can use her partially unblocked inherent energy as well as her new energy. The thin trickle of cars, in the analogy, can become several lanes moving more and more rapidly until the traffic jam disappears. Although only a quarter of Becky's energy may change—at the beginning—that change can be the start of a far greater shift than might be expected.

When giving a reading in this type of situation, be sure to stress the extremely positive effect that's possible with the new name. Clearly delineate the specific difficulties to be overcome and the specific avenues to better use of the subject's energies.

Example 3: Portion of basic energy converted to less usable energy

Our third fictitious subject, Jack Dwight Coles, was born on June 28, 1942. Although there are some conflicts in his basic chart, it's a strong chart with solid potential. There's a good deal of resemblance, as a matter of fact, between Jack's chart and Hal Allen's. For a number of years now, Jack has preferred to use his nickname and middle initial. He calls himself Jed D. Coles. Jed is a good example of *a subject who has converted a portion of the basic energy to less usable energy by changing his name*.

Let's look at the calculation sheets (Figure 25-5 on page 411 and Figure 24-6 on page 412):

> Jack Dwight Coles is an active, versatile, freedom-loving person with the potential for much excitement and adventure in his life (5 *Life Path*). He must learn to overcome his tendencies to be erratic and overindulge in physical pleasures. He must also learn to profit from his mistakes and live comfortably with change (14/5 *Karmic Debt*).
>
> He must learn to balance the exhilaration he finds in freedom (5 *Life Path*) with his inner need to be responsible and give much to others in the way of

June 28, 1942

$6 + 1 + 7 = \boxed{14/5}$

$6 - 1 = 5$
$7 - 1 = 6$
$6 - 5 = 1$ CHALLENGE

$$\frac{1}{1} + \frac{9}{9} + \frac{11}{6 \ 5} = 21 = \boxed{3}$$

JACK   DWIGHT   COLES

$$\frac{1 \ \ 3 \ 2}{6} + \frac{4 \ 5 \ \ 7 \ 8 \ 2}{(26) \ 8} + \frac{3 \ \ 3 \ \ 1}{7} = 21 = 3 \text{ SECRET SELF}$$

$$\frac{1 \ 1 \ 3 \ 2}{7} + \frac{4 \ 5 \ 9 \ 7 \ 8 \ 2}{(35) \ 8} + \frac{3 \ 6 \ 3 \ 5 \ 1}{(18) \ 9} = 24 = \boxed{6}$$

three 1's
two 2's
three 3's
one 4
two 5's
one 6
one 7
one 8
one 9

PHYSICAL	DWE	3–Strong
MENTAL	JAGHL	5–Strong
EMOTIONAL	ITOS	4–Strong
INTUITIVE	CKC	3–Strong

MATURITY NUMBER = 5 + 6 = 11/2

EFFECTIVENESS:

$\boxed{6} - \boxed{5} = 1$

$\boxed{5} - \boxed{3} = 2$

$\boxed{6} - \boxed{3} = \dfrac{3}{6}$

Figure 24-5
Calculation Sheet:
Jack Dwight Coles

$$\frac{5}{5} + \frac{0}{} + \frac{11}{6 \; 5} = \boxed{16/7}$$

JED D. COLES

$$\frac{1\,5\,4}{(10)\,1} + \frac{4}{4} + \frac{3\,6\,3\,5\,1}{(18)\,9} = \boxed{14/5}$$

two 1's
no 2 ←
two 3's
two 4's
two 5's
one 6
no 7 ←
no 8 ←
no 9 ←

PHYSICAL	EDDE	4–Strong
MENTAL	JL	2–Average
EMOTIONAL	OS	2–Average
INTUITIVE	C	1–Average

EFFECTIVENESS:

$$\boxed{5} - \boxed{5} = 10$$

$$\boxed{7} - \boxed{5} = 2$$

$$\boxed{7} - \boxed{5} = \underline{\;2\;}$$

$$14$$

Figure 24–6
Calculation Sheet:
Jed D. Coles

friendship, affection and love (*6 Expression*). He is, at times, independent (*28/1 Birthday*), but others can usually enjoy his outgoing social ways (*5 Life Path, 3 Soul Urge*), his creative expression (*3 Soul Urge*) and his original ideas (*29/1 Birthday*).

What are the changes when Jack uses Jed D. Coles?

STEP 1

COMPARE THE BIRTH CORE TO THE NEW CORE.

The 5 Expression of the new name replaces the 6 Expression of the birthname.

The 7 Soul Urge of the new name replaces the 3 Soul Urge of the birthname.

The new name contains the very discordant 5 Life Path/5 Expression aspect. The birthname has the discord of the 5 Life Path/6 Expression aspect.

The new name (effectiveness = 14) is far less effective than the birthname (effectiveness = 6).

STEP 2

COMPARE THE KARMIC DEBTS.

In the new name, the 14/5 Karmic Debt of the Expression is added to the existing 14/5 Karmic Debt of the Life Path.

A 16/7 Karmic Debt from the Soul Urge appears in the new name only.

STEPS 3 THROUGH 6

No significant changes.

STEP 7

COMPARE THE FIRST LETTERS AND FIRST VOWELS.

First Vowel: The E of Jed replaces the A of Jack.

STEP 8

COMPARE THE RELATION OF THE GROWTH NUMBER TO BOTH NAMES.

The Growth Number is 7. There's no 7 energy in the birthname, but there is the 7 Soul Urge in the new name.

> With his new name, Jed is likely to have somewhat more difficulty using freedom constructively. He would tend to be a bit more erratic with little sense of accomplishment or accountability as well as being a bit more overindulgent in physical pleasures. He's likely to scatter his energies. (*5·5 aspect. Addition of 14/5 Expression of the new name to the 14/5 Life Path.*) He's probably a little more self-centered (*3 and 6 energies of the birthname are replaced by 5 and 7 energies so that the entire new core is self-centered*) and frustrated by his inability to easily match his abilities, desires and opportunities. (*The new name is considerably less effective than the birthname.*)
>
> Jed's "different" approach is slightly more em-

phasized (*16/7 Soul Urge of new name*). His restlessness detracts somewhat from his ability to be a sensitive leader. (*The restlessness derives from the E of Jed, the sensitive leader from the A of Jack.*)

Jed is likely to appear a bit more introspective, occasionally aloof (*7 Soul Urge of the new name*).He's apt to spend somewhat more time alone — possibly studying and contemplating. This may open up some new experiences for him (*7 Soul Urge of the new name working with 7 Growth Number*).

Did you notice that Jed's reading *downplays* the negative potential of his new name—there's a repetition of phrases like "somewhat more", "a bit more", "slightly more"? That's a different emphasis than Becky's reading which so strongly *emphasizes* the *positive* direction of her new name. Why the difference?

In Becky's case, the traffic jam of her basic energy pattern would receive a significant impetus to unclog with the introduction of her married name. Without the name change, Becky would be mired in a restrictive holding pattern. With the name change (*and* the use of her free will), she may well begin a productive forward movement.

Jed's case is different. The basic energy is relatively workable, and I'd assume he'd make reasonable progress with his birthname. When Jack becomes Jed, he'll be aware of impediments which weren't there previously. But, if he's like most of us in this situation, he'll concentrate on the basic positive energy *which he's been using all along.* Jed will most likely work through the new blockages rather than fall victim to them.

Most people follow the more positive energy direction most of the time, whether that energy comes from the birthname or the new name. Becky, then, is likely to concentrate on the *new positive potential* when it appears—so *that* energy is emphasized in her reading. Jed, on the other hand, is likely to continue concentrating on the *existing positive potential*, so the new negative energy is deemphasized.

Finally, let's study the situation presented by our last fictitious subject. Abbie Dumas Jefferson was born on July 14, 1957. Abbie didn't particularly like her first or middle names. At her twenty-first birthday party, she announced that she had become Elizabeth Jefferson. In some ways, Elizabeth is similar to Becky Blake in that each woman's name change helps remove substantial restrictions to her energy flow. In addition, I feel that Elizabeth's chart also introduces some new energy. We'll look at that in more detail after we make our comparisons. Elizabeth, then, *is a subject who, (1) converts a portion of her basic energy to more usable energy and (2) introduces some new energy.*

See the calculation sheets (Figure 24-7 on page 416 and Figure 24-8 on page 417):

> Abbie Dumas Jefferson is an introspective, difficult-to-know person who tends to operate on a different wavelength than most people. She tends to depend primarily on herself (*7 Life Path*). She's apt to be extremely self-centered (*7 Life Path, 4 Expression, 8 Soul Urge, five 1's Intensity Point*) and dominating (*five 1's Intensity Point*). Although she's hard working, serious, patient and orderly (*4 Expression*), she also tends to be rigid, obstinate, dogmatic, and often obsessed with system and order. She's likely to feel limited and restricted (*13/4 Karmic Debt, 4 Expression/4 sub-element*).
>
> She does possess executive abilities (*8 Soul Urge*) and an analytical mind (*7 Life Path, 14/5 Birthday*) along with a strong sense of responsibility (*three 6's Intensity Point*). She may have to get a better perspective on handling money (*8 Modified Karmic Lesson*).

There are strong changes when she uses her new name:

STEP 1

COMPARE THE BIRTH CORE TO THE NEW CORE.

The 6 Expression of the new name replaces the 4 Expression of the birthname.
The 9 Soul Urge of the new name replaces the 8 Soul Urge of the birthname.
The new name contains the discord of the 6 and 9 energies with the 7 energy. The birthname contains the discord of the 4 and 8 energies with the 7 energy.
The new name is slightly more effective than the birthname.

STEP 2

COMPARE THE KARMIC DEBTS.

The 13/4 Karmic Debt of the Expression appears only in the birthname.

Example 4: Portion of basic energy converted to more usable energy *and* new energy introduced

July 14, 1957

$7 + 5 + 22 = 34 = 7$

$7 - 5 = 2$
$5 - 4 = 1$
$2 - 1 = 1$ CHALLENGE

$$\frac{(15)\ 6}{1\quad\ 9\,5} + \frac{4}{3\ \ 1} + \frac{(16)\ 7}{5\quad 5\quad 6} = 17 = 8$$

A B B I E   D U M A S   J E F F E R S O N

$$\frac{2\,2}{4} + \frac{4\ \ 4\ \ 1}{9} + \frac{1\ \ 66\ \ 91\ \ 5}{(28)\ (10)\ 1} = 14$$
$$= 5 \text{ SECRET SELF}$$

$$\frac{1\,2\,2\,9\,5}{(19)\ 1} + \frac{4\,3\,4\,1\,1}{(13)\ 4} + \frac{1\,5\,6\,6\,5\,9\,1\,6\,5}{(44)\ 8} = 13/4$$

five 1's
two 2's
one 3
two 4's
four 5's
three 6's
no 7 ←
no 8 ←
two 9's

PHYSICAL	EDMEE	5–Strong
MENTAL	AAJN	4–Average
EMOTIONAL	BBISRSO	7–Strong
INTUITIVE	UFF	3–Average

MATURITY NUMBER = 7 + 4 = 11/2

EFFECTIVENESS:

$7 - 4 = 3$

$8 - 7 = 1$

$$8 - 4 = \frac{4}{8}$$

Figure 24–7
Calculation Sheet:
Abbie Dumas Jefferson

$$\frac{(20)\ 2}{5\quad 9\quad 1\quad 5} \quad + \quad \frac{(16)\ 7}{5\quad 5\quad 6} \quad = \quad \textcircled{9}$$

ELIZABETH   JEFFERSON

$$\frac{5\,3\,9\,8\,1\,2\,5\,2\,8 \qquad 1\,5\,6\,6\,5\,9\,1\,6\,5}{(43)\ 7 \qquad + \qquad (44)\ 8} \qquad = 15 = \textcircled{6}$$

three 1's
 two 2's
  one 3
   no 4 ←
  five 5's
three 6's
   no 7 ←
  two 8's
  two 9's

PHYSICAL	EEEE	4–Average
MENTAL	LAHJN	5–Strong
EMOTIONAL	IZBTRSO	7–Strong
INTUITIVE	FF	2–Average

EFFECTIVENESS:

$$\textcircled{7} - \textcircled{6} = 1$$

$$\textcircled{9} - \textcircled{7} = 2$$

$$\textcircled{9} - \textcircled{6} = \frac{3}{6}$$

Figure 24–8
Calculation Sheet:
Elizabeth Jefferson

STEP 3

COMPARE THE INTENSITY TABLES.

The three 1's Intensity Point of the new name replaces the significantly divergent five 1's Intensity Point of the birthname.
The two 8's Intensity Point of the new name replaces the 8 Modified Karmic Lesson of the birthname.

STEP 4

COMPARE THE SUB-ELEMENTS.

The 4 Expression/4 sub-element appears only in the birthname.

STEP 5

COMPARE THE MATURITY NUMBER TO BOTH NAMES.

Under thirty-five years old. The comparison is unnecessary.

STEP 6

COMPARE THE TEMPERAMENTS.

No significant change.

STEP 7

COMPARE THE FIRST LETTERS AND FIRST VOWELS.

First Vowel: The E of Elizabeth (pronounced as a long E) re-places the A of Abbie.

STEP 8

COMPARE THE GROWTH NUMBER TO BOTH NAMES.

No change.

> With her new name, Elizabeth is likely to get along better with others. She'll appear more friendly, affectionate, sympathetic and understanding as well as more sensitive and giving (*6 Expression, 9 Soul Urge of the new name*). Elizabeth's approach displays just a bit more adventurousness than in the past (*First Vowel E replaces A*).
>
> She's likely to be considerably less rigid, obstinate and dogmatic (*13/4 Karmic Debt and 4 Expression/4 sub-element of the birthname are not in the new name*) and her previously extreme self-centeredness and dominant manner should be substantially reduced. (*The significantly divergent five 1's Intensity Point of the birthname became an average three 1's of the new name.*) She's likely to find it easier to handle money, too. (*The 8 Modified Karmic Lesson of the birthname is replaced by the two 8's Intensity Point of the new name.*)

Why did I mention the introduction of new energy in this case and not in Becky Blake's example? Both birth charts are strongly self-centered so that there would be little inherent energy devoted to friendship, affection or helping others. Elizabeth's new energy, from her 6 Expression and 9 Soul Urge, is primarily directed toward those missing characteristics. Since it's not basic energy, she'll have to work to make it useful to her. Because of its strength, there's a good chance that this new energy may be as important to her as the concurrent removal of restrictions.

In Becky's case, the new energy is derived from the 5 Expression and the 9 Soul Urge. The 5 potential, with it's self-centeredness, confirms the basic energy direction. The 9 Soul Urge, while a giving energy, doesn't, under these circumstances, seem strong enough to be significant. There's nothing wrong, though, in mentioning the addition of the 9 potential. As a matter of fact, it *is* mentioned in Becky's new reading, but in a manner commensurate with its importance.

The names that people use in their daily lives must clearly be taken into account. From the examples in this chapter, though, I hope it's apparent how important is the power of the birthname energy. I've done readings for some people who've *never* used their birthnames. Several of these people had to look up their names on their birth certificates because they weren't even sure of them. But all of them, even though they'd never used the names, were, without question, described by the birthname energies. You are the product of the interplay of your birth energies, your free will and your environment—along with the energy overlay of the different names you use.

CHAPTER 25

ADVANCED CHARACTER DELINEATION: THE PROCEDURE

Advanced delineations follow the same general principles discussed in Parts II and III of Volume 1. The principles are followed just as rigorously as before, but the delineation format is looser and the reading is assembled with an eye to the individual numerologist's creative input. The increased depth of the advanced reading derives from the numerologist's experience and the expanding ability to describe each subject's characteristics in the manner most meaningful to that subject.

Our basic information for the advanced delineation is, of course, derived from the core and modifiers. As you gain experience, you may choose to add additional modifiers or you may choose to pay little attention to some of the minor modifiers. Check with care that the added modifiers "make sense" *and* add significant information. Check just as carefully that the omitted modifiers don't distort the picture by their absence. In any event, use the core elements and the same group of modifiers in a consistent manner in all your delineations.

Don't adjust the reading by leaving out difficult, ambiguous or conflicting information. Don't emphasize information because it's special in *your* life. Keep the delineation as "pure" and objective as possible. Rigidity can be meaningless or harmful, but staying with the derived information for the sake of accuracy reaches to the very heart of the matter.

General premises

By all means, use your advanced understanding of the numbers and the characteristics they represent. The more you increase your awareness of the continuums represented by each number and the more understanding you have of the harmonious and discordant combination of traits, the deeper and more revealing will your readings be. Use the charts, but feel free to broaden the information from the charts with your own experience and advanced awareness.

Group the energies to produce the most intelligible delineations. By grouping each core element with similar modifier energies, you add clarity and cohesiveness and yet allow the relative importance of the different elements and modifiers to remain apparent.

The advanced procedure that I'm about to describe provides a simple general scheme for grouping energies. In this general scheme, I've grouped the descriptions of all the mental and emotional characteristics, irrespective of the elements or modifiers from which the energy is derived. I've found that this helps clarify these two important areas. Try this kind of grouping and see if it is right for you.

I expect you probably feel, as I do, that the two-part delineation procedure in Parts II and III provides a somewhat rigid format with considerable repetition. The advanced procedure that follows is easier to work with, very flexible, and not conducive to repetition. This advanced procedure, *used by a numerologist familiar with the basic precepts*, leaves room for the individual's creative juices to flow and produces a far better delineation. But take heed of the italicized phrase: the advanced procedure works *only* if you're thoroughly familiar with the basic precepts. A solid grounding in Parts II and III is imperative before proceeding to this advanced method in order to avoid transmitting distorted information.

The seven-step advanced procedure

This, then, is the advanced procedure which I use. Modify the procedure to fit your own needs, but hold fast to the basic principles.

STEP 1

CALCULATE AND ORGANIZE THE BASIC DATA.

A. PERFORM THE STANDARD CALCULATIONS.
B. GROUP THE ENERGIES ON THE ORGANIZATION SHEET.

C. PREPARE A DELINEATION OUTLINE OF THE ENERGIES.

This part of the procedure is identical to the beginning of Hal Allen's delineation in Chapter 21. Performing these steps in order will insure that all the required information is included.

STEP 2

STUDY THE CORE ELEMENTS AND MODIFIERS.

Perform these steps either in your head or by jotting down notes.
A. STUDY THE CORE ELEMENTS AND THE RELATION OF THEIR ENERGIES.
B. STUDY THE HARMONY OR DISCORD OF THE ENERGIES.
C. STUDY THE EFFECTIVENESS OR INEFFECTIVE-NESS OF THE CORE ELEMENTS.
D. DETERMINE THE STRONG MODIFIERS AND STUDY THEIR EFFECT ON THE CORE ENERGIES.

STEP 3

VISUALIZE THE SUBJECT.

Concentrate on the core elements and the strong modifiers. Based on what you determined in Step 2, do you get a clear picture of the probable type of person described by these energies?

At first, you may have to spend a good deal of time weighing the energies before you are able to the visualize the individual. With practice, you'll begin to visualize the subject as you proceed with Step 2. Take all the time you need here, until the visualization begins to develop comfortably.

This step is the heart of the advanced procedure. If this step feels too difficult, you may need more practice in the basic delineation.

STEP 4

PREPARE A FORMAT FOR THE DELINEATION BY LISTING PRINCIPAL TRAITS.

I give most of my delineations orally, but I usually work from a one- or two-page written format. When I prepare a typed reading I work from the same outline. I use the following basic format for my delineations:

DELINEATION FORMAT

LIFE PATH AND RELATED MODIFIERS
Positive traits
Traits which can be positive or negative
Negative traits or obstacles

EXPRESSION AND RELATED MODIFIERS
Positive traits
Traits which can be positive or negative
Negative traits or obstacles

SOUL URGE AND RELATED MODIFIERS
Positive traits
Traits which can be positive or negative
Negative traits or obstacles

BIRTHDAY AND RELATED MODIFIERS
Positive traits
Traits which can be positive or negative
Negative traits or obstacles

MISCELLANEOUS MODIFIERS
(Modifiers which don't group with any of the core elements)
Positive traits
Traits which can be positive or negative
Negative traits or obstacles

MIND
Positive traits
Traits which can be positive or negative
Negative traits or obstacles

EMOTIONS
Positive traits
Traits which can be positive or negative
Negative traits or obstacles

DIRECTING MODIFIERS
Negative traits or obstacles
Traits which can be positive or negative
Positive traits (Always end on a positive note.)

Rearrange the order of the main divisions of the format for each delineation if it will give that reading greater clarity. If there are two (or more) core elements with the same number, for instance, those divisions should be essentially combined. Or, if there are two core elements with similar energies—a 4 Expression along with an 8 Birthday; a 6 Life Path and a 9 Soul Urge—those divisions may well give more sense to the reading when one division follows directly after the other. Or, if there's a great deal of emphasis on emotions—say, a 6 Expression with five related modifiers—perhaps the section on emotions could either be combined with the Expression section, or follow directly. And, similarly, a great deal of emphasis on mental matters—a 7 Life Path with four related modifiers—may justify combining the section on the mind with the Life Path, or having it follow directly.

Adjust the format, then, in order to achieve the maximum of clarity and the best flow from division to division. *Always* start with the description of the lesson of the Life Path and the Life Path traits. This is the most important information in the delineation and needs the prominence of a position at the beginning for maximum emphasis. And, no matter what the order of the divisions, *always* end on a positive note!

If a characteristic relates specifically to the individual's mind or mental ability, list that characteristic in the "Mind" division rather than with its modifier. In the same way, list traits related to emotions or affection in the "Emotions" division. Each trait is listed as a word or phrase along with a note indicating from which element or modifier the trait is derived. List similar traits (and their derivations) along with the original trait listed.

The traits listed come, of course, from the charts and your experience. Refer also to the continuums on CHART 13: THE NUMBERS—ADVANCED SYMBOLISM for additional input.

The traits of the Directing Modifiers are usually listed at the end of the format. These characteristics are discussed separately and are not subject to modification by the other energies.

Insert at appropriate places in the outline phrases which mention the harmony/discord and effectiveness/ineffectiveness of the several energies.

STEP 5

DELINEATE THE BASIC CHARACTER.

Using the format prepared in Step 4 as a guide, discuss each characteristic listed in turn.

The length of the delineation of the traits of each element and its related modifiers is an indication of the importance of that particular element. The discussion of the Life Path and its related modifiers should *always* be the longest, followed by the somewhat shorter discussion of the Expression and its modifiers and shorter still discussions of the Soul Urge and Birthday. In the delineation format shown in Step 4, we list the traits of the most important element first, followed by the next important, and so on, and we place similar modifier characteristics along with traits already listed. The Life Path division, then, usually turns out to be the longest with the lengths of the rest of the divisions proportionate to their importance.

It doesn't always work out like this. Suppose there is a Life Path with one related modifier and a Soul Urge with six related modifiers. Remember that the Life Path represents about forty percent of the energy, the Soul Urge about twenty percent. To avoid distorting the reading, the description of the traits of the Life Path and its modifier should be approximately twice the length of the description of the traits of the Soul Urge and its modifiers. Although it usually feels more comfortable to fully describe each trait, here the traits of the Soul Urge and its related modifiers would be sharply abbreviated to keep the whole delineation in proportion.

STEP 6

CALCULATE AND ORGANIZE THE DATA RELATED TO NAMES OTHER THAN BIRTHNAMES.

For each name:
Prepare a partial calculation sheet (similar to Becky Blake's partial calculation sheet, Figure 24-4 on page 408, Chapter 24).

Prepare a comparision of the elements and modifiers of the new name and birthname (similar to Becky Blake's comparison, page 408, Chapter 24).

STEP 7

DELINEATE THE EFFECT OF NAMES OTHER THAN THE BIRTHNAMES.

Describe the effect of all the names commonly used and, if the subject is interested, some names previously used. Make the length of the description of each name proportional to the strength of the energy change related to that name. For some names, as you'll discover, one or two sentences may be quite enough.

Be sure to distinguish the changed inherent energy, relatively easy to use, with the more difficult-to-assimilate new energy.

In the next chapter, we follow this advanced procedure, step by step, to produce a complete advanced character delineation. Study of this reading should prove helpful in developing your own delineations.

CHAPTER 26

ADVANCED CHARACTER DELINEATION: AN EXAMPLE

"Tapwa" has been a close friend for about ten years. She's forty-three now (1981), divorced, with an eleven-year-old son and a seven-year-old daughter. She's a junior high school teacher in a large California city. Because she's grown a lot over the years and overcome many of the obstacles described in her complex chart, I felt that she would be an especially interesting subject. Tapwa was kind enough to allow me to use her delineation in this work.

To protect my friend's privacy, I've constructed a name and a birthdate with virtually all the core elements and modifiers identical with her actual core elements and modifiers. So, although Tapwa Cern Nays is a pseudonym, and although the birthday, too, has been revised, the "constructed data" represents a very real person indeed.

I asked my friend for her comments after I had completed the reading. I wanted her to give concrete examples from her life to illustrate points covered in the delineation. I asked for any additional comments, as she saw fit, to give an understanding of her personal view of some of the abstractions discussed. I think you'll appreciate Tapwa's articulate manner as you peruse a portion of her commentary appended after the delineation. I think the notes serve to indicate the general accuracy of the reading as well as its relevance to her.

The delineation, of course, follows the advanced procedure outlined in the last chapter.

Introducing my friend "Tapwa"

The
beginning
steps of the
advanced
procedure

STEP 1

CALCULATE AND ORGANIZE THE BASIC DATA.

A. PERFORM THE STANDARD CALCULATIONS (Figure 26-1, page 429).
B. GROUP THE ENERGIES ON THE ORGANIZATION SHEET (Figure 26-2, page 430).
C. PREPARE A DELINEATION OUTLINE OF THE ENERGIES (below).

LIFE PATH AND RELATED MODIFIERS

Core:	1	Life Path
Modifiers:	19/1	Karmic Debt
	four 1's	Intensity Point
	1	Prime Intensifier
	1	Secret Self
	4	Karmic Lesson
	8	Karmic Lesson
	8	Maturity Number

EXPRESSION, BIRTHDAY AND RELATED MODIFIERS

Core:	7	Expression
	7	Birthday
Modifiers:	16/7	Karmic Debt
	7	Expression/7 Birthday
	7	Expression/7 sub-element
	7	Growth Number
	two 7's	Intensity Point

SOUL URGE AND RELATED MODIFIERS

Core:	6	Soul Urge
Modifiers:	6	Modified Karmic Lesson
	2	Challenge
	one 9	Intensity Point

MISCELLANEOUS MODIFIERS

Modifiers:	none

DIRECTING MODIFIERS

Temperament:	Strong Mental
First Letter:	T
First Vowel:	A

September   16,   1938

$$9 \quad + 7 + 3 \quad = \quad \boxed{19/1}$$

$$9 - 3 = 6$$
$$7 - 3 = 4$$
$$6 - 4 = 2 \text{ CHALLENGE}$$

$$\frac{2}{1} \quad + \quad \frac{5}{1} \quad + \quad \frac{8}{5} \quad = 15 = \boxed{6}$$
$$\phantom{\frac{2}{1}}\phantom{\frac{5}{1}}\phantom{\frac{8}{}}17$$

TAPWA   CERN   NAYS

$$\frac{2 \quad 7\,5}{(14)\ 5} \quad + \quad \frac{3 \quad 95}{(17)\ 8} + \quad \frac{5 \quad 1}{6} \quad = 19 = 1 \text{ SECRET SELF}$$

$$\frac{2\,1\,7\,5\,1}{(16)\ 7} \quad + \quad \frac{3\,5\,9\,5}{22} \quad + \quad \frac{5\,1\,7\,1}{(14)\ 5} \quad = 34 = \boxed{7}$$

four 1's
one 2
one 3
 no 4 ←
four 5's
 no 6 ←
two 7's
 no 8 ←
one 9

PHYSICAL	WE	2–Average
MENTAL	APANNA	6–Strong
EMOTIONAL	TRS	3–Average
INTUITIVE	CY	2–Average

MATURITY NUMBER = 1 + 7 = 8

EFFECTIVENESS:

$$\boxed{7} - \boxed{1} = 6$$

$$\boxed{6} - \boxed{1} = 5$$

$$\boxed{7} - \boxed{6} = \underline{1}$$
$$\phantom{\boxed{7} - \boxed{6} = }12$$

Figure 26–1
Calculation Sheet:
Tapwa Cern Nays

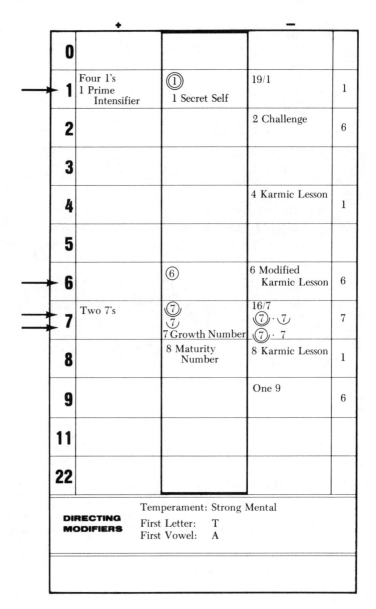

Figure 26–2
Organization Sheet:
Tapwa Cern Nays

STEP 2

STUDY THE CORE ELEMENTS AND MODIFIERS.

A. STUDY THE CORE ELEMENTS AND THE RELATION OF THEIR ENERGIES.

1 Life Path:	Independence, leadership, attainment.
7 Expression: 7 Birthday:	Good mind, studious, different, introspective, loner.
6 Soul Urge:	Responsible, sympathetic, emotional, creative.

With 1 energy aimed at outward achievement and recognition, 7 energy directed to inner peace and study, and 6 energy devoted to love and family, the three energies have little in common.

B. STUDY THE HARMONY OR DISCORD OF THE ENERGIES.

1·7:   In early years, at least, usually extremely discordant. Self-centered, dependent, inflexible.

   When the problems have been overcome, the energies may still be discordant, with the 1 wanting to move out in the world in a strong manner, the 7 tending to be introspective and different.

1·6:   Usually discordant. The 1 is involved with its own needs, the 6 in giving to others. There's probably a drastic pull between the energies.

6·7:   Usually discordant. The 6 tends to be emotional and concerned with others, the 7 is likely to be repressed and turned inward. Again, there's a drastic pull between the energies.

C. STUDY THE EFFECTIVENESS OR INEFFECTIVENESS OF THE CORE ELEMENTS

7 Expression minus 1 Life Path = 6. Abilities substantially outweigh the opportunities.

6 Soul Urge minus 1 Life Path = 5. Motivations outweigh opportunities.

7 Expression minus 6 Soul Urge = 1. Effective balance of abilities and motivations.

Although the motivations and abilities are well-balanced, there are likely to be too few opportunities for development. A good deal of frustration is likely, and probably some resentment.

D. DETERMINE THE STRONG MODIFIERS AND STUDY THEIR EFFECT ON THE CORE ENERGIES.

19/1 Karmic Debt: Problems with self-centeredness and dependence.

16/7 Karmic Debt: Problems with being "different" and self-centered.

7 Expression·7 Birthday and 7 Expression·7 sub-element: Self-contained and inflexible and/or timid and shy.

One 9 Intensity Point: Restricted point of view and little understanding of others' feelings.

A lot of substantial problems.

STEP 3

VISUALIZE THE SUBJECT.

Based on Step 2, I would visualize Tapwa like this:

> Tapwa has the potential to be independent—a leader capable of much in the way of attainment. Her responsible ways, her creative approach and her unique point of view may all prove helpful, but her introspective side and her strong emotional nature may cause conflicts.
>
> In her early years, at the very least, Tapwa will have significant obstacles to overcome. She's likely to start out in life being self-centered, dependent, "different," inflexible and timid. She may well have problems with her own and others' feelings.
>
> Even after overcoming these impediments, she will probably still have work to do to consolidate her divergent positive energies: her outgoing leadership, quiet studiousness, loving nature. She may become frustrated or resentful at all these handicaps as well as at the paucity of opportunities available for her development.

Tapwa's chart, like twenty percent of the charts you'll come across, falls into the "difficult" category. Prepare the delineation for maximum constructive effect. Emphasize the strength of the positive energies. Describe the blockages as handicaps to be overcome in order to take full advantage of the positive potential.

STEP 4

PREPARE A FORMAT FOR THE DELINEATION BY LISTING PRINCIPLE TRAITS.

In Chapter 25, I indicated that each trait should be listed as a word or phrase along with a note indicating the element or modifier from which the trait is derived. In this illustrative chapter, the traits are listed here but the derivation is noted as part of the step-by-step delineation in the following Step 5.

The format for the delineation follows the general scheme described in the last chapter with two exceptions. First, since there's a 7 Expression and a 7 Birthday, these two elements and the related modifiers are described together. Second, since all the modifiers relate directly to one or another of the core elements, there are no modifiers and no traits listed in the division marked "MISCELLANEOUS MODIFIERS."

LIST OF PRINCIPAL TRAITS

> + = positive traits
> + / − = traits which can be positive or negative
> − = negative traits or obstacles

List of principal traits to be discussed in the delineation

LIFE PATH AND RELATED MODIFIERS

1	LIFE PATH
19/1	KARMIC DEBT
FOUR 1's	INTENSITY POINT
1	PRIME INTENSIFIER
1	SECRET SELF
4	KARMIC LESSON
8	KARMIC LESSON
8	MATURITY NUMBER

+ 1. Learn the benefits of independence. Learn to stand on own two feet. Accomplish, attain.
+ 2. Leader, creator, etc.
+ 3. Attainment, satisfaction.
+ 4. Practicality.
+ 5. Organization, details.
+ 6. Working hard.
+ 7. Inner strength, ambition, self-confidence.
− 8. Self-centered.
− 9. Lack of awareness of others.
− 10. Strong personal needs.
− 11. Repressing needs.
− 12. Problems with money and material satisfactions.
− 13. Dependent.
− 14. Fearful, timid, etc.
− 15. Stubborn, self-contained.
− 16. Dominating.

EXPRESSION, BIRTHDAY AND RELATED MODIFIERS

7	EXPRESSION
7	BIRTHDAY
16/7	KARMIC DEBT
7	EXPRESSION/7 BIRTHDAY
7	EXPRESSION/7 SUB-ELEMENT
7	GROWTH NUMBER
TWO 7's	INTENSITY POINT

+ 17. Wisdom, hidden truths, technical ability.
+ 18. Spiritual awareness, psychic powers.
+ 19. Peace and faith.
+ / − 20. Introspective.
+ / − 21. Being alone.
− 22. Discordant 1·7 energy.
+ / − 23. "Different" wavelength.
− 24. Lack of trust, etc.
− 25. Deceptions.

SOUL URGE AND RELATED MODIFIERS.

6	SOUL URGE
6	MODIFIED KARMIC LESSON
2	CHALLENGE
ONE 9	INTENSITY POINT

+ 26. Responsibility.
− 27. Discordant 1·6 energy.
− 28. Discordant 6·7 energy.
+ 29. Rectifying, balancing, etc.
+ 30. Home and family.
+ 31. Creative, artistic.
− 32. Ineffectiveness of energy.

MISCELLANEOUS MODIFIERS

NONE

MIND

+ 33. Fine mind.

EMOTIONS

+ / − 34. Strong emotions, repressed in early years.
+ / − 35. Affection.
+ / − 36. Sensitivity.
+ 37. Intuition.

DIRECTING MODIFIERS

TEMPERAMENT: STRONG MENTAL
FIRST LETTER: T
FIRST VOWEL: A

+ 38. Balanced temperament.
+ 39. General approach: cautious expansion.

STEP 5

DELINEATE THE BASIC CHARACTER.

Each trait (from the list compiled in Step 4) is shown along with the element or modifier from which the trait is derived. Explanatory information about the trait and general commentary is shown in italics.

The delineation itself is shown indented.

The
delineation
for Tapwa
Cern Nays

NUMEROLOGY DELINEATION
FOR
TAPWA CERN NAYS
BORN SEPTEMBER 16, 1938

TRAIT 1

LEARN THE BENEFITS OF INDEPENDENCE. LEARN TO STAND ON OWN TWO FEET. ACCOMPLISH, ATTAIN. (1 LIFE PATH)

The lesson is placed first in the reading for maximum emphasis.

> The major number in a numerology chart is called the Life Path, and your major number, Tapwa, is a 1. There's a lesson for each Life Path—that lesson is likely to be an important focus in your life. The lesson of the number 1 is simply this: learn the benefits of independence. This is a two-part lesson—first, learn to stand on your own two feet, learn not to lean on or depend on others. Second, go on to be a leader or creator with a life of accomplishment. Some people with this Life Path spend most of their life on the first part and have little time left for accomplishment. Others with this Path, like Martin Luther King, spend little time on the first part and most of the life in a period of superior attainment.

Because of the 19/1 Karmic Debt combined with the four 1's Intensity Point and the 1 Prime Intensifier, I'm relatively certain that Tapwa will spend a good deal of her life on the first part of the lesson. I've saved this information until a little further along in the reading. At the beginning of the delineation, accentuate the positive!

TRAIT 2

LEADER, CREATOR, ETC.
    (1 LIFE PATH
     8 MATURITY NUMBER
     1 SECRET SELF)

With the obstacles, I wouldn't expect Tapwa to be able to make use of her leadership abilities until later in life. The introduction of the Maturity Number will give additional impetus to the leadership potential.

> Let's look at your positive potential. When you're operating with the power that you *can* develop, you can be a leader or creator. You have executive and administrative capability, although I suspect it won't be much noticed in the early part of your life. You're capable of taking charge, organizing, giving direction, even inspiring others. I'd expect these abilities to be particularly apparent from your mid-thirties on. (In the deep recesses of your mind, although you don't ever really expect it to happen, there's even a dream of leading in uncharted areas — perhaps as a fearless explorer.)

This is the unusual case where the Life Path and the Secret Self are the same number.

TRAIT 3

ATTAINMENT, SATISFACTION.
    (1 LIFE PATH)

A 1 who has achieved independence is usually on the way to substantial achievement, but Tapwa's ineffective combination of elements suggests less opportunity and, therefore, less achievement. This paragraph, then, is considerably toned down as compared to the same paragraph for a typical 1 Life Path.

> Once you've learned to stand on your own feet, there should be a lot of achievement that follows. You'll probably feel pleasure at your accomplish-

ments although your progress may not be as quick as you'd like. There can be praise from others as well as the possibility of financial gain.

TRAIT 4

PRACTICALITY.
  (4 KARMIC LESSON
   8 KARMIC LESSON
   8 MATURITY NUMBER)

The strong 7 energy tends to be dreamy and idealistic and causes a conflict here.

It's important that you act practically, but I suspect that you had work to do to develop a relatively realistic approach. There was probably something of a dreamy or idealistic side to you which probably conflicted. As you've gotten older, you've probably gotten far more realistic. I expect you've been aware of the benefits.

TRAIT 5

ORGANIZATION, DETAILS.
  (4 KARMIC LESSON)

7 energy tends to help here.

Organization and concern with detail are also important, but both are likely to come more readily.

TRAIT 6

WORKING HARD.
  (4 KARMIC LESSON)

It's not clear if Tapwa started out capable of hard work. At her current age of 43, I'd expect she'd learned this lesson by now and would delineate it accordingly.

There's likely to be a good deal of hard work in your life. You must be willing to work, concentrating your efforts and continuing no matter what the seeming restrictions. You probably still look at hard work as a limitation, at least part of the time. I hope you've stopped looking for easy ways out to avoid putting forward the required effort. Your growth is apt to have been severely limited until you accepted the need to work hard and patiently.

TRAIT 7

INNER STRENGTH.
    (1 LIFE PATH
    FOUR 1's INTENSITY POINT)

AMBITION, SELF-CONFIDENCE.
    (8 MATURITY NUMBER)

When you're using your positive potential, you show a great deal of inner strength. You're likely to exhibit much courage and independent feelings, even in the face of great difficulties. Now in your mature years, I expect you appear ambitious, self-confident, efficient, energetic and dependable. I suspect that these traits were being slowly developed through your growing years.

Transition paragraph from the positive potential to the negative potential of the Life Path.

You've probably found a number of obstacles to the easy achievement of independence. Because of your age, I expect that many of these hindrances have been faced and resolved. Let's look at some of these impediments.

TRAIT 8

SELF-CENTERED.
    (1 LIFE PATH)

The 7 energy emphasizes the problem.

Have you confused independence and self-centeredness? Were you concerned, in your early years especially, with your own needs almost to the exclusion of everything else? Were you aware of the self-centeredness enough to hide it under a social veneer or was it readily apparent?

TRAIT 9

LACK OF AWARENESS OF OTHERS.
    (19/1 KARMIC DEBT
    FOUR 1's INTENSITY POINT
    7 BIRTHDAY
    16/7 KARMIC DEBT)

You may have been so immersed in your own concerns that you had great difficulty becoming

aware of others' needs. You may have undone
yourself because of your inability to realistically
see yourself in relation to others. Even today, you
may still sometimes be surprised by others' negative reactions to your endeavors.

TRAIT 10

STRONG PERSONAL NEEDS.
   (1 LIFE PATH
   1 PRIME INTENSIFIER)

You probably still have strong personal needs,
material needs in particular. When you can't get
those needs met, you're likely to feel annoyed and
frustrated. Although you have the courage of your
convictions, you may be surprised at the conse-
quences of acting on those convictions. You may
still be struggling with the conflict between your
needs and your strong sense of responsibility.

*The 1·6 conflict between the self-centered portion and the giv-
ing portion is a very strong discord discussed in more detail in
the next paragraph.*

TRAIT 11

REPRESSING NEEDS.
   (6 SOUL URGE
   16/7 KARMIC DEBT)

*The 6 and 7 energies are not part of the Life Path and related
modifiers, but this is a good place to discuss the self-
centered/selfless conflict.*

You may, by now, have learned to repress at least
some of your needs in order to serve others, but
this may cause you to feel resentful. In this regard,
you may be interested to know that your chart indicates Karmic Debts, difficulties in this life as
payment for misapplication of energies in a previous life. In a past life, your selfishness caused
suffering to others. In this life, you must devote
yourself to selfless, loving ways, subordinating
your own needs, in order to repay the debt. Failure
to be selfless and loving will cause problems
which are likely to impede your achievement of independence. In the light of the previous discussion

of your strong needs, this is an area of your life requiring much work to achieve resolution.

TRAIT 12

PROBLEMS WITH MONEY AND MATERIAL SATISFACTIONS.
> (8 KARMIC LESSON
> 8 MATURITY NUMBER)

In your early years, I expect you were careless with money or felt some strain about finances. Your lack of awareness here probably affected your ability to be independent. Sometime after thirty, there was some shift in your life so that the problems of the material world, which hadn't seemed too important up to then, probably moved to center stage. The shift in your view was probably due to a reevaluation of your vocation or economic changes which affected your financial responsibility. If you have now learned to handle your finances, you can enjoy the satisfactions of the material world which come with the mastery of money.

TRAIT 13

DEPENDENT.
> (1 LIFE PATH
> 19/1 KARMIC DEBT
> 7 EXPRESSION/7 BIRTHDAY
> 7 EXPRESSION/7 SUB-ELEMENT)

Three strong modifiers emphasize the difficulties here. When there are three modifiers of this intensity, there's little question of the existence of a severe problem.

You probably started out in life in a very dependent place. In the early years, you may have been saddled with strong pressures to keep you from breaking free. I wouldn't be surprised if your efforts to stand alone were often thwarted. I'm sure you were resentful of this dependency although much of your dissatisfaction may have been hidden. You may have found solace by blaming the environment or other people. You probably wasted much time and energy because of your inability to read the realities of your situation and use them to your advantage in gaining independence.

TRAIT 14

FEARFUL, TIMID, ETC.
    (19/1 KARMIC DEBT
     7 EXPRESSION/7 BIRTHDAY
     7 EXPRESSION/7 SUB-ELEMENT
     2 CHALLENGE)

Another problem strongly emphasized. The giving quality of the 6 energy may have added to the servility.

> In your beginning years, you were probably fearful and retiring, possibly even servile. Yet, at the same time, you were brimming with feeling. It's likely that you found it difficult to work with others because of your fear of being hurt by an unkind word or action or, worse yet, by being ignored. You've probably put in much effort to learn not to worry about others' opinions of you.

TRAIT 15

STUBBORN, SELF-CONTAINED.
    (7 EXPRESSION/7 BIRTHDAY
     7 EXPRESSION/7 SUB-ELEMENT
     FOUR 1'S INTENSITY POINT
     8 MATURITY NUMBER
     FOUR 9'S INTENSITY POINT)

Still another problem strongly emphasized. Here, the adaptability of the 6 energy can help a little, but five modifiers here make this a difficult area.

> In your youth and young adulthood, you were probably self-contained. I expect that you displayed a lack of flexibility, a stubbornness and a somewhat restricted point of view. Only when you're more open and adaptable can the positive potential shine through.

TRAIT 16

DOMINATING.
    (1 LIFE PATH
     19/1 KARMIC DEBT
     FOUR 1'S INTENSITY POINT)

The 7 energy tends to be retiring, the 6 energy is concerned with harmonizing. These energies would counter the tendency to dominate.

In addition, the dependence and fear would make it probable that the dominant tendency would be relatively inexpressive.

You may, in your early years, have tended to control and dominate, if only for brief periods. You may have taken control by appearing weak and helpless. Your expressions of dominance may have been accompanied by aggressiveness and egotism.

Transition paragraph from 1 Life Path and related modifiers to 7 Expression, 7 Birthday and related modifiers.

Let's look at a completely different area of your energy.

TRAIT 17

WISDOM, HIDDEN TRUTHS, TECHNICAL ABILITY.
    (7 EXPRESSION
     7 BIRTHDAY
     TWO 7'S INTENSITY POINT)

You could be a teacher, a research worker or a philosopher—you're interested in searching for the fundamentals, the hidden truths. You could become an authority on subjects of interest to you in technical, scientific, religious or occult fields.

TRAIT 18

SPIRITUAL AWARENESS, PSYCHIC POWERS.
    (7 EXPRESSION
     7 BIRTHDAY)

The 7 Expression and 7 Birthday give the possibility of psychic powers and a good analytical mind. The two 7's Intensity Point usually emphasizes the good mind. The conflict is discussed in the delineation.

I'd expect you to have considerable interest in spiritual matters, along with some psychic ability. I'm not sure how much you use your psychic powers. You may not make the most of them because of conflicts with your strong analytical mind. (We'll discuss your powers of analysis in more detail a little later.)

TRAIT 19

PEACE AND FAITH.
    (7 EXPRESSION
    7 GROWTH NUMBER)

This paragraph discusses the 7 Growth Number and the very available energy for Tapwa's growth. Note that the discussion blends concepts related to the Growth Number with the description of other energy so that the Growth Number is discussed as part of the total picture, without undue special emphasis.

> Because of your spiritual awareness, you have the potential to retire into your very depths to find faith and peace. The peacefulness I'm talking about will come only from within—it has little to do with money or material matters. I doubt that you found this serenity in your young years—there were probably too many obstructions. I expect that you started to develop this potential about your mid-thirties.

TRAIT 20

INTROSPECTIVE.
    (7 EXPRESSION)

The introspective trait is usually a strong characteristic with a 7 core element.

> There's likely to be an introspective side to you. You probably withdraw from time to time to recharge your batteries. You might be the sort of person who needs some time alone every day, or you might just go off by yourself once a month or so. At any rate, this introspection, combined with the fear and shyness we previously discussed, may have kept you somewhat aloof from others, particularly in your early years.

TRAIT 21

BEING ALONE.
    (7 EXPRESSION
    7 BIRTHDAY
    7 GROWTH NUMBER

The 6 energy works well with others and is discussed in

the paragraph on Trait 29. Both energies appear to be strong so both are mentioned.

> One of the lessons in your life is to learn to be alone and not feel isolated. This is a lesson at which most people rebel, and you may well have the same reaction. Being alone nevertheless will provide an important coloration in your life and, if you've conquered the feeling of loneliness, your life will be far more comfortable. Ultimately, you may learn the pleasure of being alone for study and meditation. A little later, we'll discuss the other side of you—the side that works well with others.

TRAIT 22

DISCORDANT 1·7 ENERGY.

This is a good place to compare the two energies. The main purpose of this paragraph is to bring to Tapwa's attention the need to blend these conflicting potentials.

> The leadership ability that we discussed at the beginning of the reading is usually associated with an outgoing personality—the studious, introspective characteristics I've just been mentioning are of a quite different nature. I expect you've learned to blend portions of these energies to get as much as possible from both of them. Perhaps you've blended your technical ability and capability at searching for fundamentals with your hard working, organized nature to reach a degree of achievement.

TRAIT 23

"DIFFERENT" WAVELENGTH
        (7 EXPRESSION
        16/7 KARMIC DEBT
        7 EXPRESSION/7 BIRTHDAY
        7 EXPRESSION/7 SUB-ELEMENT
        TWO 7'S INTENSITY POINT)

A very strong 7 characteristic that functions both as positive and negative potential.

> You're likely to operate on a "different" wavelength than others. This is a very special quality

which may give you an unusual viewpoint and out-of-the-ordinary ideas as well as unique approaches and solutions to problems. You're apt to get a lot of benefit from your different approach.

Sometimes, though, because of that special wavelength, you may have difficulty clearly communicating your ideas to others. Others may have to work to get to know you because, at times, they may be disconcerted or confused by your point of view. This "different" wavelength, along with your introspective nature, may get in the way of permanent relations such as marriage or business partnerships.

TRAIT 24

LACK OF TRUST, ETC.
(7 EXPRESSION
7 BIRTHDAY)

This paragraph brings together a lot of the negative 7 characteristics. Tapwa has so much to deal with that I didn't want to emphasize these traits, but, in the interest of an honest reading, they should be mentioned.

In your youth and young adulthood, you may have stressed your inward-turning ways and shown little trust in others. You may have been critical, unsympathetic or intolerant. There may have been a moodiness displayed along with nervousness and irritability. A stress on perfectionism may also have been present. All of these characteristics, of course, would push others away. As you've eliminated these traits, you've undoubtedly done away with many of your early problems.

TRAIT 25

DECEPTIONS.
(16/7 KARMIC DEBT)

This negative potential is a difficult one.

Remember my mentioning your Karmic Debts? Some of the problem areas we've just been discussing are related to these debts. In addition, because of them, you may, at times, meet with strangely manifesting deceptions or losses which often appear to be mere quirks of fate. You may, for instance, have a good friend go out of your life suddenly because of some odd circumstances.

You must cultivate an optimistic understanding along with the ability to keep faith in yourself and the universe despite adversity. If you lapse into self-pity or feel victimized, your difficulties will only feel greater.

We move on to the 6 Soul Urge and related modifiers.

TRAIT 26

RESPONSIBILITY.
   (6 SOUL URGE
    6 MODIFIED KARMIC LESSON)

Responsibility is likely to play an important part in your life. You're apt to have much responsibility to carry, quite possibly more than your fair share, but I'd expect you to be willing and able to carry as much responsibility as you're given. Some people can look to family or friends for help with their responsibilities. In your case, the family and friends may well look to you for their support.

TRAIT 27

DISCORDANT 1·6 ENERGY.

In the past, you undoubtedly ran into a conflict between your responsible side and your own strong needs. I suspect that, by now, you have learned to take care of both areas.

TRAIT 28

DISCORDANT 6·7 ENERGY.

You've probably had to learn how to meet your introspective desires while still taking care of the responsibilities in your life.

TRAIT 29

RECTIFYING, BALANCING, ETC.
   (6 SOUL URGE
    6 MODIFIED KARMIC LESSON)

A strong positive potential.

Along with your strong sense of responsibility, you're capable of rectifying and balancing situations, acting as a peacemaker, when necessary. (In your younger days, you may have mistaken interfering or being too protective with being helpful.) You're most capable of working with others, and it's at these times that your harmonizing abilities are put to good use. These attributes are likely to be especially visible in marriage and parenting situations. In a marriage, you may well be the one who keeps everything balanced and running smoothly.

TRAIT 30

HOME AND FAMILY.
   (6 SOUL URGE)

As a matter of fact, one of the focuses of your life is likely to be home, family and close friends. This could mean, at different times in your life, the family revolving around your parents, or the family you start with your husband. Much of your energy is likely to be devoted to the family and much of your satisfaction (or lack of satisfaction) is probably derived here at home. Sometimes, you need the safety of home and convention; at other times, you're desirous of breaking with the very conventions that previously proved satisfying.

The break with convention is partly due to the 1 energy, even more strongly to the 7 energy.

TRAIT 31

CREATIVE, ARTISTIC.
   (6 SOUL URGE)

There's an artistic side to you—you may enjoy creative activity in music, writing or the visual arts. This is not likely to be as strong as some of your other capabilities, but it probably gives you much pleasure. You get much enjoyment from a harmonious, beautiful environment.

The one 9 Intensity Point has not been discussed with the Soul Urge and related modifiers. It's described, instead, in the paragraphs on Trait 34.

TRAIT 32

INEFFECTIVENESS OF ENERGY.
    (7 EXPRESSION MINUS 1 LIFE PATH = 6: VERY
        INEFFECTIVE
     6 SOUL URGE MINUS 1 LIFE PATH = 5:
        INEFFECTIVE
     7 EXPRESSION MINUS 6 SOUL URGE = 1:
        EFFECTIVE)

If the energy had been relatively effective, I would have used the paragraphs devoted to the effectiveness to conclude the portion of the reading prior to the description of the Directing Modifiers.

Because of the ineffectiveness of the energy, I prefer to place this information here, so that I can then conclude on a stronger positive note with the description of the mind and emotions.

As you can see, you have an extremely diverse range of abilities. You have to study your environment carefully to find the opportunities to use your natural talents. The people and situations you meet don't always present the potential for growth and inner development which you are seeking. Sometimes, the development you've expected doesn't materialize even though you've performed well. Have you learned not to demand more of your world than is realistically there? I hope you've learned to pursue your main lesson of independence and attainment at the natural pace which presents itself.

You may find that, while the experiences at hand don't often directly fulfill your inner needs, these experiences can lead to awarenesses which can help with your growth in some indirect manner. For instance, you seem to have an inner need for home and family. This need may not be satisfied in the way you would prefer—you may end up with more responsibility or more time alone than you'd

like. But, as you get more comfortable with responsibility, as you learn to feel comfortable being
alone, you're likely to find the satisfactions you
originally wanted from your home and family.

TRAIT 33

FINE MIND.
   (7 EXPRESSION
    7 BIRTHDAY
    TWO 7'S INTENSITY POINT)

The 6·7 conflict again.

You have a fine mind, capable of analyzing and
discriminating, capable of deep mental analysis
when needed. Although you're capable of a logical, rational approach, you probably don't proceed that way all the time because of the strength
of your feelings.

TRAIT 34

STRONG EMOTIONS, REPRESSED IN EARLY YEARS.
   (6 SOUL URGE
    7 EXPRESSION
    7 BIRTHDAY
    TWO 7'S INTENSITY POINT
    ONE 9 INTENSITY POINT

*The 6·7 conflict still another time. Both the 6 and 7 indicate
strong feelings, but the 7 indicates strong* repressed *feelings.
Because of Tapwa's age, I'd expect that she's gotten rid of a
good deal of the repression.*

Let's talk about your strong emotions. Early in life,
I expect you emphasized the inner person that
we've discussed so that, to a large extent, you suppressed most of those deep feelings. You probably
showed little emotion and had difficulty understanding others' emotional responses as well. You
may have shown little sympathy or compassion.

As you've grown older, I presume that you've
achieved a better balance and can now comfortably express a good deal of those strong feelings.

There's a good chance that you now appear as a sympathetic, understanding, kind and generous person.

TRAIT 35

AFFECTION.
(6 SOUL URGE
7 BIRTHDAY)

The last of the 6·7 conflict.

In your early years, although you wanted affection, you probably had difficulty knowing how to get it. Your aloof or timid attitude may have stifled the very affection you desired. As your emotional expression has matured, I expect you've learned to give and receive much in the way of friendship, affection and love.

TRAIT 36

SENSITIVITY.
(2 CHALLENGE)

You were probably extremely sensitive in those early years and often hurt because of that sensitivity. Now, with a better balance, I presume you see your sensitivity as an important strength, allowing you to be acutely aware of so much of which others have little inkling, to make significant connections between awarenesses which others can barely fathom. I hope you've learned that your extreme sensitivity doesn't make you weak and inferior, as you may have once imagined, but rather makes you strong and superior—and helps make others willing to listen and learn from you.

TRAIT 37

INTUITION.
(7 EXPRESSION
7 BIRTHDAY
7 GROWTH NUMBER)

The paragraphs discussing Traits 36 and 37 are the last portions of the delineation to deal with Tapwa's basic energy. The reading was purposefully organized so that this section ends on a positive note.

Use your fine intuition to balance your deep feelings, your excellent mind, your sensitivity. Trust your intuition to lead you in the direction of growth.

Transition paragraph to a discussion of the Directing Modifiers.

The delineation, so far, has been covering the range of your energies along with some of the hindrances to their positive use. Let's look at your disposition now to get a picture of how you tend to apply your potentials.

TRAIT 38

BALANCED TEMPERAMENT.
   (STRONG MENTAL COMPONENT)

You have a reasonably balanced disposition; you're likely to show a bit more emphasis on mental or intellectual matters than on physical, emotional or spiritual affairs. It's likely that you'll use your fine mind a good deal. Facts and logic are apt to prove significant motivating forces.

Your ability to accomplish and lead may stress these intellectual attributes. I'd expect a good deal of effort devoted to study, research and fundamentals—here you can make good use of your fine powers of analysis. Your ability to harmonize and balance is related to your deep feelings, but even here I would expect to see the working of your strong analytic capabilities.

TRAIT 39

GENERAL APPROACH: CAUTIOUS EXPANSION.
   (FIRST VOWEL A
    FIRST LETTER T)

The leadership potential of the A is in conflict with the follower potential of the T.

Although you have a strong underlying desire to expand your life and cut loose from the strictures you find, I suspect that you proceed in a relatively subdued manner. When you use your leadership potential, it's probably with a relatively quiet approach, only occasionally with clear assertiveness. Your sensitivity and idealism tend to add to this toned-down picture. You're willing to present and discuss your original ideas, but too much opposition is likely to wear you down. I expect you move with care into unknown territory.

At times, you may scatter your energy. Sometimes, you feel frustrated with your inability to marshal your forces for maximum effect.

There are times when you feel more comfortable in a subservient rather than a leadership role. Your cautiousness, along with your understanding nature, is likely to produce a slow and steady growth pattern.

Although Tapwa was divorced when I met her, she was still using her married name: Tapwa Mufil. Several years after we met, she decided to change her name completely. She had never liked her first name, anyway, and she replaced the Tapwa with Alba. She wanted to use Mufiloh, a variant of her married name, as a new last name. She also chose a new middle name. So, Tapwa Mufil became Alba Same Mufiloh. (Both Tapwa Mufil and Alba Same Mufiloh are, of course, constructed pseudonyms with elements and modifiers almost identical with the names they replace.)

To complete the reading, I'll indicate the changes in energy to be expected with both names.

STEP 6

CALCULATE AND ORGANIZE THE DATA RELATED TO THE MARRIED NAME: TAPWA MUFIL.

Look at the partial calculation sheet (Figure 26-3 on page 453):

A. COMPARE THE BIRTH CORE TO THE NEW CORE.
    The 5 Expression replaces the 7 Expression of the birth
        core.
    The 5 Soul Urge replaces the 6 Soul Urge of the birth
        core.

$$\frac{2}{1\ \ 1} \ + \ \frac{(12)\ 3}{3\ \ 9} \ = \ \boxed{5}$$

TAPWA   MUFIL   (MARRIED NAME)

$$\frac{2\ 1\ 7\ 5\ 1\quad 4\ 3\ 6\ 9\ 3}{(16)\ 7\ \ + \ \ (25)\ 7} \ = \ \boxed{14/5}$$

two 1's
one 2
two 3's
one 4
one 5
one 6
one 7
no 8 ←
one 9

PHYSICAL	WM	2–Average
MENTAL	APAL	4–Strong
EMOTIONAL	TI	2–Average
INTUITIVE	UF	2–Average

EFFECTIVENESS:

$$\boxed{5} - \boxed{1} = 4$$

$$\boxed{5} - \boxed{1} = 4$$

$$\boxed{5} - \boxed{5} = \frac{10}{18}$$

Figure 26–3
Calculation Sheet:
Tapwa Mufil

The 5 Expression/5 Soul Urge replaces the 7 Expression/7
Birthday of the birth core.

The birth core is discordant but the new core is even
more discordant.

The birth core is ineffective but the new core is even
more ineffective.

B. COMPARE THE KARMIC DEBTS.

A 14/5 Karmic Debt with the new Expression is not present in the birthname.

C. COMPARE THE INTENSITY TABLES.

One 4 replaces the 4 Karmic Lesson of the birthname.

One 6 replaces the 6 Modified Karmic Lesson of the
birthname.

D. COMPARE THE SUB-ELEMENTS.
     The new name has two 7 sub-elements in the Expression
     while the birthname has 7 Expression/7 sub-element.

E. COMPARE THE MATURITY NUMBER TO BOTH
     NAMES.
     No 8 energy in either name to relate to the 8 Maturity
     Number.

F. COMPARE THE TEMPERAMENTS.
     No change.

G. COMPARE THE FIRST LETTERS AND FIRST
     VOWELS.
     No change.

H. COMPARE THE GROWTH NUMBER TO BOTH
     NAMES.
     The 7 Expression of the birthname related to the 7
     Growth Number. There's no 7 energy in the new
     name.

STEP 7

DELINEATE THE EFFECT OF THE MARRIED NAME:
TAPWA MUFIL.

Tapwa's married name, by adding the 5·5 and 14/5, converts a
portion of the basic energy to less usable energy. This is similar
to the case of Jack Dwight Coles in Chapter 24. Let's examine
the specifics for Tapwa:

*The 5 Expression and the 5 Soul Urge of the married name are
likely to present difficulties. The new energy is considerably
different than the basic energy and not easy to assimilate.*

When you got married and started to use your
married name, Tapwa Mufil, you probably had the
feeling there would be more excitement, adventure and variety in your life. You're likely to have
been disappointed when, as time passed, you perceived little in the way of change in that direction.

*The 14/5 Karmic Debt with the Expression of the married
name presents additional difficulties.*

You're liable to have felt erratic and restless,
jumping from activity to activity with little sense

of accomplishment or satisfaction. There may even have been some fear of freedom, a fear of taking risks (even while taking them) which added to your frustration. There may have been an excessive pull toward food, drink, drugs or sex.

One 4 in the married name replaces the 4 Karmic Lesson of the birthname.

One 6 in the married name replaces the 6 Modified Karmic Lesson of the birthname.

At the same time that you felt these strong effects, there was probably a little less emphasis on hard work and responsibility.

I expect that *these* changed energies may hardly have been noticed because of the feelings of restlessness and the fear of taking risks.

No 7 energy in the married name replaces the 7 Expression of the birthname. The 7 is the Growth Number.

You may well have felt less ability to find the peace and poise which you desired than before you were married. The peace you sought wasn't easy to approach before, but, in some way, it seemed even further away when you used your married name.

Marriage, in effect, is likely to have given you the hope of a freer and more expansive life—a hope with much promise and little return which probably tantalized and frustrated you.

There is no mention of the increased discordance and ineffectiveness in the married name. These are of little consequence in comparison to the 5·5 and the 14/5.

STEP 8

CALCULATE AND ORGANIZE THE DATA RELATED TO THE NEW NAME: ALBA SAME MUFILOH.

Look at the partial calculation sheet (Figure 26-4 on page 456):

A. COMPARE THE BIRTH CORE TO THE NEW CORE.
   The 3 Expression replaces the 7 Expression of the birth core.

$$\frac{2}{1\quad 1} + \frac{6}{1\quad 5} + \frac{(18)\ 9}{3\quad 9\quad 6} = 17 = \circled{8}$$

ALBA   SAME   MUFILOH   (NEW NAME)

$$\frac{1\,3\,2\,1 \quad 1\,1\,4\,5 \quad 4\,3\,6\,9\,3\,6\,8}{7 \quad + \quad 11 \quad + \quad (39)\ (12)\ 3} = 21 = \circled{3}$$

four 1's
one 2
three 3's
two 4's
one 5
two 6's
no 7 ←
one 8
one 9

PHYSICAL	MEM	3–Average
MENTAL	ALAALH	6–Strong
EMOTIONAL	BSIO	4–Strong
INTUITIVE	UF	2–Average

EFFECTIVENESS:

$$\circled{3} - \circled{1} = 2$$

$$\circled{8} - \circled{1} = 7$$

$$\circled{8} - \circled{3} = \underline{5}$$
$$\qquad\qquad\quad 14$$

Figure 26–4
Calculation Sheet:
Alba Same Mufiloh

The 8 Soul Urge replaces the 6 Soul Urge of the birth
   core.
There are no repeated elements in the new core. There's
   a 7 Expression/7 Birthday in the birth core.
The new core is relatively harmonious; the birth core is
   quite discordant.
The new core is slightly more ineffective than the birth
   core.

B. COMPARE THE KARMIC DEBTS.
   None in either name.

C. COMPARE THE INTENSITY TABLES.
   Two 4's replace the 4 Karmic Lesson of the birthname.

Two 6's replace the 6 Modified Karmic Lesson of the birthname.

One 8 replaces the 8 Karmic Lesson of the birthname.

D. COMPARE THE SUB-ELEMENTS.

The 3 Expression/3 sub-element replaces the 7 Expression/7 sub-element of the birthname.

E. COMPARE THE MATURITY NUMBER TO BOTH NAMES.

The 8 Soul Urge in the new name relates to the 8 Maturity Number. There's no related energy in the birthname.

F. COMPARE THE TEMPERAMENTS.

No change.

G. COMPARE THE FIRST LETTERS AND FIRST VOWELS.

The only change is the omission of the First Letter T in the new name.

H. COMPARE THE GROWTH NUMBER TO BOTH NAMES.

The 7 Expression of the birthname relates to the 7 Growth Number. There's no 7 energy in the new name.

STEP 9

DELINEATE THE EFFECT OF THE NEW NAME: ALBA SAME MUFILOH.

This new name introduces some new energy, but since the new energy is similar to some of the basic potential, the new energy is relatively usable. This new energy also helps convert some of the basic potential to more usable energy. The effect of this new name is similar to the case of Abbie Dumas Jefferson in Chapter 24. Here's the delineation for Alba:

The 8 Soul Urge (and the energy associated with the 8 Maturity Number) are similar to the 1 Life Path energy.

When you use the name Alba Same Mufiloh, as you do now, you pick up some extremely positive potential. You're likely to strengthen your executive abilities along with the vision and imagination you can apply to making a success in the commercial world. You are probably feeling a bit more ambitious, self-confident, efficient and energetic. These traits are closely related to your leadership potential so they should be relatively easy to assimilate and use.

One 8 replaces the 8 Karmic Lesson of the birthname.

Two 6's replace the 6 Modified Karmic Lesson of the birthname.

Two 4's replace the 4 Karmic Lesson of the birthname.

At the same time, you probably are dealing with money with somewhat less strain. You're apt to feel less pressure of responsibility, too. Your ability to work hard and to order and systematize are likely to be somewhat improved.

The new 3 Expression added to the 6 Soul Urge of the birthname, along with deletion of part of the 7·7 birth energy, makes for more openness, friendliness, etc.

The new 3·3 aspect means the probability of difficulties with self-expression along with some frivolousness. Frivolousness is usually a negative potential, but here it may well be positive if it serves to break down the rigidity of the birth energy.

You're apt to feel more open to others—more friendly, affectionate and loving as well as a bit more capable of expressing the delight you feel. You may feel a bit frivolous at times, and that may help you act more comfortably with others. You're likely to be a bit more aware of your difficulties with self-expression and your tendency to hide your emotions from yourself and others.

Less 7 energy in the new name than in the birthname to relate to the 7 Growth Number.

Deletion of First Letter T in new name.

You may still feel, just as with your married name, that you have less ability than you had to head toward the peace and poise which you would like so much. You're likely, though, to feel less subservient and less tense with your new name.

Relatively harmonious new core replaces quite discordant birth core.

The slight difference in ineffectiveness is of little consequence and is ignored.

> You probably feel that your energies flow together somewhat more harmoniously with your new name. That feeling of harmony will make it easier to make positive use of your potentials.

After Tapwa read the above delineation, she and I discussed the reading and I made a tape recording of her comments. The following is a portion of a transcription of her remarks:

Some comments on the delineation by the subject

TRAIT 1

LEARN THE BENEFITS OF INDEPENDENCE. LEARN TO STAND ON OWN TWO FEET. ACCOMPLISH, ATTAIN.

> My lesson of learning the benefits of independence, that's really true. I'm still working on it. I'm in the process of learning that it is, in fact, absolutely vital to me. Even now I realize, like when I feel too wrapped up in my future—since I'm going to get married again—I think "Whoa! You take care that you stand on your own two feet, young lady...."

TRAIT 2

LEADER, CREATOR, ETC.

> I don't know about leader and creator.... I feel a sense of that in terms of my work, in terms of teaching.... It ties in with my feeling of competence. You're saying I'm capable of taking charge, organizing. I'm definitely capable. I do that at work. In terms of inspiring others, that's an area where I'm instrumental sometimes in making a difference, not just in my children but teachers I work with. I definitely know that I have that ability if I choose to put energy into it....

TRAIT 3

ATTAINMENT, SATISFACTION.

> I've yet to see any decent financial gain....

TRAIT 4

PRACTICALITY.

> When I was younger, I was dreamy and unrealistic....I'm much more realistic, much more, in the last several years, much more grounded in what's what. . . .

TRAIT 5

ORGANIZATION, DETAILS.

> Yes, I *am* organized. It's really true. (laughing)

TRAIT 6

WORKING HARD.

> Amen! That's exactly what there is in my life—hard work....Hard work as limitation? It really is. More of the time, I see that work is important to me. . . .Sometimes, I think it's a pain in the neck to have to work so hard to live all the time . . . but I've switched my focus and I no longer think that life's not supposed to be work . . . but I don't like it! . . .

TRAIT 7

INNER STRENGTH, AMBITION, SELF-CONFIDENCE.

> Sometimes I feel that inner strength. It's keyed to when I'm feeling positive. When I'm not feeling positive, I don't feel it. I always thought it was more or less stubbornness. . . .

TRAIT 8

SELF-CENTERED.

TRAIT 9

LACK OF AWARENESS OF OTHERS.

TRAIT 10

STRONG PERSONAL NEEDS.

> My self-centeredness has probably been pretty easy for others to spot, not for me. It makes sense to me, but it's hindsight. It's not something I'm bothered by. I feel that my self-centeredness has

been a driving force for me to change and, in that respect, I'm grateful for it. I don't look on this as a great quality of mine, but it was a good thing, it served a purpose. Hopefully, I don't have to use it any more . . . I'd like that to be different. Now, I'm putting more energy into true giving, not reciprocation. . . .

TRAIT 11

REPRESSING NEEDS.

Definitely, if I have to repress my needs I feel resentful. . . . I don't know how big my Karmic Debt is, but it feels like it must have been a whopper. . . . This was one of the hardest parts to relate to. A part of me just still screams out "This isn't fair!" I feel like I've had so much to overcome and I've done a lot of it, and *still* I have to subordinate my needs.

TRAIT 12

PROBLEMS WITH MONEY AND MATERIAL SATISFACTIONS.

I don't know if I was careless with money. I don't relate to that, but I feel like I've always had problems in relation to money. . . . I have a different attitude now. . . . I think I understand money a little bit better than I used to. I see it more as an exchange. . . . When I got divorced, I was terrified about money. I did not know how to do the accounting at all. It had to do with who was responsible for it. . . . For the last few years, I am just constantly wishing I had more money. . . .

TRAIT 13

DEPENDENT.

Absolutely! Right! This paragraph was just very, very realistic, very right on to me.

TRAIT 14

FEARFUL, TIMID, ETC.

When I was a little girl, I was very shy, I was very

---

timid. I thought that the way that you could get what you needed in life—security and love—was to be a good girl and do everything my mommy and daddy wanted of me....I was a good girl. I was extremely repressed....

TRAIT 15

STUBBORN, SELF-CONTAINED.

You bet! I'm still very stubborn....I've changed. I'm much more open and when I'm open I like myself....I can get into that stubborn, rigid place, though, when I'm upset.

TRAIT 16

DOMINATING.

I think I was dominating. I probably did that much longer than just my early years....I was burdened by being the oldest in my family. I was the only one responsible for my brothers and sisters. I had to dominate because I was so scared because I knew I didn't have any power. I was very authoritarian....When I was married, I controlled things by appearing weak and helpless....I did that in relationships with men, in a manipulative sense, up until the last few years....

TRAIT 17

WISDOM, HIDDEN TRUTHS, TECHNICAL ABILITY.

I really *am* a teacher. I do look for hidden truths and wisdom, particularly in a spiritual context ....That question, "Who am I?" has been a prevalent part of me....

TRAIT 18

SPIRITUAL AWARENESS, PSYCHIC POWERS.

Psychic—only a teeny bit. I never really talked about it because it almost sounds silly....

TRAIT 19

PEACE AND FAITH.

Yes! I certainly didn't find serenity in my young years (laughing)....I don't think I use this potential. I don't know why but I find it a little fearful....It's like reaching a boundary and pushing through the boundary. I'm not quite ready to push through.

TRAIT 20

INTROSPECTIVE.

Absolutely! I do withdraw to recharge my batteries. I also withdraw just to withdraw....The house is so small, it's real difficult. When my children leave, I'll spend a weekend alone in the house, quite content, quite peaceful...I didn't realize how vital that was....

TRAIT 21

BEING ALONE.

I'm working on it. I've been working on it for a long time. I feel like I can do that to some degree...a long time ago, lonely was a problem.

TRAIT 22

DISCORDANT 1·7 ENERGY.

I always see myself as pretty shy, although much less than I used to be, for the most part....But the arena in which I'm the least shy is my work actually. I do a lot of leading there. I'm basically pretty outspoken....

TRAIT 23

"DIFFERENT" WAVELENGTH.

I don't know about these paragraphs, I don't think so...I think that what gets in the way for me of permanent relationships or anything else is my unwillingness to be myself. In a sense, it's a problem with communication because when I'm not myself, I'm not communicating.

TRAIT 24

LACK OF TRUST.

I haven't shown trust...I've definitely been very intolerant. In ways, I'm still intolerant of other people and certainly of myself....I have a perfectionist streak and it hasn't helped me a whole lot either. It's pushed people away. . . .Often been told I was moody in boy/girl relations when I was growing up, and still in relationships I now have.

TRAIT 25

DECEPTIONS.

It's depressing to read about that Karmic Debt, but it fits for me. One of the things it's allowed me to do as I kind of integrated that more into how I see the world is that it's let me let go of certain kinds of expectations of people. . . .It's very easy for me to feel victimized . . . and, if I do that, tap into that, I'm in big trouble. If I look at things from the negative side, that's what I get. It's so true, so true.

TRAIT 26

RESPONSIBILITY.

I think I have a lot of responsibility to carry, like the children. . . .I don't look on responsibility as such a chore as I used to. I used to think it was a terrible thing but now I think it's real important, that it has to do with everything. . . .That's a real big one.

TRAIT 27

DISCORDANT 1·6 ENERGY
No comment.

TRAIT 28

DISCORDANT 6·7 ENERGY
No comment.

TRAIT 29

RECTIFYING, BALANCING, ETC.

I do act as a peacemaker, definitely. It's most apparent in parenting and marriage. . . .I sometimes balance by making trouble and then resolving it.

TRAIT 30

HOME AND FAMILY.

The home and family are really a very good focus in my life. When I was young, until about eighteen, and went away to college, the home was *the* most important part of my life . . . I'm a real nester. Even when my husband had flown, my children were my nest. . . . In any way that I can be extremely upset, it will come from my home. Other things can bother me but that rocks me right down to the bottom.

TRAIT 31

CREATIVE, ARTISTIC.

Yes, I think there's an artistic side, but I'm only beginning to do that. . . .

TRAIT 32

INEFFECTIVENESS OF ENERGY.

It bothers me at school. I am really quite competent but nobody sees me as that, not really, and I don't toot my horn, maybe that's a part of it. . . . I feel like I have a dedication and a commitment that is extremely strong and that it is rarely picked up by anyone as being of any value. . . . I feel like I don't always know what's best for me, that, sometimes, something that may not seem to be right on the money really turns out to be something important. . . .

TRAIT 33

FINE MIND.
No comment.

TRAIT 34

STRONG EMOTIONS, REPRESSED IN EARLY YEARS.

I'm starting to change and deciding I don't want to be 100% on my feelings. It seems like years ago I was always either angry, depressed, or sad—a little bit of happy in relation to the children. . . . I feel like my feelings totally dominate my existence at times. I do not like that. It doesn't serve me that well. I feel like I'm coming to the middle of the road, where the feelings can be there but don't have to totally sway me. Boy, that's a hard middle of the road to get to and I'm nowhere near it.

TRAIT 35

AFFECTION.

Definitely had trouble knowing how to get affection. . . .My mother always told me that if you weren't nice, people wouldn't like you. What I discovered recently is that I'm often not nice—I'm nice sometimes—and I don't care if everyone doesn't like me. It's a burden to have to be nice.

TRAIT 36

SENSITIVITY.

Definitely was. I still am very sensitive. . . .As a child, my mother said to me *"You're too sensitive!"* and, in my being, I knew she was wrong. It's the only strength, I think, that's I've carried from my childhood. I knew I wasn't too sensitive, and that to be this sensitive wasn't a bad thing. I don't ever feel that it makes me weak and inferior. I do feel that I'm very strong from that place. . . .

TRAIT 37

INTUITION.

I do, now, trust my intuition. I've learned through therapy in the last seven or eight years. I didn't ever know I had intuition before.

TRAIT 38

BALANCED TEMPERAMENT.

I definitely tend to intellectualize even my feelings. I'm moving into a physical sphere for the first time. I do my exercises, and even that came from my bad back. . . .Even when I'm heavily in my emotions, I'm in an emotional-mental place.

TRAIT 39

GENERAL APPROACH: CAUTIOUS EXPANSION.

I don't cut loose and go for it in life. I'm real cautious. . . . Opposition doesn't change my mind; I just stop presenting. . . . I *do* feel frustrated because I don't focus myself. . . . It's easier for me not to make a big issue. I don't want to hassle it. . . .

TAPWA'S COMMENTS ON HER MARRIED NAME, TAPWA MUFIL:

The married name was my depressed place. All I did was get depressed. When I got married, I lost my feelings of independence. . . . I don't remember too well, but I remember a definite fear of freedom. . . .

I definitely didn't have any feeling of peace or poise for a long time. I don't know that I ever had it with that name. . . . I felt it somewhat when the children were born, for a short period of time. . . .

So hard for me to give anything to that name. I felt there was this big life opening up for me . . . and nothing happened good except the children. And, as for me, who I had been before that marriage, it was horrible, a devastation of me. I felt that I was a pretty strong, capable, independent person when I met my ex-husband. By the time we were divorced, I used to say I was a carrot, most of me underground, a few leaves on top. I had totally submerged my being. I had no clear picture of who I was at all.

AND FINALLY, HER FEELINGS ABOUT HER NEW NAME, ALBA SAME MUFILOH:

The new name is really very significant to me. I wanted more of a feeling of self than I had . . . . When I started therapy I decided to change my name, and that was a big step. . . . This was the beginning for me of my opening up. I felt like I was just starting to be a person then. I was definitely more aware of my feelings. All the pieces started to be put together in a better way.

By now, you're probably not surprised at the overall accuracy of the reading. I found Tapwa's comments, like the comments of many others who have had delineations, to be extremely useful. Tapwa's feedback illuminates various portions of the reading and gives a new, often broader, view to some of the characteristics under discussion. For instance:

In paragraph 7, Tapwa questions whether what I call inner strength may be what she calls stubbornness.

In paragraph 16, Tapwa felt that she was much more dominant in the early part of her life than indicated in the reading. Here, I had weighed the effect of the several conflicting energies and delineated the *probable* outcome. The actual outcome differed and, in this particular case, surprised me. (Be sure to delineate the subject matter broadly if you have any doubts about the probable resultant of several energies.)

In paragraph 19, I enjoyed Tapwa's view of her approach to peace and faith as "reaching a boundary and pushing through the boundary." I may want to use that description the next time I'm dealing with a similar potential.

In paragraph 29, I was delighted with Tapwa's view that she sometimes balances situations by "making trouble and then resolving it."

Your advanced delineations should be of considerable interest to the people receiving the readings. By learning from the subject's feedback, as here in Tapwa's example, your readings can become more subtly attuned to the intricacies of the personality.

PART V:
PROGRESSED
DELINEATION

CHAPTER 27

INTRODUCTION TO
PROGRESSED DELINEATION

At certain times in your life, you've probably had the feeling that the opportunities are available for exactly what you want to do. At other times, you've undoubtedly experienced the feeling that *nothing*'s going right, that you don't seem to be able to make the contacts you need and that you can't find a satisfactory outlet for the strong capabilities you have.

At any particular time in your life, there are specific energies and influences in operation which are not directly related to your basic characteristics. These energies and influences can be mapped by numerology. You can determine in advance the times of greatest opportunity. You can foresee problems and the areas in which they're likely to occur. Or, you can look back and get a clear picture of why some past experiences were so satisfying while others were so uncomfortable.

The mapping of these forces is accomplished by preparing a progressed delineation, a reading describing the probable events and opportunities at any specified time in the life. Some students are especially delighted at this point. "Aha!" they say, "now I'll be able to foretell the future." I'm sorry to say this isn't true. The progressed delineation *won't* allow you to predict your future or anyone else's, but it *will* allow you to:

> determine the influences operating at any time in an individual's life;
>
> determine when an individual's various energies can each be put to the best use;
>
> determine the times when obstacles to the use of various energies may be present;

determine the best times to convert negative energies to positive energies;

pinpoint the specific times when special opportunities are available.

What each individual does with this information is dependent on that individual's free will. Many of us, of course, learn how to make the most of the opportunities when they occur, as well as learning how to prepare for the difficulties when *they* occur. The information determined by the progressed delineation can be remarkably helpful but, ultimately, your life depends on what you choose to do with the energies you have in the circumstances in which you find yourself.

Definitions

A PROGRESSED DELINEATION, A DELINEATION FOR A PARTICULAR TIME PERIOD IN A SUBJECT'S LIFE, IS A SYNTHESIS OF THE SUBJECT'S PROGRESSED CYCLES FOR THAT PARTICULAR TIME PERIOD.

EACH PROGRESSED CYCLE DESCRIBES THE SEQUENCE OF PROBABLE INFLUENCES, EVENTS, OPPORTUNITIES AND/OR DESIRABLE APPROACHES FOR GROWTH DURING A SEQUENCE OF SPECIFIED TIME PERIODS.

The time spans of the different progressed cycles

There are between eight and eleven progressed cycles operating concurrently in any individual's life. The specified time periods, or phases, are of various durations. The shortest phase is one day. The phase of some of the longer cycles may be thirty or forty years. Some of the cycles make more of an impact on the life than others. Some of the phases of some cycles make more of an impact on the life than others.

There are two long term cycles, with phases lasting many years. They set the background tone of a subject's life.

There are between four and seven medium term cycles (the number varies with the individual), with phases lasting from one to nine years. They are often extremely significant, occasionally most dramatic in describing the influences on the subject's life.

There are two short term cycles, one with a phase lasting a month, one with a phase lasting a day. These cycles are important in pinpointing precise times for specific actions.

In Chapters 28 and 29, we'll introduce the long term cycles. We'll show how they're calculated, describe their duration, their particular effect and their significance.

In Chapter 30, we'll discuss the synthesis of the two long term cycles.

In Chapters 31 and 32, we'll examine the medium term cycles in similar detail and, in Chapter 33, we'll synthesize these cycles.

In Chapters 34 and 35, we'll describe the short term cycles.

Finally, in Chapter 36, we'll illustrate the synthesis of all the progressed cycles covered in the preceding chapters.

Our plan of study for progressed cycles

An individual's response to a cycle depends, among other things, on the energy available to that individual, the energy described by the individual's core and modifiers. Karen, for instance, with strong energy devoted to carrying responsibility, is likely to find many opportunities in a cycle requiring the carrying of responsibility. Given the desire to take advantage of the available opportunities, Karen is likely to find much in the way of growth and expansion. On the other hand, Arthur, with strong energy devoted to the expression of freedom, may find that same cycle full of obstacles and restrictions.

The response to a cycle probably will vary with age as well as desire for development. A child of ten usually reacts differently to a cycle emphasizing rest and meditation than an adult of twenty-five. A twenty year old is apt to react differently to a cycle stressing hard work than a forty year old. A person eager for growth is likely to use whatever influences are available and, in his own unique way, turn them to advantage. The individual less interested in growth may use only those influences which are harmonious with his own energies. He will probably struggle or rebel against influences less directly related to his energies.

The progressed delineation, then, should include not only the influences operating on an individual at a given time, but a description of the individual's probable reaction to those influences. I usually delineate the subject's probable approach to the events and opportunities expected, but, if possible, I also indicate alternate approaches which may bring less problems along with additional growth.

How an individual responds to the influences of the progressed cycles

The progressed cycles are derived from the birthdate and

Progressed
cycles derived
from the
birthdate and
birthname

the birthname. The subject's energies which determine the probable approach are, of course, also derived from the birthdate and birthname as previously described in Parts II and III of Volume 1, and from the new name(s) as previously described in Chapter 24, Part IV, of this volume.

Progressed
chart

Just as it was in character delineation, it's important to collect all the data completely and organize it carefully in preparing a progressed delineation. There is, as a matter of fact, a reason to be especially careful here—some of the very important medium term cycles run from January 1 to December 31 while others run from birthday to birthday. Unless the beginning and ending dates of a particular cycle are clearly distinguished, significant errors in the timing of probable influences may result.

I organize the progressed data on the progressed chart form (Figure 27-1 on page 475). (At the end of this chapter, on page 483, Figure 27-9 is a blank progressed chart form suitable for copying for your own use.) The form may look a bit complex at first, but I'm sure that, with a little practice, you'll find it easy to use and remarkably helpful.

First, look at the columns:

> Column I, marked "YEAR" provides the space to list the years under consideration.
> Column A, marked "AGE" provides the space to list the subject's ages in the years under consideration.
> The long term cycles are listed in columns J and K.
> The medium term cycles are listed in columns B through H.
> The short term cycles are not shown here.

Now, let's look at the horizontal rows. Each row represents one year of a person's life. The data covering *36* years can be included on one chart.

"But," you might say at even the first glance, "the rows don't go all the way across the chart. How come?" That break—between columns F and G—is the feature that makes the chart so useful.

The easiest way to understand that break is to look at the beginning steps in filling out the chart. Assume we're doing a progressed delineation for Edna Walker, born on June 30, 1958. We'll start by listing the years of Edna's life in the column marked "YEAR," beginning with 1958, Edna's year of birth.

When we've listed the years, the chart would look like Figure 27-2, page 476.

You can see that the rows on the right-hand side, up to the break at least, do indeed each represent one year. Let's look at this just a little more closely.

As the years proceed down the chart, the line at the top of each row represents the beginning of the year and the line at the bottom of the row represents the end of the year.

The first row represents 1958. Line L represents the beginning of the year, January 1, 1958. Line M represents the end of the year, December 31, 1958.

Age	Medium Term					Year	Long Term	
	Transits				Essence	Personal Year	Universal Year		Period	Pinnacle

Figure 27–1
Progressed Chart

The second row represents 1959. Line M *now* represents the beginning of this year, January 1, 1959 and line N represents the end of the year, December 31, 1959.

Line M, then, represents *both* December 31, 1958 and January 1, 1959. And line N represents both December 31, 1959 and January 1, 1960—and so on down the chart. Each horizontal line on the right-hand side of the chart represents December 31 of one year *and* January 1 of the succeeding year.

The space between the top and bottom lines of each row represents all the days in the year. If there were enough room, we could divide each row into 365 spaces, each representing one

Age	Medium Term					Year	Long Term	
	Transits		Essence	Personal Year	Universal Year		Period	Pinnacle
						1958		
1						1959		
						1960		
						1961		
						1962		
						1963		
						1964		
						1965		
						1966		
						1967		
						1968		
						1969		
						1970		
						1971		
						1972		
						1973		
						1974		
						1975		
						1976		
						1977		
						1978		
						1979		
						1980		
						1981		
						1982		
						1983		
						1984		
						1985		
						1986		
						1987		
						1988		
						1989		
						1990		
						1991		
						1992		
						1993		

Figure 27–2
Progressed Chart
Showing Year

day. We could, without too much trouble, actually divide each row into 12 spaces, each representing one month. We'll do just that for 1958 and label the spaces with the name of each month. We'll enlarge the row so it's easier to see what we're doing. Here's the result:

Remember that Edna was born on June 30, 1958. In the diagram above, her day of birth would be represented by line P. (That line would also represent July 1, 1958.) If you look back at Figure 27-2 on page 476, line P, on the left side of the chart, is the same line P as in the enlarged diagram above. In both cases, line P, halfway between line L and line M, represents Edna's day of birth.

On Figure 27-2, line Q, halfway between the beginning and end of 1959, represents Edna's first birthday, and line R, halfway between the beginning and end of 1960, represents Edna's second birthday. Between her first and second birthday, Edna is one year old, so we place a "1" in the "AGE" column in the row between lines Q and R.

Does it sound strange that Edna is *one* year old in the *second* year of her life? (When you say that a child is one year old, that's really a short way of indicating that the child has now lived one year and is now in the second year.) If Edna is one year old in her second year, then she would be two years old in her third year, three years old in her fourth year, and so on.

We take note of this in the progressed chart by writing the numbers 1, 2, 3, etc., one in each row, down the "AGE" column to the left (Figure 27-3 on page 478). For each age, the birthday representing the start of that age would be the line marking the top of the row with that age noted. In other words, the horizontal line between the row marked "26" and the row marked "27" represents the 27th birthday, and the horizontal line between the row marked "30" and the row marked "31" represents the 31st birthday.

But what about the first year of life? If Edna is two years old in her third year and one year old in her second year, then she is *zero* years old in her first year. (Looking at it another way, if your first birthday indicates you've lived one year and are one year old, then on the day you're born you've lived *zero* years and are *zero* years old.) A zero is placed in the first row of the "AGE" column to denote this situation.

Age	Medium Term					Year	Long Term	
	Transits			Essence	Personal Year	Universal Year		Period	Pinnacle
0							1958		
1							1959		
2							1960		
3							1961		
4							1962		
5							1963		
6							1964		
7							1965		
8							1966		
9							1967		
10							1968		
11							1969		
12							1970		
13							1971		
14							1972		
15							1973		
16							1974		
17							1975		
18							1976		
19							1977		
20							1978		
21							1979		
22							1980		
23							1981		
24							1982		
25							1983		
26							1984		
27							1985		
28							1986		
29							1987		
30							1988		
31							1989		
32							1990		
33							1991		
34							1992		
35							1993		

Figure 27-3
Progressed Chart
with Age Added

THE LEFT-HAND ROWS, THEN, THE ROWS DIFFER-
ENTIATED BY AGE, EACH REPRESENT A YEAR RUN-
NING FROM BIRTHDAY TO BIRTHDAY. THE RIGHT-
HAND ROWS, THE ROWS DIFFERENTIATED BY THE
CALENDAR YEARS, EACH REPRESENT A YEAR START-
ING ON JANUARY 1 AND ENDING ON DECEMBER 31.
THE BREAK OCCURS BECAUSE, IN GENERAL, THE
BIRTHDAY-TO-BIRTHDAY YEAR DOESN'T COINCIDE
WITH THE CALENDAR YEAR.

Now, Edna was conveniently born on June 30, exactly in the
middle of the year. If she'd been born on July 28 or April 14,
the rows on the left side of the chart would, theoretically, be a
little lower or higher in relation to the rows on the right side. In
practice, though, the progressed chart, as shown, works just
fine. The lines at the top and bottom of the rows at the left
always represent the birthdays, no matter whether the birthdays fall early or late in the year.

In the rest of Part V, we'll be completing the progressed chart
and interpreting the data. But even without filling out the rest
of the chart, we can surmise that changes in the influences in a
subject's life occur (1) at the beginning of each calendar year
(when changes occur in the cycles on the right side of the
chart), and (2) at each birthday (when changes occur in the
cycles on the left side of the chart).

When changes occur in the influences on a subject's life

There are a few special times when the birthday year and the
calendar year coincide (or virtually coincide). If Edna had been
born on January 1, 1958, the beginning of the chart should look
like Figure 27-4 on page 480.

As you can see, the lines representing the birthdays here are a
continuation of the lines representing January 1, and the rows
are continuous across the entire chart. Since we're using a progressed chart form with a break in the middle, we indicate this
special case by drawing short diagonals at the break line, as on
Figure 27-5 on page 480.

We delineate the progressed cycles, in this case, knowing
that changes in the influences occur only once a year on
January 1.

Special case: Birthday on January 1

Age	Medium Term					Year	Long Term	
	Transits			Essence	Personal Year	Universal Year		Period	Pinnacle
0							1958		
1							1959		
2							1960		
3							1961		
4							1962		
5							1962		

Figure 27–4
Progressed Chart:
Special Case

Special case: Birthday in the first half of January

If a subject is born anytime in the first half of January, the birthday year and the calendar year are *virtually* coincident. I delineate these charts in the same manner as if the subject had been born on January 1, with the changes in the influences occurring only once a year on January 1.

Special case: Birthday on December 31

Now suppose, instead, that Edna had been born on December 31, 1958. The beginning of the chart should look like Figure 27-6 on page 481.

In this case, the lines representing the birthday are virtually coincident with the lines representing January 1 *of the succeeding year.* We are still using the same progressed chart form, so we indicate this condition by again drawing short diagonals at the break line, this time slanting the other way, as on Figure 27-7 on page 481.

Here, again, changes in the influences occur only once a year, on December 31/January 1. Note that the row representing age zero on the left coincides with the row representing the year *1959* on the right even though the date of birth is in *1958.*

Age	Medium Term					Year	Long Term	
	Transits			Essence	Personal Year	Universal Year		Period	Pinnacle
0							1958		
1							1959		
2							1960		
3							1961		
4							1962		
5							1963		

Figure 27–5
Progressed Chart:
Special Case

Age	Medium Term					Year	Long Term	
	Transits			Essence	Personal Year	Universal Year		Period	Pinnacle
							1958		
0							1959		
1							1960		
2							1961		
3							1962		
4							1963		

Figure 27-6
Progressed Chart:
Special Case

If a subject is born anytime in the last half of December, the birthday year is *virtually* coincident with the succeeding calendar year. I delineate these charts as if the subject were born on December 31, with the changes in the influences just once a year on December 31/January 1.

Special case: Birthday in the last half of December

In this chapter, we'll begin the progressed chart for Harlan William Allen, the fictitious subject first introduced in Volume 1. You may want to refresh your memory about Harlan's energies by reading his complete character delineation on pages 198–217 of Chapter 21, Volume 1, or a summary of his character delineation on pages 217–218 of the same chapter.

Harlan William Allen (or Hal Allen, as we'll call him for short) was born on May 12, 1941. We can fill in the "YEAR" and "AGE" columns just as we did previously for Edna Walker (Figure 27-8 on page 482).

If we wanted Hal's chart past age 35, we'd paste 2 sheets together or continue on another sheet. Later, on pages 566–568 in Chapter 33, we'll discuss a short-cut to determine the influences at any age without having to figure all the years in between.

Beginning a progressed chart for Hal Allen

Age	Medium Term					Year	Long Term	
	Transits			Essence	Personal Year	Universal Year		Period	Pinnacle
0							1958		
1							1959		
2							1960		
3							1961		
4							1962		
5							1963		

Figure 27-7
Progressed Chart:
Special Case

Preview
of the
succeeding
chapters in
Part V

In the succeeding chapters in Part V, we'll keep adding to Hal's progressed chart until it's completed. As we add specific data for each cycle to the chart in Chapters 28 through 35, we'll also do the portion of Hal's progressed delineation described by that data.

In Chapter 36, we'll do a complete delineation for two years in the life of Hope Edythe Lynch, a fictional construct like Hal. This complete delineation, like the partial delineations in the previous chapters, will be annotated to indicate the derivation of the information included.

HARLAN WILLIAM ALLEN
MAY 12, 1941

Age	Medium Term					Year	Long Term	
	Transits				Essence	Personal Year	Universal Year		Period	Pinnacle
0								1941		
1								1942		
2								1943		
3								1944		
4								1945		
5								1946		
6								1947		
7								1948		
8								1949		
9								1950		
10								1951		
11								1952		
12								1953		
13								1954		
14								1955		
15								1956		
16								1957		
17								1958		
18								1959		
19								1960		
20								1961		
21								1962		
22								1963		
23								1964		
24								1965		
25								1966		
26								1967		
27								1968		
28								1969		
29								1970		
30								1971		
31								1972		
32								1973		
33								1974		
34								1975		
35								1976		

Figure 27-8
Progressed Chart:
Hal Allen

Age	Medium Term					Year	Long Term	
	Transits				Essence	Personal Year	Universal Year		Period	Pinnacle

Figure 27–9
Blank Progressed Chart Form

CHAPTER 28

LONG TERM CYCLES, PART 1: THE LIFE PATH PERIODS

The two long term cycles, the Life Path Periods and the Pinnacles, set the background tone for long phases of the life. They produce no abrupt or insistent effect, but, rather, are strong determinants of the general influences. They are important cycles.

THE THREE LIFE PATH PERIODS IN EACH PERSON'S LIFE DESCRIBE THE PROBABLE GENERAL INFLUENCES IN THE THREE PHASES OF THE LIFE AS ASPECTS OF THE LIFE PATH DIRECTION. (The Life Path Periods—or Periods, for short—are also often called Cycles, but the term "Cycles" is not used here to avoid confusion with the general term "cycles.") When we discussed the Birthday element in Chapter 6 of Volume 1, we described the many different lanes of the Life Path highway. Here, we have a similar analogy. If you again think of the many-laned highway of the Life Path, the Period is the lane on which the subject is traveling at a particular time. The lane describes the general influences acting on the individual. Since there are three Periods, most people occupy three different lanes—or live under three different general influences—during the course of their lives. From a description of these probable influences, a subject can determine which of his energies will be most useful. **Definition**

The First Period, or Developmental Period of the Life Path, covers youth and young adulthood. The important childhood **First Period** and adolescent influences, the character of the family, the prevalent influences as the young person moves out into the world are all described here. In addition to dealing with the current influences, the subject would be well advised to prepare a foundation for the next Period in the later years of this one. The First Period often appears to be the restrictive because the youth or young adult usually has less ability than the mature adult to convert any negative potential to positive as well as less ability to deal with the negative influences present.

Second Period

The Second Period, or Productive Period of the Life Path, covers the important middle years, the time when a person is likely to be moving forward in his chosen work as well as in raising a family. Here, the individual often has the potential of operating at the height of his powers, expanding his life, delighting in the opportunities coming his way, receiving recognition from his peers. In addition to dealing with the influences of this period, the subject should again lay a foundation for the next Period in the later years of this one.

Third Period

The Third Period, or Integrative Period of the Life Path, covers the later years of life: the closing of the career (sometimes accompanied by the culmination of the career) and the retirement period, years often devoted to reflection and integration of all that has gone before. The "feel" of the Third Period is heavily dependent on the growth and satisfactions of the previous Period. Lack of development in that middle Period may leave a residue of pain, guilt or resentment which may strongly affect this time.

Calculation

The Periods, being aspects of the Life Path, are described by the three sub-elements that combine to form the Life Path:

THE FIRST PERIOD IS DESCRIBED BY THE SUB-ELEMENT OF THE *MONTH* OF BIRTH.

THE SECOND PERIOD IS DESCRIBED BY THE SUB-ELEMENT OF THE *DAY* OF BIRTH.

THE THIRD PERIOD IS DESCRIBED BY THE SUB-ELEMENT OF THE *YEAR* OF BIRTH.

The sub-element has, of course, been reduced to a single digit or master number.

If there's a karmic number behind the sub-element—19 behind the 1, 13 behind the 4, 14 behind the 5, 16 behind the 7—the karmic number should be noted because it will probably strongly affect the Period.

If Patty was born on October 18, 1951, her Life Path cal-   **Examples**
culation would look like this:

```
October   18,   1951
   1      (9)    7   = 17 = (( 8 ))
```

Her First Period is 1, the sub-element of the month.
Her Second Period is 9, the sub-element of the day.
Her Third Period is 16/7, the sub-element of the year.
    The 16/7 notation expresses the karmic number
    behind the year sub-element.

A few more examples:

```
December   14,   1950
   3       (5)    6   = (( 14/5 ))
```

First Period = 3

Second Period = 14/5
    The 14/5 notation expresses the karmic number
    behind the day sub-element.

Third Period = 6

```
August   29,   1800
   8     (11)    9   = 28 = 10 = (( 1 ))
```

First Period = 8

Second Period = 11/2
    The 11/2 notation expresses a Period with a master
    number.

Third Period = 9

The First Period starts at birth.   **Time span**
    The Second Period starts on January 1 of the 1 Personal Year
closest to the 28th birthday.
    The Personal Year is a medium term cycle described in

Chapter 31. To calculate the Personal Year, add the month of birth, day of birth and year under consideration (all reduced to a single digit or master number), then reduce the sum to a single digit or master number.

Example: Ross was born on July 18, 1923. What's his Personal Year in 1981?

Month of birth:	July $= 7$
Day of Birth:	$18 = 1 + 8 = 9$
Year under consideration:	1981
	$= 1 + 9 + 8 + 1$
	$= 19 = \underset{17}{1}$
	$= 1 + 7$
	$= 8$ Personal Year

The Third Period starts on January 1 of the 1 Personal Year closest to the 56th birthday and continues the rest of the life. Here's a chart for convenience:

TIME SPAN OF LIFE PATH PERIODS

Time
Span
Chart

Life Path	First Period	Second Period	Third Period
	age:	age:	age:
1	0-26	27-53	54 on
2 or 11/2	0-25	26-52	53 on
3	0-24	25-51	52 on
4 or 22/4	0-23	24-59	60 on
5	0-31	32-58	59 on
6	0-30	31-57	58 on
7	0-29	30-56	57 on
8	0-28	29-55	56 on
9	0-27	28-54	55 on

Transition
between
Periods

The transition between Periods tends to be gradual. Even though the new Period starts in a 1 Personal Year, it usually is felt to a limited degree two or three years before the 1 Personal Year. The old Period doesn't stop abruptly at the 1 Personal Year, either, but its influence gradually fades away over the next two or three years.

Example:
Hal Allen's
calculation

We'll return to Hal Allen and determine his Periods and their time spans.

Hal was born on

May   12,   1941
5   ⌣3⌣   6   =   ⦿14/5⦿

Hal has a 5 First Period.
    From the Time Span Chart, Hal's First Period
    extends from birth to age 31.
He has a 3 Second Period.
    From the Time Span Chart, Hal's Second Period
    extends from age 32 to 58.
He has a 6 Third Period.
    From the Time Span Chart, Hal's Third Period
    extends from age 59 on.

We can show this information on our calculation sheet like
this:

May   12   1941
5   ⌣3⌣   6   =   ⦿14/5⦿
(0-31)   (32-58)   (59 on)

These notations are shorthand for the following:

Hal's 5 First Period starts at birth and continues, in full
force, to the end of 1972 (age 31). It then fades out over the
next two or three years.
    Hal's 3 Second Period is in full force from the beginning of
1973 (the year in which Hal turns 32) to the end of 1999 (age
58). It is probably first felt to a limited degree at the start of
1970 (three years before 1973). It doesn't completely fade out
until the end of 2002 (three years after 1999).
    Hal's 6 Third Period is in full force from the beginning of
2000 (the year in which Hal turns 59) through the rest of his
life. It is probably first felt to a limited degree at the start of
1997 (three years before 2000).

Adding the Period data to Hal Allen's progressed chart

For ease in delineation, we'll transfer all this information to
Hal Allen's progressed chart which we started in Chapter 27.
With the information added, the chart would look like Figure
28-1 on page 490. Note especially the strong horizontal lines at
the start of the Second and Third Periods. The transition from
one phase to another in *any* cycle is important. It's emphasized
on the chart by a horizontal line.

HARLAN WILLIAM ALLEN
MAY 12, 1941

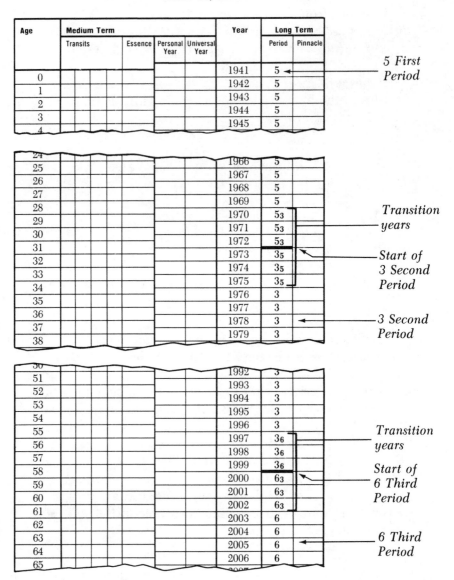

Age	Medium Term					Year	Long Term	
	Transits			Essence	Personal Year	Universal Year		Period	Pinnacle
0							1941	5
1							1942	5
2							1943	5
3							1944	5
4							1945	5

5 First Period

24							1966	5
25							1967	5
26							1968	5
27							1969	5
28							1970	5$_3$
29							1971	5$_3$
30							1972	5$_3$
31							1973	3$_5$
32							1974	3$_5$
33							1975	3$_5$
34							1976	3
35							1977	3
36							1978	3
37							1979	3
38								

Transition years

Start of 3 Second Period

3 Second Period

50							1992	3
51							1993	3
52							1994	3
53							1995	3
54							1996	3
55							1997	3$_6$
56							1998	3$_6$
57							1999	3$_6$
58							2000	6$_3$
59							2001	6$_3$
60							2002	6$_3$
61							2003	6
62							2004	6
63							2005	6
64							2006	6
65							2007	

Transition years

Start of 6 Third Period

6 Third Period

Figure 28–1
Progressed Chart
with Periods:
Hal Allen

CHART 14: THE LIFE PATH PERIODS, on page 696, describes the three different Periods for each of the single digits and master numbers. In general terms, the First Period usually displays limiting influences, the Second Period usually produces influences and opportunities for expansion, and the Third Period sometimes describes influences supportive of reflection and retirement, sometimes influences supportive of bustling activity.

The strong negative influence of the karmic number is described in the bottom row of the chart. The negative impact would modify the general description of the particular Period. A 13/4 Second Period, for example, would be described by combining the general description of the 4 Period from the top row of the chart, the description of the 4 Second Period from the third row of the chart, and the description of the 13/4 karmic Period from the bottom row. The First Period, usually limiting enough, is never a karmic Period.

Chart 14: Life Path Periods

A delineation of any Period includes the following:

A. The general description of the influences along with the specific description of the First, Second or Third Period (FROM CHART 14: THE LIFE PATH PERIODS), *expressed as an aspect of the subject's Life Path*. It's easier, of course, to read the general and specific description and ignore the Life Path, but the distortion that results should be apparent. Consider, for instance, a 5 Second Period on a 7 Life Path as compared to a 5 Second Period on a 5 Life Path. In the first example, the activity and change of the Period are likely to provide an uncomfortable backdrop for studious, meditative or introspective activities while, in the second case, the freedom and variety of the Period provide a fine stage for the individual's expansive approach.

  With a 22 Period, describe both the 22 and 4 Periods, and with the 11 describe both the 11 and 2. (There's never a 22 First Period, and although the 11 First Period can exist mathematically, it always reduces to a 2 First Period.) The influences of both the higher and lower levels of the master number would probably be present, subject to the individual's desire or ability to use them.

B. The karmic Period description, from the bottom row of CHART 14: THE LIFE PATH PERIODS, if applicable. The negative potential, along with suggestions for overcoming the obstacles, should be included.

C. The subject's potentials—both from the birthname and current name(s), as well as the birthday. A knowledge of the subject's potentials provides insight into the individual's

Delineation description

ability to operate with the current influences. The core elements, Karmic Debts and Karmic Lessons may be of importance, along with any other strong modifiers which either flow or conflict with the influences. Usually, the elements or modifiers with a number matching the Period number are of particular import.

D. Preparation for the next Period. This is usually of importance only in the last few years of the current Period. Sometimes, though, when a Period is considerably different than the previous Period or when the influences of the Period may strongly conflict with the subject's potentials, a longer period of preparation may be helpful.

Hal Allen's Period delineation

Below are the delineations of Hal Allen's three Periods along with the description of his transition years. (We're assuming here that Hal's birthname is also his current name—that there are no additional energies from new names.) Each portion of the delineation is written in the present tense. In an actual delineation, of course, you would usually be discussing the current Period only.

Hal Allen's calculation sheet (Figure 28-2 on page 493) and organization sheet (Figure 28-3 on page 494) are repeated from Chapter 21 of Volume 1. We'll need to refer to these sheets in collecting the data on Hal's potentials.

5 FIRST PERIOD

1941–1972 (birth to the end of the year in which Hal turned 31).

THE DATA:
A. 5 First Period on a 5 Life Path.
B. No karmic Period.
C. 14/5 Karmic Debt on Life Path
   5 Life Path/5 sub-element
   6 Expression and 6 Modified Karmic Lesson conflicting with 5 energy
D. Prepare for 3 Second Period.

The body of the paragraph is from the general 5 Period description and the 5 First Period description on Chart 14.

As a child and young adult, you probably find yourself in a constantly changing environment with much uncertainty and travel. This is probably

May 12, 1941

$5 + 3 + 6 = \boxed{14/5}$

$$5 - 3 = 2$$
$$6 - 3 = 3$$
$$3 - 2 = 1 \text{ CHALLENGE}$$

$$\frac{2}{1 \quad 1} + \frac{(19)\ 1}{9 \quad 9\,1} + \frac{6}{1 \quad 5} = \boxed{9}$$

HARLAN WILLIAM ALLEN

$$\frac{8 \quad 9\,3 \quad 5}{(25)\ 7} + \frac{5 \quad 3\,3 \quad 4}{(15)\ 6} + \frac{3\,3 \quad 5}{11} = 24$$
$$= 6 \text{ SECRET SELF}$$

$$\frac{8\,1\,9\,3\,1\,5}{(27)\ 9} + \frac{5\,9\,3\,3\,9\,1\,4}{(34)\ 7} + \frac{1\,3\,3\,5\,5}{(17)\ 8} = 24 = \boxed{6}$$

four 1's
no 2 ←
five 3's
one 4
four 5's
no 6 ←
no 7 ←
one 8
three 9's

PHYSICAL	WME	3–Average
MENTAL	HALANLLAALLN	12–Strong
EMOTIONAL	RII	3–Average
INTUITIVE		0–Weak

MATURITY NUMBER $= 5 + 6 = 11/2$

Figure 28-2
Calculation Sheet:
Hal Allen

a difficult atmosphere for you or any young person because of the continual feeling of restlessness, possibly accentuated by a fluctuating money supply. It may seem like a good environment in which to learn the exhilaration of the constructive use of freedom (5 *Life Path*). At this early stage in your life, though, your tendencies to be erratic and proceed with little sense of accomplishment (*14/5 Karmic Debt and 5·5*), your problem with excessive

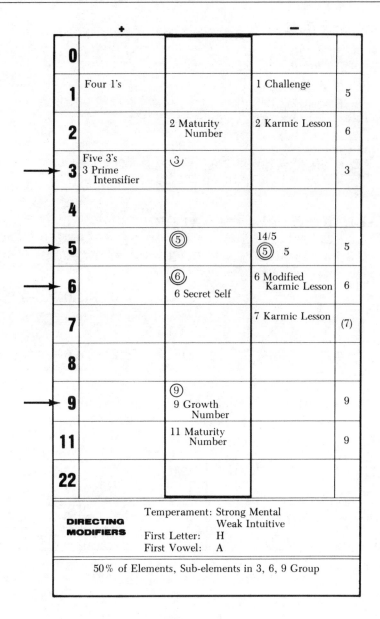

	+		−	
0				
1	Four 1's		1 Challenge	5
2		2 Maturity Number	2 Karmic Lesson	6
3	Five 3's 3 Prime Intensifier	③		3
4				
5		⑤	14/5 ⑤ 5	5
6		⑥ 6 Secret Self	6 Modified Karmic Lesson	6
7			7 Karmic Lesson	(7)
8				
9		⑨ 9 Growth Number		9
11		11 Maturity Number		9
22				

DIRECTING MODIFIERS	Temperament: Strong Mental 　　　　　　　　Weak Intuitive First Letter:　H First Vowel:　A
50% of Elements, Sub-elements in 3, 6, 9 Group	

Figure 28–3
Organization Sheet:
Hal Allen

physical appetites (*14·5 Karmic Debt and 5·5*), your difficulty in learning the lesson of change: to begin, nurture, experience and detach (*14/5 Karmic Debt*)—all are likely to be emphasized in this environment. Although you're capable of carrying much responsibility (*6 Expression, 6 Modified Karmic Lesson*), you're not likely to encounter much of it at this time.

From 1963 through 1972 (age 22-31), the last ten years of the First Period, I'd add the following in preparation for the next Period. Usually, the next Period would only be mentioned within four or five years of the end of the current Period, but, because of the nature of the Second Period, the preparation is likely to take longer.

> You're going to spend most of your productive years in a rather permissive atmosphere and you're likely to get more out of those years if you learn to curb your appetites and your restless nature. Failure to make headway in these important areas in the next few years may limit your pleasures and accomplishments later. (*See the second paragraph of the 3 Second Period on Chart 14.*)

From 1970 through 1972 (age 29-31), the 3 Second Period is felt to a limited degree.

> You're likely to feel somewhat more interest in friendships, artistic pursuits and verbal activities now than you did previously. (*See the 3 Second Period description on Chart 14*).

3 SECOND PERIOD

1973-1999 (beginning of year in which Hal turned 32 to end of year in which Hal turned 58)

THE DATA:
A. 3 Second Period on a 5 Life Path.
B. No karmic period.
C. 3 Birthday (Birthday always same as Second Period)
    Five 3's Intensity Point
    3 Prime Intensifier
D. Prepare for 6 Third Period.

The body of the paragraph below is from the general 3 Period description and the 3 Second Period description on Chart 14.

> If you've made some headway in controling your restless nature and in using freedom constructively (*5 Life Path*), this may well be a time of delight and pleasure. There's likely to be much social life and

entertainment along with artistic pursuits and verbal activities such as acting or writing. With your adaptability and verve (5 *Life Path*), social skills, imagination, creative talents and verbal abilities (3 *Birthday, five 3's Intensity Point, 3 Prime Intensifier*), you may even find recognition and financial gain. There's likely to be much activity and possibly travel, but there's apt to be less of the frenetic quality of your younger years. You may still have some tendency to waste your energies or to act capriciously or self-indulgently (3 *Birthday, five 3's Intensity Point*). Unless these tendencies are controlled, there's likely to be frustration and loss of time and direction.

From 1973 through 1975 (age 32-34), the 5 First Period is fading out.

You may notice, although there's still lots of activity in your life, that the erratic quality seems to be lessening. (*See the 5 First Period description on Chart 14*).

From 1990 through 1999 (age 49–58), the last ten years of the Second Period, I'd add the following in preparation for the 6 Third Period. This, again, is a long period of preparation, but the sharp contrast between the middle and last Periods warrants it.

In the later years of your life, you may have substantial responsibilities which are likely to feel particularly limiting after the freedom you've enjoyed until then. Begin to consider how to deal with your restlessness in a restricted environment, how to express freedom constructively despite the limitations. (*See the 6 Third Period description on Chart 14.*)

From 1997 through 1999 (age 56-58), the 6 Third Period is felt to a limited degree:

There may be more responsibility in your life now

than previously, or you may become aware of some responsibilities that may be yours in the next few years. You may find the pace of activity beginning to slow. (*See the 6 Third Period description on Chart 14.*)

6 THIRD PERIOD

2000 on (beginning of year in which Hal turns 59, and on)

THE DATA:
A. 6 Third Period on a 5 Life Path.
B. No karmic Period.
C. 6 Expression
    6 Modified Karmic Lesson
    5 Life Path conflicting with 6 energy
D. This is last Period, no preparation required for another Period.

The body of the paragraph below is from the general 6 Period description and the 6 Third Period description in Chart 14.

In these later years of your life, there's a possibility of a supportive environment centered around home and family, an atmosphere of love and caring. With your restless nature, you may not be able to take full advantage of the opportunities and, instead, may feel restricted and tied down (*conflict with the 5 Life Path*). There are likely to be responsibilities here, but you have substantial capabilities in that direction (*6 Expression, 6 Modified Karmic Lesson*). After the relatively loose environment of your early and middle years, this far more structured situation may be much less to your liking.

From 2000 through 2002 (age 59-61), the 3 Second Period is fading out.

You may feel a slowdown in the pace of activities now. There's likely to be a quieter social life than previously. (*See the 3 Second Period description on Chart 14.*)

For Hal, as for most of us, the ability to pursue the lesson of his Life Path in his First Period will strongly affect his dealings in the Second Period. And, similarly, his mastery (or lack of mastery) of the lesson in the first and middle Periods will certainly mark his last. The numerologist has no way of knowing when (or even if) the lesson is learned, so the Period delineation must be rendered broadly to cover the many possibilities.

CHAPTER 29

LONG TERM CYCLES, PART 2: THE PINNACLES

THE FOUR PINNACLES DESCRIBE THE GENERAL IN- **Definition**
FLUENCES DURING EACH OF THE FOUR PINNACLE
PHASES OF THE LIFE. The Pinnacles have no direct relation
to the Life Path like the Periods, but they are, nevertheless, important in the description of the tone of the individual's
background.

The First Pinnacle, or Developmental Pinnacle, covers youth **First**
and young adulthood. It describes some of the influences **Pinnacle**
strongly affecting the young person's development. It's particularly important to build a foundation here in the First Pinnacle for the Second and Third Pinnacles. The First Pinnacle,
like the First Period, often appears limiting.

The Second and Third Pinnacles are two shorter phases (nine **Second**
years each) which together span the important middle years. **and**
Both are involved with what is often the most productive **Third**
period of the life, so they may be thought of as Productive Pin- **Pinnacles**
nacles A and B. The influences described are very important
and usually overshadow the influences of the concurrent
Period. The Third Pinnacle, more often than not, is more ex-
pressive and more productive than the Second, so that it may
be well to devote a good deal of energy in the Second Pinnacle
to preparation for the Third. A bit of attention should be given
in the Third Pinnacle to preparation for the Fourth.

The Fourth Pinnacle, or Integrative Pinnacle, is similar to the **Fourth**
Integrative Period in covering the later years of life. The "feel" **Pinnacle**
of this last Pinnacle is heavily dependent on the growth and

satisfactions of the productive period of life, the previous *two* Pinnacles. The influences of the period affect the subject about as much as the satisfied (or dissatisfied) sense of development he brings to the start of the Pinnacle.

Calculation

The Pinnacles are found by simple addition. The sum is reduced to a single digit or master number.

THE FIRST PINNACLE IS THE SUM OF THE MONTH AND DAY SUB-ELEMENTS OF THE LIFE PATH.

THE SECOND PINNACLE IS THE SUM OF THE DAY AND YEAR SUB-ELEMENTS OF THE LIFE PATH.

THE THIRD PINNACLE IS THE SUM OF THE FIRST AND SECOND PINNACLES.

THE FOURTH PINNACLE IS THE SUM OF THE MONTH AND YEAR SUB-ELEMENTS OF THE LIFE PATH.

Time span

The First Pinnacle starts at birth. To determine the subject's age at the end of the First Pinnacle, subtract the Life Path from 36. (If the Life Path is a master number, reduce it to a single digit before subtracting.) The First Pinnacle ends on December 31 of the year in which the subject reaches the determined age.

The Second Pinnacle starts on January 1 of the following year and lasts nine years.

The Third Pinnacle starts on January 1 of the year after the Second Pinnacle ends and lasts nine years.

The Fourth Pinnacle starts on January 1 of the year after the Third Pinnacle ends and continues the rest of the life.

We can sum this up in a simple chart:

Time Span Chart

TIME SPAN OF PINNACLES

Life Path	First Pinnacle	Second Pinnacle	Third Pinnacle	Fourth Pinnacle
	age:	age:	age:	age:
1	0-35	36-44	45-53	54 on
2 or 11/2	0-34	35-43	44-52	53 on
3	0-33	34-42	43-51	52 on
4 or 22/4	0-32	33-41	42-50	51 on
5	0-31	32-40	41-49	50 on
6	0-30	31-39	40-48	49 on
7	0-29	30-38	39-47	48 on
8	0-28	29-37	38-46	47 on
9	0-27	28-36	37-45	46 on

The transition between Pinnacles tends to be relatively abrupt. The influence of a new Pinnacle may be felt three to six months before the completion of the existing Pinnacle, but usually in a substantially reduced form. When a Pinnacle ends, its influence rarely lingers more than a month or so. The sudden changes that sometimes occur in a life—the gain or loss of interest in a job, an avocation or a relation—may sometimes be due to the sharp change of Pinnacles.

Transition between Pinnacles

Lenore was born on July 13, 1963.

Example

$$\begin{array}{cccc} \text{July} & 13, & 1963 & \\ 7 & 4 & 1 & = 12 = \boxed{3} \end{array}$$

First   = month sub-element + day sub-element
Pinnacle   7   +   4   = $\underline{\underline{11/2}}$

> The 11/2 notation expresses a Pinnacle with a master number.
>
> The First Pinnacle is from birth to age 33 (from the chart of the Time Span of Pinnacles, page 500).

Second   = day sub-element   + year sub-element
Pinnacle   4   +   1   = $\underline{\underline{5}}$

> The Second Pinnacle is from age 34 to 42.

Third   = First Pinnacle   + Second Pinnacle
Pinnacle   11   +   5   = $\underline{\underline{16/7}}$

> The 16/7 notation expresses a karmic Pinnacle.
> The Third Pinnacle is from age 43 to 51.

Fourth   = month sub-element + year sub-element
Pinnacle   7   +   1   = $\underline{\underline{8}}$

> The Fourth Pinnacle is from age 52 on.

A summary of Lenore's Pinnacles:

11/2	First Pinnacle	(0-33)
5	Second Pinnacle	(34-42)
16/7	Third Pinnacle	(43-51)
8	Fourth Pinnacle	(52 on)

Example:
Hal Allen's
calculation

Using calculations similar to the example just shown and the chart of the Time Span of Pinnacles, page 500, Hal Allen's Pinnacles would be summarized as follows:

8	First Pinnacle	(0-31)
9	Second Pinnacle	(32-40)
8	Third Pinnacle	(41-49)
11/2	Fourth Pinnacle	(50 on)

Hal's 8 First Pinnacle starts at birth in 1941 and continues to the end of 1972 (the year in which Hal turns 31).

Hal's 9 Second Pinnacle starts at the beginning of 1973 (the year in which Hal turns 32) and continues to the end of 1981 (the year in which Hal turns 40).

Hal's 8 Third Pinnacle starts at the beginning of 1982 (the year in which Hal turns 41) and continues to the end of 1990 (the year in which Hal turns 49).

Hal's 11/2 Fourth Pinnacle starts at the beginning of 1991 (the year in which Hal turns 50) and continues the rest of his life.

Adding the
Pinnacle data
to Hal Allen's
progressed
chart

We'll transfer this information to the progressed chart (Figure 29-1 on page 503) and again, as we did with the Periods, indicate the start of new Pinnacles with emphasized horizontal lines. Since the transitions are relatively abrupt, there is no need to note them on the progressed chart.

Chart 15:
Pinnacles

CHART 15: THE PINNACLES, on page 710, describes the four different Pinnacles for each of the single digits and master numbers. In general terms, the First Pinnacle usually displays limiting influences, the Second and Third Pinnacles usually produce influences and opportunities for expansion, and the Fourth Pinnacle sometimes describes influences supportive of reflection and retirement, sometimes influences supportive of bustling activity.

The strong negative influence of the karmic number—19/1, 13/4, 14/5, 16/7—is described in the bottom row of the chart. The negative impact would strongly modify the description of the particular Pinnacle. A 16/7 Third Pinnacle, for example, would be described by combining the general description of the 7 Pinnacle from the top row of the chart, the description of the 7 Third Pinnacle from the third row of the chart, and the description of the 16/7 karmic Pinnacle from the bottom row of the chart. The First, Second, Third or Fourth Pinnacles may, at times, each be a karmic Pinnacle.

HARLAN WILLIAM ALLEN
MAY 12, 1941

Age	Medium Term				Year	Long Term	
	Transits	Essence	Personal Year	Universal Year		Period	Pinnacle
0					1941		8
1					1942		8
2					1943		8← ⎯ 8 First
3					1944		8 Pinnacle
27					1969		8
28					1970		8
29					1971		8
30					1972		8
31					1973		9 ← Start of
32					1974		9 Second
33					1975		9 Pinnacle
34					1976		9← ⎯ 9 Second
35					1977		9 Pinnacle
36					1978		9
37					1979		9
38					1980		9
39					1981		9 Start of
40					1982		8 ← Third
41					1983		8 Pinnacle
42					1984		8← ⎯ 8 Third
43					1985		8 Pinnacle
44					1986		8
45					1987		8
46					1988		8
47					1989		8
48					1990		8 Start of
49					1991		11/2 ← Fourth
50					1992		11/2 Pinnacle
51					1993		11/2← ⎯ 11/2 Fourth
52					1994		11/2 Pinnacle
62					2004		11/2
63					2005		11/2
64					2006		11/2
65					2007		11/2
66					2008		11/2
67							

Figure 29–1
Progressed Chart
with Pinnacles:
Hal Allen

A delineation of any Pinnacle includes the following:

Delineation description

A. The general description of the influences of the environment along with the specific description of the First, Second, Third or Fourth Pinnacle (from CHART 15: THE PINNACLES).

    With a 22 Pinnacle, describe both the 22 and 4 Pinnacles, and with the 11, describe both the 11 and 2. The influences of both the higher and lower levels of the master number would probably be present, subject to the individual's desire or ability to use them.

B. The karmic Pinnacle description, from the bottom row of CHART 15: THE PINNACLES, if applicable. The negative potential, along with suggestions for overcoming the obstacles, should be included.

C. The subject's potentials—both from the birth name and current name(s), as well as the birthdate. A knowledge of the subject's potentials provides insight into the individual's ability to operate with the current influences. The core elements, Karmic Debts and Karmic Lessons may be of importance, along with any other strong modifiers which flow or conflict with the influences. Usually, the elements or modifiers with a number matching the Pinnacle number are of particular import.

D. Preparation for the next Pinnacle.
    The First Pinnacle should prepare for the Second and Third.
    The Second should prepare strongly for the Third.
    The Third should prepare sparingly for the Fourth.
    The preparation is important in the last ten years or so of the First Pinnacle, all of the Second, the last two or three years of the Third.

Hal Allen's Pinnacle delineation

Following are the delineations for Hal Allen's four Pinnacles. (We're assuming here that Hal's birthname is also his current name—that there are no additional energies from new names). The transitions are not mentioned, but, in a reading for the appropriate year they should be touched on briefly. Each portion of the delineation is written in the present tense. In an actual delineation, of course, you would usually be discussing the current Pinnacle only. For data relating to Hal's potentials, consult his calculation sheet and organization sheet shown on pages 493 and 494 of Chapter 28.

8 FIRST PINNACLE

1941-1972 (birth to the end of the year in which Hal turned 31).

THE DATA:
A. 8 First Pinnacle.
B. No karmic Pinnacle.

C. No 8 energy. Little energy devoted to business affairs except
    four 1's Intensity Point to some extent.
D. Prepare for 9 Second Pinnacle and 8 Third Pinnacle in last
    ten years of this Pinnacle.

*The body of the paragraph below is from the general 8 Pin-
nacle description and the 8 First Pinnacle description on Chart
15.*

> As a child and young adult, you're likely to find
> yourself in an environment with emphasis on busi-
> ness and commercial activity, organizational and
> managerial abilities, pragmatic approaches. You
> may be involved in business activity at an early
> age, but, whatever your age, you're likely to feel
> restricted unless you can find a situation making
> use of your cleverness and adaptability (5 *Life
> Path*). Your restless nature (*14/5 Karmic Debt, 5·5*)
> will probably be limited and your free-wheeling
> approach and need for constantly changing stim-
> ulii (*14/5 Karmic Debt, 5·5*) is likely to be repressed,
> causing you much resentment. You probably ex-
> hibit little of the logical, rational approach or
> balanced judgment about people and finances
> which would allow you to make the most of your
> opportunities (*no 8 energy*).

*From 1963 through 1972 (age 22-31), the last ten years of the
First Pinnacle, I'd add the following in preparation for the
middle Pinnacles.*

In Preparation for the 9 Second Pinnacle:

> Become aware of your loving, giving side, your
> sympathetic, compassionate self which gives with-
> out need for reward (*6 Expression and 9 Soul Urge*).
> You may not have much need for this giving side
> now, but, when you do, give as freely as you can
> and sense the deep satisfaction you receive. You
> may find more need for tolerance from ages 32 to
> 40. (*See the general description of the 9 Pinnacle on
> Chart 15*).

In preparation for the 8 Third Pinnacle:

> Between ages 41 and 49, you'll probably be in an

environment very similar to the one you're in now. I doubt that this current period is especially comfortable or satisfying, but, at least become aware of the situations where your capabilities fit in effectively in the business world. Keep these situations in mind for the future. With the experience and maturity that comes with time, you may be able to take better advantage of the commercial opportunities later. (*See the general description of the 8 Pinnacle on Chart 15.*)

9 SECOND PINNACLE

1973–1981 (year in which Hal turns 32 to year in which Hal turns 40).

THE DATA:

A. 9 Second Pinnacle.
B. No karmic Pinnacle.
C. 9 Soul Urge, 9 Growth Number
    6 Expression, 6 Modified Karmic Lesson.
D. Prepare strongly for 8 Third Pinnacle during the entire Second Pinnacle.

The body of the paragraph below is from the general 9 Pinnacle description and the 9 Second Pinnacle description on Chart 15.

There's apt to be much drama and high emotion in your life. There are probably many times when you need to show tolerance and compassion as you avail yourself of opportunities related to humanistic, philanthropic or artistic endeavors. You may be asked to be friendly or loving with little expectation of any return. Although there is a strong side of you that is loving and giving and capable of foregoing your own needs (*9 Soul Urge, 6 Expression*), that side is probably at odds with the restless side of your nature. If you can manage to concentrate on your ability to give, you may substantially develop your natural potential in that area and lead to considerable growth (*9 Growth Number*). Some highly emotional endeavor—a love affair or a close personal relationship—is likely to be completed during this time. You may not even want the completion, but it's likely to prove a stepping stone to freedom. Your responsibilities and accomplishments will depend on your ability to respond to the humanistic opportunities that beckon.

In preparation for the 8 Third Pinnacle, add the following during the entire 9 Second Pinnacle. See the general description of the 8 Pinnacle on Chart 15.

Between ages 41 and 49, you're likely to be in a business or commercial environment similar to what you may have experienced before your 32nd birthday. I don't think there's much you can do now in preparation for this coming period except keep aware of your abilities—your creative approach (5 *Life Path*) as well as your humanistic leanings (9 *Soul Urge*, 6 *Expression*). See if you can discern a place for these abilities later on when the opportunities probably will primarily emphasize business matters and organizaiton.

8 THIRD PINNACLE

1982-1990 (year in which Hal turns 41 to year in which Hal turns 49)

THE DATA:
A. 8 Third Pinnacle.
B. No karmic Pinnacle.
C. No 8 energy. Little energy devoted to business affairs except four 1's Intensity Point to some extent.
Much 5 energy conflicting with the influences.
D. Prepare sparingly for 11/2 Fourth Pinnacle the last two or three years of the Third.

The body of the paragraph below is from the general 8 Pinnacle description and the 8 Third Pinnacle description on Chart 15.

Here, as in your younger years, you're in a period emphasizing business and commercial activity, organizational and management abilities. When you were in a similar environment previously, I suspect that, with your youthful ideas, you felt limited and unable to use the free-wheeling approach which you enjoyed. By now, though, if you've learned to use freedom constructively (*5 Life Path*), if you've learned to curb your physical appetites (*14/5 Karmic Lesson and 5·5*), if you've learned something of the lesson of change: to begin, nurture, experience and detach (*14/5 Karmic Lesson*), you may be able to use some of the business opportunities to your advantage. If you can find a situation which allows you to use your creative, imaginative ways (*5 Life Path*), you may achieve success and recognition.

In preparation for the 11/2 Fourth Pinnacle, add the following from ages 47 through 49: (From the general description of the 2 Pinnacle and the description of the 2 Fourth Pinnacle on Chart 15. The influence of the 11 Fourth Pinnacle is relatively weak and is not mentioned here).

From age 50 on, you'll find that your sensitivity and receptivity are likely to be more important than your business acumen. At the present time, you may not find too many opportunities to promote harmony, but when you do, be prepared to give of yourself and to note the satisfaction you receive.

11/2 FOURTH PINNACLE

1991 on (year in which Hal turns 50, and on)

THE DATA:
A.   11/2 Fourth Pinnacle.
B.   No karmic Pinnacle.
C.   11/2 Maturity Number, 2 Karmic Lesson, related 6 and 9 energies.
D.   This is the last Pinnacle, no preparation for next Pinnacle.

The paragraph below is from the general description of the 11 Pinnacle on Chart 15. The influence of the 11 Fourth Pinnacle is relatively weak since the only 11 energy comes from the 11/2 Maturity Number.

At this time, you may find there's emphasis on philosophic, religious or metaphysical studies. I doubt that you'll have much desire to use these kinds of opportunities. You may feel a heightened awareness, perhaps a bit more nervous tension than previously.

The body of the paragraph below is from the general 2 Pinnacle description and the 2 Fourth Pinnacle description on Chart 15.

At the same time, you're apt to find that your sensitivity and receptivity are of special importance now (*6 Expression, 9 Soul Urge*). You may have developed your ability to be tactful, diplomatic and considerate (*2 Karmic Lesson*) and that may be helpful now. Your ability to promote harmony and to be friendly and affectionate are likely to be much appreciated (*6 Expression, 9 Soul Urge*). You may feel a little restless and limited in this environment (*5 Life Path, 14/5 Karmic debt, 5·5*), but there is a strong giving side of you that may find satisfaction, although not as much excitement as you would prefer (*6 Expression, 9 Soul Urge*). If you want, a pleasant full or partial retirement time is probably possible.

For Hal, the First and Third Pinnacles present opportunities for which he has little inherent energy. The influences of the Second and Fourth Pinnacles give him more possibilities, but never deal directly with his strongest energy, the 5 potential. Being aware of the Pinnacle's influences, even if one's own energies are not directly called into play, can be of considerable importance. If Hal, for instance, can learn to use his 5 energy to meet the influences of the First and Third 8 Pinnacles, he can substantially assist his growth. An awareness of the Pinnacles can help everyone in promoting their own development.

CHAPTER 30

LONG TERM CYCLES, PART 3: THE SYNTHESIS

By combining the descriptions of the Period and Pinnacle operating at any given time in a subject's life, we receive a picture of the general influences and, often, particular emphases. In a delineation, I usually describe the current long term cycles, then discuss any Period or Pinnacle which begins operating within the next three or four years, and finally describe any previous Period or Pinnacle which ended within the last few years.

Relative importance of the concurrent Period and Pinnacle

We have to determine the relative importance of the background cycles so that the importance is reflected in the synthesis:

IF ONE OF THE LONG TERM CYCLES CLEARLY HAS MORE OF THE SUBJECT'S ENERGY AVAILABLE THAN THE OTHER, THAT CYCLE'S INFLUENCES TEND TO DOMINATE THAT PHASE. As an example, Hal Allen's 5 First Period, with energy from Hal's 5 Life Path, 14/5 Karmic Debt and 5 Life Path/5 sub-element, receives a good deal of energy, even though a substantial portion is negative energy. There's virtually no energy related to Hal's 8 First Pinnacle and, in addition, the 5 energy is heavily conflicted with the 8 influences. When these two cycles are operating, the influence of the 5 First Period is likely to dominate. The 8 influences need be mentioned only in passing.

IF SIMILAR LEVELS OF ENERGY ARE AVAILABLE IN A CONCURRENT PERIOD AND PINNACLE, THE

STRONGER MODIFIER NUMBER TENDS TO DOMINATE THAT PHASE.

> 1, 4, 5, 8, and 22 tend to be strong.
> 3, 6, and 9 tend to be average.
> 2, 7, and 11 tend to be weak.

The influence of a 4 Period, for instance, would tend to dominate the influences of a 2 Pinnacle if their energy levels were similar. Or, a 6 Pinnacle would tend to dominate a 7 Period.

IF SIMILAR LEVELS OF ENERGY ARE AVAILABLE IN A CONCURRENT PERIOD AND PINNACLE:

The First Period tends to be
> more influential than the First Pinnacle,
> less influential than the Second Pinnacle.

The Second Period tends to be
> more influential than the First Pinnacle,
> less influential than the Second Pinncle,
> less influential than the Third Pinnacle,
> more influential than the Fourth Pinnacle.

The Third Period tends to be
> less influential than the Third Pinnacle,
> more influential than the Fourth Pinnacle.

Commentary   If a concurrent Period and Pinnacle have the same number, it emphasizes the particular influence of that number. If the subject is lucky enough to have positive energy to take advantage of the emphasized opportunities, he may find that this time in the life is of particular importance.

If a karmic Period and karmic Pinnacles occur at the same time, this is likely to be a significantly difficult time of the life. If the same karmic number is involved in both cycles, the negative impact is likely to be strong.

The first few years of a new Period or Pinnacle are especially significant as the subject becomes acclimatized to the different direction and learns how best to use the new influences. If the Period and Pinnacle change at the same time, the transition has increased importance because all of the background influences in the individual's life are shifting simultaneously. The subject should be given information about this change as much as five years before the shift so that he can prepare adequately.

Looking at Hal Allen's progressed chart (Figure 30-1 on page 514), we find five separate phases of his life: five different combinations of Periods and Pinnacles.

Hal Allen's progressed chart

Following is the synthesis of the long term cycles for each of Hal's five phases. We'll analyze all the phases and give a complete delineation of the first two. By describing Hal's background influences at twelve year intervals starting at age 20, all the phases will be covered. You'll get a good idea of how the cycles are blended as well as an awareness of the probable ebb and flow of Hal's life.

Synthesis of Hal Allen's long term cycles

1961: AGE 20

5 First Period on a 5 Life Path (birth–age 31)
8 First Pinnacle (birth–age 31)

ANALYSIS:

There's a lot of 5 energy available, little 8 energy. The influences of the 5 First Period are likely to dominate this phase.

DELINEATION:

> You're probably in a constantly changing environment with much uncertainty and travel. This is likely to be a difficult atmosphere for you, with its continual feeling of restlessness, possibly accentuated by a fluctuating money supply. It may seem like a good environment in which to learn the exhilaration of the constructive use of freedom, but your age works against you. Your tendencies to be erratic and proceed with little sense of accomplishment, your problem with excessive physical appetites, your difficulty in learning the lesson of change: to begin, nurture, experience and detach—all are likely to be emphasized in this environment (5 *First Period with 5 Life Path, 14/5 Karmic Debt, 5 Life Path/5 sub-element*).

> There's likely to be some emphasis on business and commercial activity. You may be working now, but the business world is likely to feel restrictive and limiting to your free-wheeling nature un-

HARLAN WILLIAM ALLEN
MAY 12, 1941

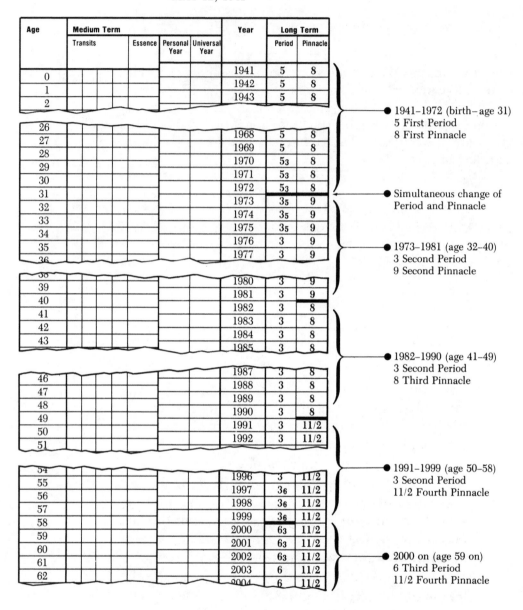

Figure 30–1
Progressed Chart
with Long Term Cycles:
Hal Allen

less you find just the right position (8 *First Pinnacle with no 8 energy*).

(With twelve years to go to the new Period and Pinnacle, there is no mention of preparation and no concern with transitions.)

1973: AGE 32

Start of 3 Second Period on a 5 Life Path (age 32–58)
Start of 9 Second Pinnacle (age 32–40)

ANALYSIS:

There's a good deal of 9 energy available along with related 6 energy. There's some 3 energy present. The influences of the 9 Second Pinnacle are likely to dominate this phase. (Even if there were similar levels of 3 energy and 9 energy available, the Second Pinacle tends to be more influential than the First Period.)

DELINEATION:

This year is likely to have special importance. The influences which have been with you since birth —the restlessness and the emphasis on business—are making way now for other influences, leading to an environment emphasizing social, artistic and humanistic values (*simultaneous start of new Period and new Pinnacle*).

There's apt to be much drama and high emotion at this time. There are probably many times when you need to show tolerance and compassion as you avail yourself of opportunities related to humanistic, philanthropic or artistic endeavors. You may be asked to be friendly or loving with little expectation of any return. After your free-wheeling years, you will probably now be expected to concentrate on your ability to give to others. Development of your giving abilities will lead to considerable growth. Some highly emotional endeavor—a love affair or a close personal relation—is likely to end at this time or in the next few years, although this may not be what you necessarily want. The completion, though, may prove a stepping stone to freedom (9 *Second Pinnacle with 9 Soul Urge, 9 Growth Number, 6 Expression, 6 Modified Karmic Lesson*).

You may find opportunities now for much social life, travel, artistic pursuits and verbal activities such as acting or writing. There's potential here for pleasure and achievement. You may lose time and direction if you waste your energies or act capriciously or self-indulgently (3 *Second Period with 3 Birthday, five 3's Intensity Point, 3 Prime Intensifier*).

Stay aware of your abilities—your creative approach and your humanistic leanings. Consider where you can use these abilities in the relatively ordered business world you'll probably be in from age 41 through 49 (*preparation for the 8 Third Pinnacle with no 8 energy*).

You may notice, although there's still lots of activity, that the erratic quality of your early years seems to be lessening (5 *First Period fading out*).

1985: AGE 44

3 Second Period on a 5 Life Path (age 32–58)
8 Third Pinnacle (age 41–49)

ANALYSIS:

There's some 3 energy available (3 *Birthday, five 3's Intensity Point, 3 Prime Intensifier*), but no 8 energy. The influences of the Second Period are likely to dominate this phase. (At age 32, our last example, the 3 Second Period was weak compared to the concurrent 9 Pinnacle, but now, the 3 energy can come into its own. Although the 3 Second Period runs for 27 years, only between ages 41 and 49 is it likely to be especially effective.)

IN THE DELINEATION, DISCUSS:

3 Second Period: the 3 potential is not extremely strong, but
   it's the strongest energy in this phase.
8 Third Pinnacle: briefly mentioned.
(There are no preparations for future Periods or Pinnacles at
   this time. There are no transitions to be noted, either.)

1997: AGE 56

3 Second Period on a 5 Life Path (age 32–58)
11/2 Fourth Pinnacle (age 50 on)

ANALYSIS:

There's some 3 energy available (*3 Birthday, five 3's Intensity Point, 3 Prime Intensifier*), little 11 energy. (*11 Maturity Number*). There's some 2 energy (*2 Maturity Number, 2 Karmic Lesson*), but a great deal of related 6 and 9 energy (*6 Expression, 6 Modified Karmic Lesson, 9 Soul Urge, 9 Growth Number*). The influences of the 2 Fourth Pinnacle are likely to dominate this phase. (In other contexts, the 6 and 9 energy would also be helpful to the 3 energy. In the 3 Period, the emphasis on social activity doesn't really stress the deep feelings of the 6 and 9 potential. The 6 and 9 energy, with emphasis on creativity, might be of some help with the 3 verbal activities, but the lightness of the 3 Period is usually relatively unreceptive to the high level artistic emphasis of the 6 and 9.)

IN THE DELINEATION, DISCUSS:

2 Fourth Pinnacle: the influences (including the 6 and 9 potential) are strong.
3 Second Period: a lesser influence, but certainly there.
11 Fourth Pinnacle: briefly mentioned.
Preparation for the 6 Third Period: the 6 Third Period is in sharp contrast to the 3 Second Period, but the 2, 6, and 9 energies associated with the 2 Fourth Pinnacle can help with the preparation.
Transition to the 6 Third Period: Felt to a limited degree, it should be briefly mentioned.

2009: AGE 68

6 Third Period on a 5 Life Path (age 59 on)
11/2 Fourth Pinnacle (age 50 on)

ANALYSIS:

2, 6, and 9 energy is available for the 6 Third Period *and* the 2 Fourth Pinnacle (*2 Maturity Number, 2 Karmic Lesson, 6 Expression, 6 Modified Karmic Number, 9 Soul Urge, 9 Growth Number*). Little 11 energy (*11 Maturity Number*) is available. The influences of the 6 Third Period *and* the 2 Fourth Pinnacle are likely to dominate the period.

IN THE DELINEATION, DISCUSS:

6 Third Period: the influences are strong, but there is also conflict with the 5 energy.
2 Fourth Pinnacle: strong influences, too.
11 Fourth Pinnacle: briefly mentioned.
(There are, of course, no preparations for future Periods or
Pinnacles and no transitions to come.)

Looking at all the phases of the life for an overview

Although it's much easier to look at only the current Period
and Pinnacle, I think the importance of looking (even ever so
quickly) at *all* the phases cannot be overestimated. Back in
Chapters 7 and 21 in Volume 1, we discussed the strong conflict
between Hal's restless 5 energy and his loving, giving 6·9
energy. By examining the potential flow of Hal's entire life, we
can see that there's a place for both energies.

From birth to age 31, Hal is likely to indulge his restless free-
wheeling appetites.

From 32 to 40, I'd expect a simmering down of the frenetic
pace with the onset of maturity. A lot of activity still, artistic
pursuits, social life, more interest in others—a more balanced
potential possible than in the early years.

From 41 to 49, a probable transition period. Perhaps an approach to the business world with a better understanding of his
creativity, a more mature approach to people.

From 50 to 58, perhaps with the restlessness in balance, there
may be a flowering of the loving, responsible, giving Hal.
There may also be the pleasures of travel, social life, artistic
pursuits.

And finally, from 59 on, a loving supportive environment
with friends and quiet social activities.

Hal has the possibility of developing from a restless youngster
to a mature loving man with a creative, free-wheeling bent.
We can't be sure what Hal will do with his energies in the different periods of his life, but as numerologists, we can guide
him to the most positive use of his energies with the various influences present.

Most lives have a sense of flow and development similar to
Hal's—a relatively clear direction mapped by the Periods and
Pinnacles. Use these important tools—the indicators of the
background life influences.

CHAPTER 31

MEDIUM TERM CYCLES, PART 1:
THE UNIVERSAL YEAR
THE PERSONAL YEAR
THE EPICYCLE

While the long term cycles set the general tone for extended periods, the medium term cycles indicate influences, approaches and events for a much shorter span of time. There are from five to seven medium term cycles in a person's life, each lasting from one to nine years. (Strictly speaking, an Essence may last more than nine years, but this is a rare occurrence.) The cumulative effect of these cycles usually shifts at least a portion of the influences, approaches and events at almost every birthday as well as at the beginning of each year. The medium term cycles are more important to the individual than the more diffused long term cycles or the more concentrated short term cycles. A careful reading of these medium term cycles provides vital information allowing preparations for or defense against the probable influences and events to come.

THE UNIVERSAL YEAR IS A MEDIUM TERM CYCLE DESCRIBING THE GENERAL YEARLY TREND OF WORLD INFLUENCES. The general influences in the world are substantially modified by the energy put forth by the earth's population. Although the trend of the influence can be indicated, the direction of the influence *plus* the activated

Definition of the Universal Year

energy cannot be described in advance. I don't, therefore, find the Universal Year particularly useful in discussing the trend of the events in the world. Rather, I see it as a kind of broad background tone for a given year. It's a cycle of distinctly lesser importance.

Calculation of the Universal Year

At any given time the Universal Year is the same for everyone. IT'S CALCULATED BY ADDING THE DIGITS OF THE YEAR AND REDUCING THE SUM TO A SINGLE DIGIT OR MASTER NUMBER.

Examples:

$$1958 = 1 + 9 + 5 + 8 = 23$$
$$= 2 + 3$$
$$= 5 \text{ Universal Year}$$

$$1960 = 1 + 9 + 6 + 0 = 16$$
$$= 1 + 6$$
$$= 7 \text{ Universal Year}$$

Universal Years don't register karmic influences. 1960 is a 7 Universal Year—there is no 16/7 Universal Year.

$$1966 = 1 + 9 + 6 + 6 = 22/4 \text{ Universal Year}$$

Universal years with master numbers describe the influence of both the higher and lower levels—a 22/4 year has 22 and 4 influences; an 11/2 year has 11 and 2 influences.

Time span and transitions of the Universal Year

The Universal Year lasts one year, from January 1 to December 31. It may be felt to some degree from October through December of the previous year. Its fading influence manifests slightly through January and February of the following year.

Chart 16: Personal Year/ Universal Year

CHART 16: THE PERSONAL YEAR/THE UNIVERSAL YEAR, on page 724, describes the different Universal Years in the bottom row. The influences, as you can see, are extremely broad.

The influences described by the Universal Year are important in a reading only if the number of the Universal Year (1) is the same as the Personal Year, or (2) is in sharp conflict with the Personal Year. If the two are the same, we would expect that the individual's approach would feel in harmony with world influences, increasing the possibility of productive development. If, instead, the two are in conflict, the individual is likely to feel some resistance as he uses his approach in a world heading in a different direction.

The Universal Year influence, whether positive or negative, is never particularly large. It should be covered in one or two sentences of the delineation at most. If the Universal Year is neither the same as nor in conflict with the Personal Year, its effect can be ignored.

Commentary on the Universal Year

THE PERSONAL YEAR DESCRIBES THE YEARLY APPROACH TO EVENTS LIKELY TO PRODUCE GROWTH AND DEVELOPMENT. By using the described approach, the subject is in the best posture to take advantage of the events and opportunities presented, as well as to avoid or alleviate the confusions and difficulties attendant on the experiences encountered. The Personal Year is a very important cycle.

Definition of the Personal Year

THE PERSONAL YEAR IS THE SUM OF THE BIRTH MONTH, BIRTH DAY AND UNIVERSAL YEAR OF THE YEAR IN QUESTION, EACH REDUCED TO A SINGLE DIGIT OR MASTER NUMBER. THE SUM IS LIKEWISE REDUCED TO A SINGLE DIGIT OR MASTER NUMBER.

Calculation of the Personal Year

Examples:

Rachel was born on June 15, 1938. What's her Personal Year in 1983?

Birth Month	+	Birth Day	+	Universal Year		
June		15		1983		
6	+	6	+	3	=	15
					=	1 + 5
					=	6 Personal Year

As you can see, the year of birth is of no consequence in calculating the Personal Year. If two people have the same birth month and birth day, even if they're born in different years, they have the same Personal Year.

Paul was born on August 23, 1914. What's his Personal Year in 1977?

Birth Month	+	Birth Day	+	Universal Year		
August		23		1977		
8	+	5	+	6	= 19	
					= 1 + 9	
					= 1 Personal Year	

The Personal Years, like the Universal Years, don't register karmic influences. In this example, we have a 1 Personal Year, not a 19/1 Personal Year.

Edwina was born on April 19, 1960. What's her Personal Year in 1968?

Birth Month	+	Birth Day	+	Universal Year	
April		19		1968	
4	+	1	+	6	= 11/2 Personal Year

The 11/2 Personal Year describes the 11 and 2 approach; the 22/4 Personal Year describes the 22 and 4 approach.

Robert was born on November 4, 1970. What's his Personal Year at birth?

Birth Month	+	Birth Day	+	Universal Year		
November		4		1970		
11	+	4	+	8	= 23	
					= 2 + 3	
					= 5 Personal Year	

The first Personal Year in everyone's life is the same number as the Life Path.

Time span and transitions of the Personal Year

The Personal Year, like the Universal Year, lasts one year, from January 1 to December 31. It may be felt to some degree from October through December of the previous year. Its fading influence can be felt through January and February of the following year. (The first Personal Year in an individual's life is usually shorter than a full year, extending only from the birthday to December 31. Only if a person is born on January 1, does the first Personal Year last a complete year.)

Actions predicated on the approach described by the Personal Year are more powerful between March and September because the influences are operating in a pure form, without the overlay of previous or coming approaches. If an action or event of importance can be scheduled, schedule it for maximum impact in those middle seven months.

Chart 16: Personal Year/ Universal Year

If you turn to CHART 16:PERSONAL YEAR/UNIVERSAL YEAR, on page 724, you'll find the description of the Personal Years in the top row. The capitalized words or phrases emphasize the chief characteristic of each year's approach.

Commentary on the Personal Year

Although there may be only one or two parts to the main approach for the Personal Year, there are often a few other constituents which add to that approach. Occasionally, an individual will find a year developing so that he has possibilities for growth along a number of different avenues. In a 1 Personal Year, for instance, he may find opportunities to clarify his goals, start a new venture, become more independent and develop his individuality—with all those opportunities, it's likely to be an exciting and significant year. In most years, though, an individual will probably find only one or two doors opening. He should concentrate on growth in those areas with the most potential—it certainly isn't necessary to work on all the possibilities for each year to feel that progress is being made.

The chart presents the approaches, of course, in general terms. It shouldn't be expected to be followed rigidly every day of the year. By all means, take a month's vacation in a 4 Personal Year. It's true that the primary direction emphasizes work, but other activities are not only acceptable but desirable. Similarly, don't use a 5 Personal Year, with its emphasis on freedom, as an excuse to avoid all work or duty. Freedom—especially the constructive use of freedom—implies an acute awareness of other directions.

Interpret each year's tactics broadly. A person weighed down with responsibility may find a 6 Personal Year a good time to clarify those responsibilities and possibly even dispense with a few of them. A too responsible individual may end a 6 Personal Year with less obligations than at the start of the year—that's not a "standard" approach, but it's undoubtedly a step in a positive direction. A strong individualist, to cite another example, may find a 1 Personal Year a fine time to abandon some of those traits that alienate and confuse others.

Again, not the usual approach, but, nevertheless, a move to be applauded.

Definition of the Epicycle

The Personal Years run in consecutive order from 1 to 9 except for the occasional substitution of 11/2 for 2 or 22/4 for 4. (When figuring the second and fourth years, always do the complete calculation to determine if a master number is present.)

THE ONGOING FLOW OF THE PERSONAL YEARS FORMS A VERY IMPORTANT REPEATING NINE YEAR CYCLE CALLED THE EPICYCLE. THE EPICYCLE IS THE VITAL CONNECTION BETWEEN THE LONG TERM AND MEDIUM TERM CYCLES. IN A SENSE, IT'S THE BASIC BUILDING BLOCK ON WHICH THE ENTIRE PROGRESSED CYCLE STRUCTURE RESTS.

Epicycles and Periods

For most of us, the first Epicycle in our life is abbreviated. (Only those with a 1 Life Path start life with a 1 Personal Year and a complete Epicycle.) After this abbreviated start, the First Period then extends for an additional two or three Epicycles. The important Second Period starts in a 1 Personal Year and lasts three or four complete Epicycles. The Third Period also starts in a 1 Personal Year as the Epicycles continue.

Epicycles and Pinnacles

The First Pinnacle extends for an additional three complete Epicycles after the abbreviated beginning Epicycle. (Only a person with a 1 Life Path starts with a complete Epicycle so that the First Pinnacle, in this case, is four Epicycles long.) The Second and Third Pinnacles start in a 1 Personal Year and each has a duration of one complete Epicycle. The Fourth Pinnacle also starts in a 1 Personal Year as the Epicycles continue.

The long term background cycles, then, are composed of a finite number of Epicycles. (Epicycle is a word of ancient Greek origin defined as a cycle within a larger cycle.) Since all but the First Period and First Pinnacle *must* start in a 1 Personal Year, three distinct patterns emerge:

Epicycles with Life Path 1, 2, 11/2 and 3

With Life Path 1, 2, 11/2 and 3 (Figure 31-1 on page 525), the Third Period and Fourth Pinnacles start at the same time, denoting a strong change in the background tone at ages 52, 53, or 54. There may be a distinct change of interest and direction in middle age, sometimes surprising because of its abruptness. This is sometimes a difficult transition with much to work out in the ensuing years.

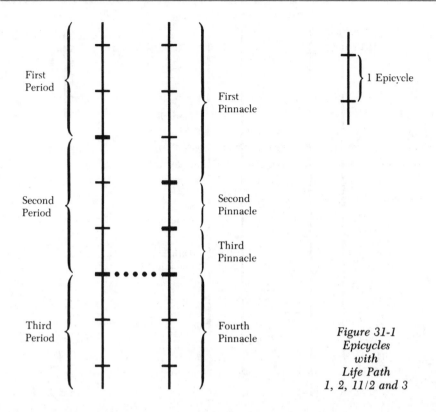

First
Period

First
Pinnacle

1 Epicycle

Second
Period

Second
Pinnacle

Third
Pinnacle

Third
Period

Fourth
Pinnacle

Figure 31-1
Epicycles
with
Life Path
1, 2, 11/2 and 3

With a 4 and 22/4 Life Path (Figure 31-2 on page 526), the Periods and Pinnacles never change at the same time. This is the only pattern in which the Second Period lasts four Epicycles rather than three and encompasses all four Pinnacles. The influence of the Second Period, lasting from age 24 to 59, is likely to be significant.

Epicycles with Life Path 4 and 22/4

With Life Path 5 through 9 (Figure 31-3 on page 526), the Second Period and Second Pinnacle start at the same time, indicating a strong change in the background tone somewhere between the ages of 28 and 32. This is, as a matter of fact, Hal Allen's pattern and was discussed in Chapter 30. This configuration is sometimes an indicator of a sudden maturation—a slow starter who, out of the blue, begins to move, or a steady developer who, at this point in the life, begins a dramatic upsurge.

Epicycles with Life Path 5 through 9

We'll examine the Epicycle in more detail. Let's become aware, not so much of the individual years but rather of the *flow* from year to year.

Commentary on the Epicycle

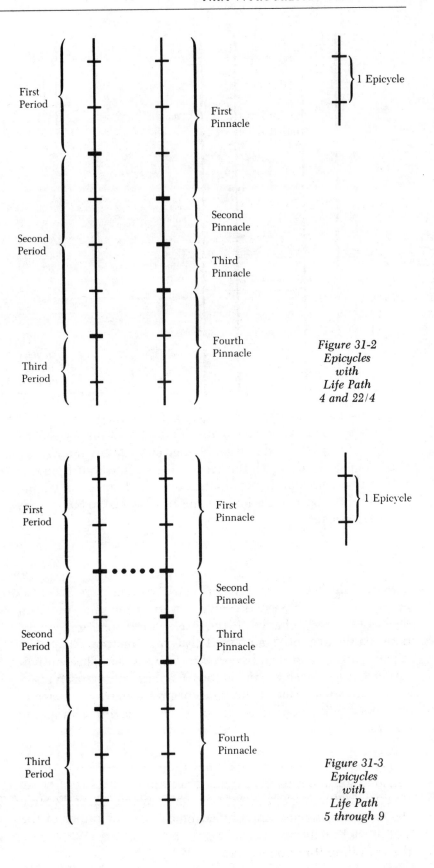

Figure 31-2
Epicycles
with
Life Path
4 and 22/4

Figure 31-3
Epicycles
with
Life Path
5 through 9

THE EPICYCLE

PERSONAL YEAR	APPROACH	COMMENTS
1	Plan and begin. Make changes, expand.	Take action. Be prepared for important change.
2	Wait, cooperate. Stay in the background.	Be receptive. (Receptive 11 Personal Year is sometimes substituted.)
3	Express the joy of living. Concentrate on self-improvement.	Take action.
4	Work hard, take care of details. Put everything in order.	Take action only in order to consolidate. (Active 22 Personal Year is sometimes substituted.)
5	Make changes, expand. Seek new directions.	Take action. Be prepared for important change.
6	Take care of family responsibilities. Work for harmony.	Be receptive.
7	Study past, present—plan for the future. Reflect, analyze, meditate.	Be receptive.
8	Act dynamically. Accomplish, advance, achieve recognition.	Take action.
9	Complete experiences. Contemplate future plans.	Take action only in order to complete. Be receptive. Be prepared for important change.

The flow, as you can see, is not a direct one. There are diversions, meanderings, detours. There are dramatic forward thrusts and times for patient waiting. You can be sure only that the endeavors started in the 1 Personal Year will come to some sort of fruition in the 8 Personal Year and will fade or change in the transition 9 Personal Year.

However redundant and confusing, the flow of the Epicycle does eventually bring endeavors to completion. More important, I suspect, is the growth and development of the individual that comes with the Epicycle flow. The Epicycle has a place for all levels, intensities and qualities of experience. It also allows for careful timing of proposed action for maximum impact.

Begin to think of life as a series of Epicycles. Begin to sense the ebb and flow of this important indicator. Check where you are in your own Epicycle and check those close to you, too. Look at the Personal Year in relation to previous activities and the potentials being developed. Is Paul taking advantage of his 5 Personal Year to expand his plans and move forward with his enterprises? Is Judy waiting patiently through her 7 Personal Year, contemplating her past endeavors and planning for future ones? And, is Ellen phasing out parts of her life in her 9 Personal Year and looking into new projects to begin in the coming year? An understanding of the Epicycle and its component Personal Years gives a sense of structure and balance to the life.

Think of each Epicycle as flowing into the next. The 9 Personal Year does not bring the Epicycle to an abrupt halt; rather, it provides a transition year whose energies move uninterruptedly into the 1 Personal Year at the beginning of the subsequent Epicycle.

The Universal Years follow their own Epicycle, but the pattern here is of less importance. In Chapters 34 and 35, you'll see that the Personal Month and Personal Day, the short term cycles, maintain a similar configuration.

Personal Year delineation description

A delineation of any Personal year in an Epicycle includes the following:

A. An awareness of the long term cycles. The tone set by the background cycles would affect the Personal Year even though the description of the current Period and Pinnacle might be described separately. A 1 Personal Year with a 3 Period and 2 Pinnacle, for instance, has a different connotation than a 1 Personal Year with an 8 Period and a 1 Pinnacle.

B. An awareness of the Epicycle. If you think of an individual's life as a series of Epicycles, with each Epicycle on a potentially more evolved level than the last, the particular Epicycle in which the Personal Year is placed is of importance. The fifth Epicycle of life has more potential, for instance, than the first or second. In the delineation, we're particularly concerned with the location of the Epicycle within the background cycles. For example, we have a Second Period made up of three Epicycles. The first Epicycle has a beginning quality, the third a sense of more accomplishment. A 4 Personal Year, for instance, with its emphasis on work, would read somewhat differently in each Epicycle.

C. A description of the Universal Year (from Chart 16). One or two sentences is sufficient if the Universal Year is the same or in conflict with the Personal Year. Otherwise, ignore it.

D. A description of the Personal Year (from Chart 16). With a 22 Personal Year, clarify the option to revert to a 4 Personal Year, or to operate with both the 22 *and* 4 approaches. I usually ignore the 22 approach unless the subject is over thirty years old, except for mention of the nervous tension. With an 11 Personal Year, describe both the 11 and the 2. I don't usually read the 11 approach unless the subject is over twenty, except, again, to note the nervous tension.

E. The subject's current potentials—both from the birthname and current name(s), as well as the birthdate. The subject's energies define the ability to enhance, deflect or mute the approach described by the Personal Year. The core elements, Karmic Debts, Karmic Lessons and Challenge, may be of importance, along with any other strong modifiers which either flow or conflict with the approach. Usually, the elements or modifiers with a number matching the Personal Year number are of particular concern.

F. Preparation for the next Personal Year. A brief description of the approach for the subsequent year provides some understanding of the ongoing flow.

Example: Hal Allen's progressed chart

We'll delineate a few of Hal Allen's Personal Years. We can fill in the Personal Year and the Universal Year columns on his progressed chart using the calculations outlined at the beginning of this chapter (Figure 31-4 on page 530).

Note that the Universal Year has recurring 22/4 rather than 4 Years. This is typical of most of the twentieth century, but won't occur at all in the twenty-first.

Hal has a recurring 11/2 Personal Year. Hal has little 11 energy but the 11 approach should be briefly mentioned when the 11/2 Personal Year occurs.

The start of each Epicycle is marked with a strong horizontal line in the Personal Year column. (The Universal Year Epicycle *isn't* marked because the weakness of the cycle gives little reason to call attention to its beginning.)

HARLAN WILLIAM ALLEN
MAY 12, 1941

Age	Medium Term					Year	Long Term	
	Transits				Essence	Personal Year	Universal Year		Period	Pinnacle
0						5	6	1941	5	8
1						6	7	1942	5	8
2						7	8	1943	5	8
3						8	9	1944	5	8
4						9	1	1945	5	8
5						1	2	1946	5	8
6						11/2	3	1947	5	8
7						3	22/4	1948	5	8
8						4	5	1949	5	8
9						5	6	1950	5	8
10						6	7	1951	5	8
11						7	8	1952	5	8
12						8	9	1953	5	8
13						9	1	1954	5	8
14						1	2	1955	5	8
15						11/2	3	1956	5	8
16						3	22/4	1957	5	8
17						4	5	1958	5	8

Age	Medium Term					Year	Long Term	
31						9	1	1972	35	8
32						1	2	1973	35	9
33						11/2	3	1974	35	9
34						3	22/4	1975	35	9
35						4	5	1976	3	9
36						5	6	1977	3	9
37						6	7	1978	3	9
38						7	8	1979	3	9
39						8	9	1980	3	9
40						9	1	1981	3	9
41						1	2	1982	3	8
42						11/2	3	1983	3	8
43						3	22/4	1984	3	8
44						4	5	1985	3	8
45						5	6	1986	3	8
46						6	7	1987	3	8
47						7	8	1988	3	8
48						8	9	1989	3	8

Figure 31–4
Progressed Chart
with Personal Year and Universal Year:
Hal Allen

Let's look at Hal in 1956, 1976 and 1986. Each portion of the Personal Year delineations is written in the present tense. We're assuming here that Hal's birthname is also his current name—that there are no additional energies from new names.

Hal Allen's Personal Year delineations

1956: 11/2 PERSONAL YEAR

Hal turns 15.

Delineation: 1956

THE DATA:

A.   5 First Period on a 5 Life Path, 8 First Pinnacle. See complete description, page 513 of Chapter 30.

B.   The second complete Epicycle of the 3½ Epicycles in this Period and Pinnacle.

C.   3 Universal Year.

D.   11/2 Personal Year.

E.   Hal's related potentials:
     2 Karmic Lesson
     6 Expression
     6 Modified Karmic Lesson
     Conflict with 5 Life Path, 14/5 Karmic Debt, 5·5.

F.   Prepare for following 3 Personal Year.

THE DELINEATION:

You're likely to be in an environment filled with activity, variety and uncertainty. Since you tend to jump from activity to activity and since your youth probably precludes a desire for accomplishment, you may be content enough with this state of affairs. You may be involved, even at your young age, in some sort of work but I suspect it makes you feel restricted (5 *First Period, 8 First Pinnacle*).

This year is apt to present some frustrating aspects to a person with your restless nature. You may have to wait longer than you'd like for activities to develop. You should be prepared for delays, detours and stoppages. This is a good time to develop more patience, although you may not be much interested in making the effort (2 *Personal Year and second Epicycle in this Period and Pinnacle with 2 Karmic Lesson, conflict with 5 energy*).

If you have a job or if you're working at home or with friends, concentrate on working with others in a spirit of cooperation. Try to relate to others tactfully and with consideration. Emphasize harmony.

Take care of the details when necessary. Give time and effort to further another's work (*2 Personal Year*). There's a responsible, understanding side to you which hasn't had much chance to develop in the uncertain atmosphere around you, but this is a good time to work on these important abilities (*6 Expression, 6 Modified Karmic Lesson*).

Emotions and sensitivity need to be kept in balance. If you don't practice self-control—and there are likely to be many situations not to your liking—there may well be substantially heightened nervous tension. It's likely to provoke disharmony and distract from your ability to absorb new awarenesses (*2 Personal Year and 11 Personal Year*).

Next year, you'll be happy to know, will probably be full of much more in the way of fun, social life and entertainment and much less in the way of lessons and responsibility (*preparation for 3 Personal Year*).

The delineation is primarily based on the 2 Personal Year description rather than the 11 Personal Year, since Hal is only fifteen years old. The 11 nervous tension, though, is noted. The reading is modified to accentuate Hal's youth.

CHART 16: THE PERSONAL YEAR/THE UNIVERSAL YEAR is intended for ages eighteen and up. Descriptions of Personal Years for children and teenagers have to be rephrased to account for activities to be expected at younger ages.

Delineation: 1976

1976: 4 PERSONAL YEAR

Hal turns 35.

THE DATA:
A. 3 Second Period on a 5 Life Path, 9 Second Pinnacle. See complete description, page 515 of Chapter 30.
B. The first Epicycle of the Second Period.
C. 5 Universal Year.
D. 4 Personal Year
E. Hal's related potentials:
   Conflict with 5 Life Path, 14/5 Karmic Debt, 5·5.
F. Prepare for following 5 Personal Year.

THE DELINEATION:

You're likely to be in an environment stressing social, creative and verbal activities. You may be involved in philanthropic, humanistic or artistic endeavors (*3 Second Period, 9 Second Pinnacle*). This is a good year to stabilize your ventures, to establish a secure base for future development (*4 Personal Year*).

Concentrate on hard work, mental and/or physical. Work to put a solid base under your endeavors. Search out and strengthen the weak areas. Take care of all the details. Put everything in order, ready for potential growth (*4 Personal Year*). Use your creativity, versatility, and enthusiasm in getting the job done (*5 Life Path*). You're likely to feel a sense of excitement in the air and be irritated that you have to spend so much time working (*5 Universal Year emphasized by 5 Life Path*). This is a fine time to solidify your humanistic or philanthropic ideas. You may want to begin solidifying your artistic ideas now, too (*4 Personal Year with 9 Pinnacle and the first Epicycle of the 3 Period*).

Make an effort to meet your obligations. If work is shirked, the resulting leisure isn't likely to be enjoyable. Work may be long and unremitting, but there's much satisfaction to be obtained from its completion. Progress is apt to be slower than you expect. Don't depend on luck or dreams—they're not much help at this time (*4 Personal Year*). I hope you've worked through your restlessness and tendency to jump from activity to activity. If you haven't, you're likely to have difficulty meeting your obligations (*5 Life Path, 14/5 Karmic Debt, 5·5*).

Be efficient, economical, rational with financial matters. Establish a solid foundation here, too, for the future (*4 Personal Year*).

Counteract any feelings of limitation or restriction by periodically interspersing some play to relieve the pressure of the work load. Get in some freewheeling activities when you can to relieve those restless feelings (*4 Personal Year with 5 Life Path*).

> Check on health matters when necessary (*4 Personal Year*).
>
> Next year will probably be a lot more exciting for you. There's likely to be much change and variety—new friends and opportunities (*preparation for 5 Personal Year*).

The 4 Personal Year description is tempered because of Hal's 5 energies. Because of his age, it's assumed that he's made some progress in handling the negative 5 potentials.

Delineation: 1986

1986: 5 PERSONAL YEAR

Hal turns 45.

THE DATA:

A.   3 Second Period on a 5 Life Path, 8 Third Pinnacle. See analysis, page 516 of Chapter 30.
B.   The second Epicycle of the Second Period.
C.   6 Universal Year.
D.   5 Personal Year.
E.   Hal's related potentials:
    5 Life Path
    14/5 Karmic Debt
    5·5
    Conflict with 6 Expression, 6 Modified Karmic Lesson.
F.   Prepare for following 6 Personal Year.

THE DELINEATION:

> You're likely to be in an environment stressing social, creative and verbal activities along with the enjoyment of life's pleasures. There's apt to be some emphasis on business or commercial activity, too (*3 Second Period, 8 Third Pinnacle*).
>
> This is a year to expand horizons, to grow and change, to delight in the variety of experience. Enjoy the new friends, new opportunities, the adventure and excitement. Enjoy the social activities. Revel in the freedom (*5 Personal Year*). If possible, take advantage of opportunities to continue developing your artistic skills (*Second Epicycle of the 3 Second Period*).

Concentrate on feeling loose and free. Move away from old routines, but do it constructively. If you're bogged down, seek out new directions. The opportunities lie with the new and progressive. Involvement with detail work will probably feel confining (5 *Personal Year*). Your versatility, cleverness and enthusiasm should make it easy for you to enjoy all the activity (5 *Life Path*).

Don't scatter your energy in all directions. In the past, you've tended to be restless and impulsive. If you're more careful in using freedom, if you have a better balance here, there will be less interference with the free-wheeling opportunities (5 *Personal Year with 14/5 Karmic Debt, 5·5*).

There may be an important change in this year—a change of residence, work or family situation. You may not initiate the change, but the ultimate effect is dependent on your ability to take advantage of it and use it to help in forward movement (5 *Personal Year*).

Be sure to take care of your responsibilities, particularly related to family and friends (6 *Expression*, 6 *Modified Karmic Lesson*, 6 *Universal Year*). After the whirl of this year, you may look forward to next year with its quieter emphasis on family and domestic matters (*preparation for 6 Personal Year*).

Because of his age, there's a good chance that Hal's 5 energy is in good balance. If so, it contributes to the pleasures of a 5 Personal Year.

In our three examples, Hal's age and energies along with the balance of those energies significantly affect his approach to his life experiences. We *can't* predict what he'll do or how he'll feel. We can, though, expect that his 5 Personal Year, at ages 44 and 45, will probably give him a good deal of opportunity, excitement and adventure, while his 4 Personal Year, at ages 43 and 44, is likely to be filled with the pressures of work and service. What transpires is up to Hal—if he chooses to loaf through the 4 year and labor through the 5 year, he's not likely to feel much sense of satisfaction, but, if he uses his energies judiciously, he can benefit in both years.

The Epicycle and the Personal Year give us a remarkable opportunity for focusing our diverse energies from year to year. Become aware of the meaningful effect on your life and the lives of those close to you.

CHAPTER 32

MEDIUM TERM CYCLES, PART 2:
THE TRANSITS
THE ESSENCE

Definition

THE TRANSITS AND THE ESSENCE ARE MEDIUM TERM CYCLES DESCRIBING PROBABLE EVENTS OR THE PROBABLE TREND OF EVENTS. The events relate to the individual's personal and professional life, the use of the talents, the personal relationships—friendships, romances, marriages, families—travel and health. The Transits and Essence describe the events to which the approach, described by the Personal Year, is directed. These three cycles are very important, the most significant of all the progressed cycles.

Calculation of the Transits

All the cycles we've discussed so far and the additional cycles in Chapter 34 and 35 are derived from the birthdate. The Transits and Essence are the only cycles derived from the birthname.

Each letter of each name in the birthname describes the events in specific periods of the life. THE INFLUENCE OF EACH LETTER, CALLED THE TRANSIT, LASTS A GIVEN NUMBER OF YEARS EQUIVALENT TO THE MODIFIER NUMBER OF THE LETTER. The modifier number is, of course, the letter's place in the alphabet reduced to a single digit. For instance:

A, the first letter, has a 1 year Transit.
B, the second letter, has a 2 Year Transit. . . .

K, the eleventh letter, has a 2 year Transit.
(11 = 1 + 1 = 2; master numbers do not apply to the duration of the Transits.)

L, the twelfth letter, has a 3 year Transit.
(12 = 1 + 2 = 3). . . .

N, the fourteenth letter, has a 5 year Transit.
(14 = 1 + 4 = 5). . . .

Z, the twenty-sixth letter, has an 8 year Transit.
(26 = 2 + 6 = 8).

The number of years each Transit lasts, then, is as follows:

A	J	S	......	1 year
B	K	T	......	2 year
C	L	U	......	3 year
D	M	V	......	4 year
E	N	W	......	5 year
F	O	X	......	6 year
G	P	Y	......	7 year
H	Q	Z	......	8 year
I	R		......	9 year

Here is the method for calculating the Transits for the many years in an individual's life. We'll use the name of a fictitious lady:

DALE LEE SANDER, born on October 11, 1952

On Dale's progressed chart, we first fill in the Age and Year columns as discussed in Chapter 27.

We work with one name at a time. We start with the first name, Dale, and show its Transits in the first Transit column to the left (Figure 32-1 on page 539).

The letters of this first name express their influence, one after the other, each lasting its specific number of years.

D, the first letter in Dale, has a 4 year Transit. We print the D to cover 4 years: age 0 (year of birth), age 1, 2, and 3.

A, the second letter in Dale, has a 1 year Transit. A expresses its influence only at age 4.

L, the third letter, has a 3 year Transit, covering ages 5, 6 and 7.

E, the fourth and last letter has a 5 year Transit. The chart shows the influence of E at ages 8, 9, 10, 11, 12.

The influence of the first name lasts thirteen years—from age 0 through age 12. Having finished this first Transit of Dale, we start the second:

D, with a 4 year Transit, influences age 13, 14, 15, 16.
A, with a 1 year Transit, influences age 17.
L, with a 3 year Transit, influences age 18, 19, 20.
E, with a 5 year Transit, influences age 21, 22, 23, 24, 25.

We can continue with additional Transits of Dale as far as we're interested in going. A light horizontal line is placed at the end of each letter's Transit. We have now completed the calculation of the Transits of the first name.

DALE LEE SANDER
OCTOBER 11, 1952

Age	Medium Term					Year	Long Term	
	Transits			Essence	Personal Year	Universal Year		Period	Pinnacle
0	D						1952		
1	D						1953		
2	D						1954		
3	D						1955		
4	A						1956		
5	L						1957		
6	L						1958		
7	L						1959		
8	E						1960		
9	E						1961		
10	E						1962		
11	E						1963		
12	E						1964		
13	D						1965		
14	D						1966		
15	D						1967		
16	D						1968		
17	A						1969		
18	L						1970		
19	L						1971		
20	L						1972		
21	E						1973		
22	E						1974		
23	E						1975		
24	E						1976		
25	E						1977		
26	D						1978		
27	D						1979		
28	D						1980		
29	D						1981		
30	A						1982		
31	L						1983		
32	L						1984		
33	L						1985		
34	E						1986		
35	E						1987		

Figure 32–1
Progressed Chart
with Transits of First Name:
Dale Lee Sander

The Transits of Lee, the second name, are placed in the second Transit column in a similar manner (Figure 32-2 below on this page).

First, the 3 year L Transit, followed by the 5 year E Transit which is, in turn, followed by another 5 year Transit for the second E.

The first Transit of Lee lasts 13 years from age 0 (birth) to age 12. It's just a coincidence that both the Dale and Lee Transits end at the same age.

DALE LEE SANDER
OCTOBER 11, 1952

Age	Medium Term						Year	Long Term	
	Transits			Essence	Personal Year	Universal Year		Period	Pinnacle
0	D	L					1952		
1	D	L					1953		
2	D	L					1954		
3	D	E					1955		
4	A	E					1956		
5	L	E					1957		
6	L	E					1958		
7	L	E					1959		
8	E	E					1960		
9	E	E					1961		
10	E	E					1962		
11	E	E					1963		
12	E	E					1964		
13	D	L					1965		
14	D	L					1966		
15	D	L					1967		
16	D	E					1968		
17	A	E					1969		
18	L	E					1970		
19	L	E					1971		
20	L	E					1972		
21	E	E					1973		
22	E	E					1974		
23	E	E					1975		
24	E	E					1976		
25	E	E					1977		
26	D	L					1978		
27	D	L					1979		
28	D	L					1980		
29	D	E					1981		
30	A	E					1982		
31	L	E					1983		
32	L	E					1984		
33	L	E					1985		
34	E	E					1986		
35	E	E					1987		

Figure 32-2
Progressed Chart
with Transits of First and Middle Names:
Dale Lee Sander

We continue with additional Transits of Lee. The second Transit ends at age 25, the third ending at age 38, is off the chart.

The Transits of the last name, Sander, are placed in the third Transit column in a similar manner (Figure 32-3 below on this page). (If there was a fourth name, its Transits would, of course, be placed in the fourth Transit column.)

DALE LEE SANDER
OCTOBER 11, 1952

Age	Medium Term			Essence	Personal Year	Universal Year	Year	Long Term	
	Transits							Period	Pinnacle
0	D	L	S				1952		
1	D	L	A				1953		
2	D	L	N				1954		
3	D	E	N				1955		
4	A	E	N				1956		
5	L	E	N				1957		
6	L	E	N				1958		
7	L	E	D				1959		
8	E	E	D				1960		
9	E	E	D				1961		
10	E	E	D				1962		
11	E	E	E				1963		
12	E	E	E				1964		
13	D	L	E				1965		
14	D	L	E				1966		
15	D	L	E				1967		
16	D	E	R				1968		
17	A	E	R				1969		
18	L	E	R				1970		
19	L	E	R				1971		
20	L	E	R				1972		
21	E	E	R				1973		
22	E	E	R				1974		
23	E	E	R				1975		
24	E	E	R				1976		
25	E	E	S				1977		
26	D	L	A				1978		
27	D	L	N				1979		
28	D	L	N				1980		
29	D	E	N				1981		
30	A	E	N				1982		
31	L	E	N				1983		
32	L	E	D				1984		
33	L	E	D				1985		
34	E	E	D				1986		
35	E	E	D				1987		

Figure 32–3
Progressed Chart
with All Transits:
Dale Lee Sander

As you can see, the first Transit of Sander runs 25 years from age 0 (birth) to 24. The second Transit ends off the chart at age 49.

We've now calculated Dale's complete Transits from birth to age 35.

Calculation of the Essence

THE ESSENCE FOR EACH YEAR IS CALCULATED BY ADDING UP THE MODIFIER NUMBERS OF THE TRANSITS FOR THE YEAR AND REDUCING THE SUM TO A SINGLE DIGIT OR MASTER NUMBER (Figure 32-4 on page 543).

At Dale's birth (age 0), the Transits are D, L and S.

$$D + L + S$$
$$= 4 + 3 + 1 = 8 \text{ Essence}$$

At age 1, the Transits are D, L and A.

$$D + L + A$$
$$= 4 + 3 + 1 = 8 \text{ Essence}$$

Even though the Transits for the two years are different, the Essence is the same.

At age 2, the Essence is

$$D + L + N$$
$$= 4 + 3 + 5 = 12$$
$$= 1 + 2 = 3$$
$$= 12/3 \text{ Essence}$$

The Essence at age 2 is written as 12/3 because the number "behind" the Essence, in this case the 12 "behind" the 3, adds its own subtleties. For Dale's first two years, there are no numbers "behind" the Essence.

We proceed down the chart, adding the Transits to find the Essence and recording the Essence in its column. A horizontal line is placed at the end of the time span of each Essence.

Time span

The Transits last between one and nine years. They start on the subject's birthday (rather than on January 1 like most cycles) and end on the day before the birthday (rather than December 31 like most cycles).

The Essence lasts a minimum of one year and occasionally as much as nine or ten years. They usually don't last more than three or four years. Like the Transits, the Essence starts on the subject's birthday and ends on the day before the birthday.

There's little in the way of transition from Transit to Transit or Essence to Essence. Sometimes, the Transit or Essence is felt to some degree about a month before the birthday beginning and about a month after the birthday ending. Often, partic-

Transitions

DALE LEE SANDER
OCTOBER 11, 1952

Age	Medium Term						Year	Long Term	
	Transits			Essence	Personal Year	Universal Year		Period	Pinnacle
							1952		
0	D	L	S	8			1953		
1	D	L	A	8			1954		
2	D	L	N	12/3			1955		
3	D	E	N	14/5			1956		
4	A	E	N	11/2			1957		
5	L	E	N	13/4			1958		
6	L	E	N	13/4			1959		
7	L	E	D	12/3			1960		
8	E	E	D	14/5			1961		
9	E	E	D	14/5			1962		
10	E	E	D	14/5			1963		
11	E	E	E	15/6			1964		
12	E	E	E	15/6			1965		
13	D	L	E	12/3			1966		
14	D	L	E	12/3			1967		
15	D	L	E	12/3			1968		
16	D	E	R	18/9			1969		
17	A	E	R	15/6			1970		
18	L	E	R	17/8			1971		
19	L	E	R	17/8			1972		
20	L	E	R	17/8			1973		
21	E	E	R	19/1			1974		
22	E	E	R	19/1			1975		
23	E	E	R	19/1			1976		
24	E	E	R	19/1			1977		
25	E	E	S	11/2			1978		
26	D	L	A	8			1979		
27	D	L	N	12/3			1980		
28	D	L	N	12/3			1981		
29	D	E	N	14/5			1982		
30	A	E	N	11/2			1983		
31	L	E	N	13/4			1984		
32	L	E	D	12/3			1985		
33	L	E	D	12/3			1986		
34	E	E	D	14/5			1987		
35	E	E	D	14/5					

Figure 32–4
Progressed Chart
with Transits and Essences:
Dale Lee Sander

ularly with the longer Transits, it may be a few months after the start of the Transit before the individual is fully aware of the new influences, even though they've been operational since the birthday.

Chart 17: Essence

Turn to CHART 17: THE ESSENCE, on page 738. The top row gives a general description of the Essence, listing the events and opportunities to be expected. Capitalized words or phrases in the description of each Essence emphasize the probable type of activity. Sometimes, desirable means of dealing with the activities are also included. They are not integral to the Essence, but indicate specific characteristics and energies which, if available, are helpful in appropriately developing the opportunities.

Commentary

All of the Essences may indicate significant times in the life, but some seem to make a more dramatic impact than others. The 1 Essence, with its feeling of change and new direction, often marks an auspicious period. The 4 Essence usually indicates some limitations or restrictions strongly affecting the subject while the 5 Essence usually emphasizes impressive breakthroughs to freedom. The 8 Essence sometimes signifies important business developments with far-reaching effects while the 9 Essence, more often than not, introduces high drama and high feeling.

An 11 Essence always indicates the possibility of events of both the 11 and 2 Essences and a 22 Essence the possibility of events of both the 22 and 4 Essences. Essences with master numbers often have a strong impact on the life. Even when it's difficult to live up to the positive potential of the master number, as it is most of the time, the accompanying nervous tension is likely to impress itself on the subject.

The second row on Chart 17 describes the additional emphasis to an Essence because of the number "behind" the Essence. Some of these additional emphases are of minor import, some are extremely important. Most important of all the numbers "behind" are the karmic numbers—the 19/1, 13/4, 14/5 and 16/7.

Although a 7 Essence, or a 25/7 or 34/7 usually marks a period of quiet growth, the 16/7 Essence very often demarcates a period of great intensity and tension, a time with superior possibilities disguised by confusing circumstances. It's not too uncommon to find the 16/7 Essence denoting an especially vital transition in the life.

The 19/1 Essence is usually a bit less intense than the 16/7—but just a bit. The dramatic potential of the 19/1 is usually far clearer than the possibilities of the 16/7. The 19/1 usually indicates the possibility of a substantial and difficult developmental period, often a transition to a significant maturation.

Usually less productive and almost as difficult as the 19/1 and 16/7 is the 13/4 Essence. There's a feeling here of suffocating and seemingly never-ending restriction. Though the limitations are present, they're often there because of the subject's unclear view or tunnel vision, rather than because of outside circumstances. This period may actually present the opportunities to lift the restrictions, but the shift of view to accomplish this may be lost in the pressures of work and duty.

The 14/5 Essence is likely to be more frustrating than difficult. The individual may feel overwhelmed by a deluge of opportunity, adventure and experience. Sometimes, as a matter of fact, he has the time of his life with all the unusual, exciting activity, but may have great difficulty learning to handle freedom, learning to make the most of opportunities, learning to grow and develop. Potentials with major future possibilities are often lost or unseen until far too late for appropriate action.

The next to last row on Chart 17 describes the effect of a long period—five or more years—of a single Essence. If the right energies are present, an extended period may be a time of unparalleled development. Usually, though, that single emphasis for a long time tends to have a wearying effect. If the Essence is one of the more dramatic ones—the karmic Essences or the 1, 5, 9, 11, 22 especially—that long period will need much effort and concentration by the individual to stay on track to reap the potential benefits.

We'll discuss the bottom row of the chart, the Essence and Personal Year with the same number, in Chapter 33.

Chart 18: Transits

Now turn to CHART 18: THE TRANSITS, on page 752. Here you'll find the events and opportunities described by the twenty-six Transits. Important events can occur with any Transit, but some of the Transits seem to have a stronger impact than others. The one year Transits—A, J, S; the five year Transits—E, N, W; and the nine year Transits—I and R—make the most dynamic impression.

Commentary

When a particular Transit is repeated in a given year—R and R in the same year, for instance—the overbalance of a single energy presents problems and obstacles. Chart 18 also describes the negative potential to be expected with doubled Transits. The description of the events of a year with, say, T·T Transits would indicate the negative potential, but the events to be expected with the T Transit alone would also be included.

The Transits with strong individual impacts have strong impacts when repeated, too. A, J and S, because of their short period, are rarely doubled, but when the doubling does occur, the year is difficult. E, N and W are occasionally doubled, leading to the likelihood of a frustrating chaotic time with energy scattered. I and R, because of their nine year period, are doubled more frequently than other Transits, describing periods of high drama and intense emotion. Transits repeated three (or even four) times in a year are occasionally found. These Transits intensify the descriptions given for the doubled energy.

Far more common than the doubled letter Transits are Transits with the same modifier number occurring in a given year. E·N, E·W and N·W occur often and I·R occurs even more frequently. The descriptions for these combinations are shown in the top row of the chart. If there's an E·N Transit, the E·N description along with the E events and the N events would be included for the year. If there are three or four Transits with the same modifier number, the description is intensified.

If you look back on Dale Sander's progressed chart, you'll see that she has an E·E Transit from ages 8 through 10, 21 through 25 and 34, 35. She even has an E·E·E Transit at ages 11 and 12. She also has an E·N Transit from ages 3 through 7 and 29 through 31. *19* of Dale's 36 years shown contain E·E, E·E·E or E·N. An unusual and difficult chart configuration!

Relative impact of Transits and Essence

The Essence and the Transits all contribute to the description of the events for a given year. The contribution of each to the total description depends on the importance of their respective impacts.

If there's a karmic Essence, its very strong impact takes precedence over the information derived from the Transits. If there's a 16/7 Essence, as an example, the events of the year would probably be dominated by the 16/7 Essence description. The 7 Essence events would also be strongly noted. The events described by the Transits would be added to the 16/7 Essence and 7 Essence descriptions, if appropriate, or listed in a secondary capacity.

If there isn't a karmic Essence with its very important impact present, there are several Essences and doubled (or multiple) Transits with important impacts that take precedence. If a 1, 5, 9, 11 or 22 Essence is present, it takes precedence over the Transits. If a doubled (or multiple) A, J, S; E, N, W; I or R Transit is present, it takes precedence over the Essence and other Transit(s).

If the 1, 5, 9, 11 or 22 Essence *and* a doubled (or multiple)

A, J, S; E, N, W; I or R Transit are present, they both, together, take precedence over the other Transit(s). Events other than the ones described by the governing Essence or Transit would be added to their description, if appropriate, or listed in a secondary manner.

If none of these very important or important Essences or Transits are present in a given year, there are other Essences and Transits with above average or average impact which take precedence in a similar manner. If even these are not present, the below average Essence and Transits that *are* present describe the year's events with neither Essence nor Transits taking precedence.

The following chart summarizes these impacts:

RELATIVE IMPACT	ESSENCE	TRANSITS
Very Important	19/1, 13/4, 14/5, 16/7	—
Important	1, 5, 9, 11, 22	Multiple or double A, J, S; E, N, W; I, R
Above average	4, 6, 8	Multiple or double 1, 5, 9 modifier numbers; Below average Transits repeated more than twice; A
Average	—	Below average Transits repeated twice; J, S; E, N, W; I, R
Below average	2, 3, 7	The rest of the Transits

Relative impact chart

Let's see how this works in practice:

From Figure 32-4, page 543, when Dale Sanders is ten years old, she has a 14/5 Essence and E, E, D Transits.

Using the relative impact chart

> The very important 14/5 Essence takes precedence.
> The important E·E Transit events are added to the 14/5 description.
> The below average D Transit is also mentioned.

When Dale is sixteen years old, she has an 18/9 Essence and D, E, R Transits.

> The important 18/9 Essence takes precedence.
> The average E and R Transit events are added to the 18/9 description.
> The below average D Transit is also mentioned.

When Dale is twenty-seven years old, she has a 12/3 Essence and D, L, N Transits.

> The average N Transit takes precedence.
> The below average 12/3 Essence and D, L Transits are added to the N Transit.

Commentary on relative impact

Don't be misled by the phrase "relative impact." The relative impact is used here *only* in determining that some events have a greater probability of occurring in a given period than others.

In numerology terms, years don't have very important or important impacts as much as they have the *potential* for very important or important impacts. A year with a very important Essence or an important Essence or Transit is *not* necessarily a more significant year for an individual than a year with only average or below average Essence and Transits. The significance of a year can only be determined by the *actual* developments in a person's life. This, of course, depends on the person's *actual* actions in relation to the events on hand.

Let's examine this critical point in greater detail.

In a year with a very important 16/7 Essence, there are likely to be events with the potential to effect important changes in the life. If the individual has the ability and the desire, he may take advantage of the events to produce dramatic transitions and make that year a very important one in the life. If, on the other hand, the individual lacks the ability or desire, there may be little change or growth and the year may seem of little significance.

Now in a year with only below average Essence and Transits present, say a 3 Essence with B, O, D Transits, what are some of the possibilities? Love affairs, marriage, travel, creative work! The B, O, D Transits would be of less significance if a 16/7 Essence were present and, similarly, the 3 Essence would be of less consequence if E·E Transits were present—BUT, when just the 3 Essence and B, O, D Transits are present, they obviously can present strong, exciting possibilities. If the individual takes advantage of the potential, he may begin a beautiful marriage, take a Mediterranean cruise or compose and publish some original music, making the year extremely significant. He may, for whatever reason, not take advantage of the potential so that little of consequence may take place.

In a progressed delineation, you'll find that the events or trend of events themselves, as described by the Essence and Transits, automatically indicate the potential significance of the year. In the reading, then, no mention need be made of relative impacts. It's up to the individual whether he rises above or falls below the potential importance described by the delineation.

There are a few subtleties worth noting. If a specific event is mentioned twice in the Essence and Transits for a given year, that event has more possibility of occurring than if only mentioned once. If it's mentioned more than two times, the possibility increases. In a year with a 3 Essence and B, O, D Transits, for example, love affairs are mentioned three times (3 Essence and B, O Transits). There's more possibility of love affairs than if it was a year with a 3 Essence and J, Y, D Transits, where the love affairs would relate only to the 3 Essence.

Some Transits are repeated frequently in a particular life and the repetition weakens the impact considerably. Occasionally, for example, you'll run into a person with a middle initial but no middle name. Harry S. Truman, for instance, has no middle name. This means that the S Transit appeared in every year in his life. With continuous repetition like that, no attention need be paid to the description of the S Transit.

You'll find that some people have many I's and R's in their name. Since each I and R has a 9 year Transit, the progressed chart is likely to show an I or R in many, or even most, years. The I or R usually produces much emotion and drama, but if an individual has so many repetitions of I and R, he'll take the high drama he encounters for granted and it needs little specific mention.

Delineation description of Transits and Essence

A delineation of probable events or the trend of events includes the following:

A. An awareness of the long term cycles. The tone set by the background cycles would affect the events even though the description of the current Period and Pinnacle might be described separately. A 6 Essence or an F Transit, for instance, would operate with more impact in a 6 Period than a 7 Period.

B.   The events or trend of events described by the Essence (from Chart 17) and the Transits (from Chart 18). It's important to group the events for clarity.

Separate the events into the following groups:

> General
> Professional
> Financial
>
> Personal
>   Friendships
>   Romance
>   Marriage
>   Home/Family
>
> Travel
> Health

Rearrange the groups for the delineation in the order of impact:

> If a group contains events from a karmic Essence with its very important impact, that group is placed at the beginning of the reading and emphatically emphasized. (See Hal's delineation at age twenty-five, page 553.)

> If there's no karmic Essence, place the groups with events from Essences or Transits with important impacts at the beginning of the reading and emphasize. (See Hal's delineation at age thirty-five, page 556.)

> If there's no very important or important Essence or Transits, place the groups so that the above average events get a bit more emphasis than the average events. Mention the below average events in passing. (See Hal's delineation at age fifteen, page 552.)

> The number of sentences devoted to each group is a good measure of the group's importance.

C.   Preparation for important events, if any, coming within the next three or four years.

The subject's energies don't modify the events themselves, but they do indicate the subject's ability to deal with the events. In the next chapter, when we synthesize the medium term cycles, we'll deal with this important issue.

We'll delineate several years in Hal Allen's life to show the probable events. Let's first return to his progressed chart. We can fill in the Transits and Essence columns using the calculations outlined at the beginning of the chapter (Figure 32-5 below).

We'll look at the probable events in Hal's life at ages 15, 25 and 35. The years under consideration are shaded in the progressed chart for ease of reference. Each portion of the delineation is written in the present tense.

Example: Hal Allen's progressed chart

Hal Allen's delineation of Transits and Essence

HARLAN WILLIAM ALLEN
MAY 12, 1941

Age	Medium Term					Year	Long Term	
	Transits			Essence	Personal Year	Universal Year		Period	Pinnacle
0	H	W	A	14/5			1941	5	8
1	H	W	L	16/7			1942	5	8
2	H	W	L	16/7			1943	5	8
3	H	W	L	16/7			1944	5	8
4	H	W	L	16/7			1945	5	8
5	H	I	L	20/2			1946	5	8
6	H	I	L	20/2			1947	5	8
7	H	I	E	22/4			1948	5	8
8	A	I	E	15/6			1949	5	8
9	R	I	E	23/5			1950	5	8
10	R	I	E	23/5			1951	5	8
11	R	I	E	23/5			1952	5	8
12	R	I	N	23/5			1953	5	8
13	R	I	N	23/5			1954	5	8
14	R	L	N	17/8			1955	5	8
15	R	L	N	17/8			1956	5	8
16	R	L	N	17/8			1957	5	8
17	R	L	A	13/4			1958	5	8
18	L	L	L	9			1959	5	8
19	L	L	L	9			1960	5	8
20	L	I	L	15/6			1961	5	8
21	A	I	L	13/4			1962	5	8
22	N	I	L	17/8			1963	5	8
23	N	I	L	17/8			1964	5	8
24	N	I	E	19/1			1965	5	8
25	N	I	E	19/1			1966	5	8
26	N	I	E	19/1			1967	5	8
27	H	I	E	22/4			1968	5	8
28	H	I	E	22/4			1969	5	8
29	H	A	N	14/5			1970	5₃	8
30	H	M	N	17/8			1971	5₃	8
31	H	M	N	17/8			1972	5₃	8
32	H	M	N	17/8			1973	3₅	9
33	H	M	N	17/8			1974	3₅	9
34	H	W	A	14/5			1975	3₅	9
35	A	W	L	9			1976	3	9

Figure 32–5
Progressed Chart
with Transits and Essences:
Hal Allen

Delineation: Age 15

AGE 15: 1956–1957

THE DATA:

A. 5 First Period on a 5 Life Path, 8 First Pinnacle. See complete description, page 513.

B. 17/8 Essence, R, L, N Transits.
    In order of impact:
    Above average: 17/8 Essence
    Average: R, N Transits
    Below Average: L Transit

C. Prepare for 13/4 Essence at age 17 and L·L·L Transits at ages 18 and 19.

THE DELINEATION:

LONG TERM CYCLES

> You're likely to be in an environment filled with activity, variety and uncertainty. Since you tend to jump from activity to activity and since your youth probably precludes a desire for accomplishment, you may be content enough with this state of affairs. You may be involved, even at your young age, in some sort of work, but I suspect it makes you feel restricted (5 *First Period, 8 First Pinnacle*).

GENERAL

> There are a lot of possibilities this year (*No Essence or Transit with very important or important impact*). There may be some significant events with much drama and the possibility, too, of delays. Strong emotions are apt to need self-discipline for positive results (*R Transit*). There's likely to be the constant change and activity you like along with sudden, unexpected, unusual or exciting happenings (*N Transit*). Extravagant or self-indulgent actions may create difficulties (*L Transit*).

PROFESSIONAL

> If you're working, there may be chances for advancement. Your schoolwork may also hold opportunities for advancement and improvement of your standing and reputation. (*17/8 Essence. Since a fifteen year old's primary work is usually school, the description of the Essence is extended to include that activity*). Unique or unusual ideas may lead to more independence (*17/8 Essence*). Your work or school-

ing may involve humanitarian or philanthropic endeavors (*R Transit*).

FINANCIAL

There's some chance of financial gain for you or your family, but finances may have a tendency to fluctuate (*17/8 Essence, N Transit, extended, because of Hal's age, to include his family*).

TRAVEL

There's a good chance of travel, possibly related to school or work activities (*8 Essence, N and L Transits*).

PERSONAL

This is probably a good year to enjoy both new friends and old, although your interest in freedom may bring separation from some old friends. (*N and L Transits*). There's even a chance for romance although it's likely to be sudden, unusual and short-lived (*R and N Transits*). There may be much pleasure and happiness at home (*L Transit*).

PREPARATION FOR THE FUTURE

You should be prepared for either some hard work and/or some feeling of restriction at age seventeen. At age eighteen and nineteen, if you're feeling indolent and selfish, you'll block opportunities for advancement (*preparation for 13/4 Essence at age seventeen, L·L·L at ages eighteen and nineteen*).

The delineation emphasizes the above average 17/8 Essence and the average R, N Transits with only a little comment on the below average L Transit. Since there is no outstanding impact, there is a rather diffused quality in the reading for this year. Hal may choose, if he so desires, to stress one or another of the possibilities open to him.

Because of his youth, events related to marriage were omitted and events related to business were downplayed. Health wasn't mentioned in the Essence or any of the Transits.

AGE 25: 1966–1967
THE DATA:
A.   5 First Period on a 5 Life Path, 8 First Pinnacle. See complete description, page 513.

Delineation:
Age 25

B.   19/1 Essence, N, I, E Transits.
     In order of impact:
          Very important: 19/1 Essence
          Above average: E·N Transit
          Average: I Transit
C.   Prepare for additional similar year at age 26 and 22/4 Essence at ages 27 and 28.

THE DELINEATION:

LONG TERM CYCLES

You're likely to be in an environment filled with activity, variety and uncertainty. You may be learning to deal with your continued feeling of restlessness, your tendency to be erratic and your excessive physical appetites. You're likely to be involved in the business world and struggling with the restrictive and limiting effect on your free-wheeling nature. (5 *First Period, 8 First Pinnacle. Note that the description is considerably different than at age fifteen.*)

GENERAL

The years from your twenty-fourth to your twenty-seventh birthday form what could be an extremely important time in your life. There are opportunities to achieve independence by changing existing limiting situations. The achievement of independence is likely to take a lot of effort and you may feel beset with obstacles and problems. You may have to struggle to learn the important lessons leading to development and growth (*19/1 Essence*).

This period emphasizes beginnings, change and progress, the development of new ideas (*1 Essence*). Be prepared for sudden, unexpected, unusual, and/or exciting events (*E and N Transits*). Remember that haste, impulsiveness and the scattering of energy may impede potential benefits (*E·N Transits*). There's likely to be much drama in the important events, possibly delays to reckon with (*I Transit*). Try to balance the strong emotions that are likely. Sensitivity, loving and giving will usually help; emotional confusion is apt to hinder progress (*I Transit*).

PROFESSIONAL

This three year period is a good time to develop or expand business interests. You may meet new business associates and you may find possibilities for increasing your status and having your abilities recognized (*1 Essence*). The business opportunities may relate to humanitarian or philanthropic endeavors (*I Transit*).

PERSONAL

You may find new friends in your life and you may feel the desire for freedom leading to separation from old friends (*1 Essence, E, N Transits*). There may be exciting, unusual, but probably short-lived romances (*E, N Transits*). Marriage may be close if unsettled areas have been resolved, but high emotions can cause problems. A sudden marriage or separation and a change of home is possible (*E, N Transits*).

TRAVEL, FINANCIAL, HEALTH

There's a possibility of travel although fluctuating finances may keep you on edge (*E, N Transits*). Attend to matters of health, particularly when emotions are running high (*I Transit*).

PREPARATION FOR THE FUTURE

You may want to prepare for the possibility of some extremely significant ventures and the nervous tension that goes with it at ages twenty-seven and twenty-eight (*preparation for 22/4*).

The delineation stresses the very important 19/1 Essence and accompanying 1 Essence events by placing them at the beginning of the reading (the paragraphs related to General and Professional matters) and devoting the most space to them. The events described by the E, N and I Transits, with only above average or average impact, are condensed in a few short paragraphs. Although the events of the E, N and I Transits are similar to the events of the N and R Transits at age fifteen, the emphasis on the events in the two delineations is markedly different, primarily because of the extreme importance of the 19/1 Essence in the reading at age twenty-five.

Delineation: AGE 35: 1976–1977
Age 35   THE DATA:
              A. 3 Second Period on a 5 Life Path. 9 Second Pinnacle. See
                 complete description, page 515.
              B. 9 Essence, A, W, L Transits
                 In order of impact:
                     Important: 9 Essence
                     Above average: A Transit
                     Average: W Transit
                     Below average: L Transit
              C. Preparation isn't necessary for the 17/8 Essence and R, W,
                 L Transits at ages 36 through 38 since these years prob-
                 ably don't present any major difficulties. These years are
                 not shown on the progressed chart since it ends at age 35,
                 but they can be calculated easily.

              THE DELINEATION:

              LONG TERM CYCLES

                   You're likely to feel much drama and emotion in
                   your life at this time. Your ability to act tolerantly
                   and compassionately as you deal with opportuni-
                   ties related to humanistic, philanthropic or artistic
                   endeavors is likely to be important. There are the
                   possibilities here, too, for much pleasure in social
                   life, travel, artistic pursuits and verbal activities
                   such as acting or writing (3 *Second Period, 9 Second
                   Pinnacle*).

              GENERAL

                   This year certainly seems to emphasize drama and
                   emotion. There are likely to be significant events
                   involving much feeling—the tolerance and com-
                   passion necessary in this entire period will certain-
                   ly be of importance now. This year may mark an
                   important ending in your life, the end of a mean-
                   ingful experience or close personal relation. (End-
                   ings usually mean that someone moves or interests
                   change, only occasionally does an ending mean
                   death. The ending will probably give you more
                   freedom, but that's probably not apparent at the
                   time the ending occurs. The unexpectedness of the
                   ending is liable to be unsettling, too (9 *Essence*).
                   There may be a change in residence or in the work
                   situation. There may be important decisions to

make with implications for the future (*A Transit*). There's likely to be much change and activity, punctuated by sudden, unexpected, unusual or exciting events (*W Transit*). Extravagance or self-indulgence will probably cause difficulties (*L Transit*).

ROMANCE

Highly emotional love affairs involving great confusion are possible (*9 Essence*). They may be sudden, exciting and short-lived (*W Transit*). You may have to learn the difficult lesson that ultimate love doesn't restrict but rather supports freedom. The freedom involved may be your freedom or the freedom of the one you love (*9 Essence*).

PROFESSIONAL

Business opportunities may relate to humanitarian or philanthropic ventures (*9 Essence*). There may be business opportunities involving the creative talents (*L Transit*) as well as new business contacts (*A Transit*).

FRIENDSHIP, MARRIAGE, HOME/FAMILY, TRAVEL, HEALTH

There's the possibility of new friends (*A, W Transits*). There may be a feeling of restlessness about marriage (*W Transit*) but if emotions are balanced, there could be pleasure and happiness at home (*W, L Transits*). There's a good chance of travel (*A, W, L Transits*). Be sure to take care of your health (*W Transit*).

This delineation emphasizes the important impact of the 9 Essence, uses the above average A and average W Transits as back-up and mentions only a little about the below average L Transit. The paragraphs related to general, romantic and professional matters, all stressed by the 9 Essence, make up three-quarters of the reading.

Hal, at fifteen, may advance in school or on his job, or may, through lack of effort, show little movement at all. At age twenty-five, he may break through to a new level of independence, significantly changing the direction of his life—or, he

may make some changes in his dependent relationships, pro-
gressing slightly—or, he may not change at all or may even
move backwards. He may, at age thirty-five, learn to handle
his feelings well and understand the relation between love and
freedom, or he may negate the potential and become mired in
emotional confusion.

The subject's free will is the ultimate determinant of the use
made of the events that transpire and, therefore, the *actual* impact made on the life.

CHAPTER 33

MEDIUM TERM CYCLES, PART 3: THE SYNTHESIS

By synthesizing the medium term cycles—the Universal Year, the Personal Year, the Epicycle, the Essence and the Transits—we delineate the probable events or trend of events and the approach to them most likely to lead to growth and development. In addition to a reading for the current year, I often discuss some of the previous years if it's of interest to the subject. I rarely read more than one or two years ahead in detail. Although you can describe the *probable* events and desirable approach even ten or twenty years ahead, the *actual* approach is heavily dependent on the progress to that date. A detailed reading too far into the future has little meaning.

In the synthesis, a number of points must be kept in mind:

DELINEATE THE MEDIUM TERM CYCLES IN RELATION TO THE LONG TERM CYCLES

Relating medium term cycles and long term cycles

The long term cycles don't directly influence the medium term cycles, but they do indicate probable broad directions of growth. The Period and Pinnacle are of some significance in the years when important changes may be expected—the 1, 5 and 9 Personal Years—or when promising activity is likely—the 3, 4, 8 and 22 Personal Years. In those years, an awareness of the background tone may be helpful in distinguishing favorable opportunities. In the receptive years—the 2, 6, 7 and 11 Personal Years—there are apt to be more in the way of detours or wanderings and the long term cycles are of less interest. Begin the progressed delineation with a description of the long term cycles to set the stage for the more specific medium term cycles.

Relating current year to Epicycle

DELINEATE THE CURRENT YEAR IN RELATION TO THE EPICYCLE.

The Epicycle is a nine year repeating cycle of the Personal Years. Although the Essence and Transits don't usually repeat a pattern in the same way that the Personal Years do, their influence is also an important part of the Epicycle. The addition of the probable trend of events adds dimension to the description of the Epicycle.

Let's look at a couple of Hal Allen's Epicycles (Figure 33-1 on page 561). We've circled the Essence and Transits that take precedence each year and, for the purpose of this discussion, we'll ignore the other Essences and Transits.

The first Epicycle we will examine runs from 1964 through 1972. This Epicycle is the end of both Hal's 5 First Period and 8 First Pinnacle. Hal's lessons relating to freedom and his relation to the business world will probably provide the background tone.

The Epicycle starts with a 1 and 2 Personal Year stressing the 17/8 Essence and the N and I Transits—the emphasis here is on the excitement and emotions related to business. There are three 19/1 Essences in a row at age twenty-four through twenty-six—possibilities here for achieving more independence. Following are two 22/4 Essences at ages twenty-seven and twenty-eight. Because of Hal's energies, I'd expect the years to stress the 4 potential of work and limitation with some 22 nervous tension and a small possibility of 22 significant ventures. A 14/5 Essence is next with its emphasis on using freedom. The Epicycle closes with a 17/8 Essence and an N Transit—excitement related to business.

This Epicycle, which could be considered marking the end of Hal's formative years, flows from business emphasis at the beginning to business emphasis at the end, with time to explore independence, hard work and freedom in between. Can you see that the business years at the end of the Epicycle are likely to be significantly different than the business years at the beginning because of the explorations in the middle years?

Hal's Epicycle from 1982 through 1990 has a somewhat different flow. This Epicycle covers his 8 Second Pinnacle with its business emphasis. The R, I Transits open the period—emotions are likely to run high. Then, four years of a 23/5 Essence—exploring freedom—are followed by three years of a 17/8 Essence with accompanying I, E or I, N Transits—business emphasis with excitement and emotions. The Epicycle ends with a 9 Essence—drama, emotion, completion—and a 13/4 Essence—work and limitation. I get the sense here of delight in freedom at the beginning of the period (although there are the emotional R and I Transits along with the 23/5 Essence), then a commitment to business interests followed by drama and feelings of limitation. I suspect that Hal may still be struggling to balance his free-wheeling approach with the need to earn a living.

HARLAN WILLIAM ALLEN
MAY 12, 1941

Age	Medium Term			Personal Year	Universal Year	Year	Long Term	
	Transits		Essence				Period	Pinnacle
0	H	W	A	14/5	5	6	1941	5	8
1	H	W	L	16/7	6	7	1942	5	8
2	H	W	L	16/7	7	8	1943	5	8
					8	9	1944	5	8

Age	Medium Term			Personal Year	Universal Year	Year	Long Term	
20	L	I	L	15/6					
21	A	I	L	13/4	8	9	1962	5	8
22	N	I	L	17/8	9	1	1963	5	8
23	N	I	L	17/8	1	2	1964	5	8
24	N	I	E	19/1	11/2	3	1965	5	8
25	N	I	E	19/1	3	22/4	1966	5	8
26	N	I	E	19/1	4	5	1967	5	8
27	H	I	E	22/4	5	6	1968	5	8
28	H	I	E	22/4	6	7	1969	5	8
29	H	A	N	14/5	7	8	1970	5_3	8
30	H	M	N	17/8	8	9	1971	5_3	8
31	H	M	N	17/8	9	1	1972	5_3	8
32	H	M	N	17/8	1	2	1973	3_5	9

Age	Medium Term			Personal Year	Universal Year	Year	Long Term	
39	R	I	L	21/3					
40	R	I	L	21/3	9	1	1981	3	9
41	R	I	E	23/5	1	2	1982	3	8
42	R	I	E	23/5	11/2	3	1983	3	8
43	R	I	E	23/5	3	22/4	1984	3	8
44	R	I	E	23/5	4	5	1985	3	8
45	L	I	E	17/8	5	6	1986	3	8
46	L	I	N	17/8	6	7	1987	3	8
47	L	I	N	17/8	7	8	1988	3	8
48	A	L	N	9	8	9	1989	3	8
49	N	L	N	13/4	9	1	1990	3	8
					1	2	1991	3	11/2

Figure 33-1
Progressed Chart:
Hal Allen

As you can see, reading the current year as part of the Epi-cycle flow rather than as an isolated year can dramatically connect significant periods of the life.

Relating Personal Year, Essence and Transits

THE PERSONAL YEAR ALONG WITH THE ESSENCE AND/OR TRANSITS ARE REQUIRED FOR EACH YEAR'S DESCRIPTION.

You need the Personal Year to determine the desirable approach. You need the Essence and/or Transits to determine the probable trend of events. Some years seem governed more by one cycle than the others but all should be mentioned. (Strictly speaking, an occasional Essence or Transit is of little significance in a given year and can be omitted, but, at least one Transit *or* Essence should be included in any year's description).

The Personal Years can be rated for relative impact in a manner similar to the rating of the Essence and Transits in Chapter 32. The 1, 5, 8, 9, 11 and 22 Personal Years have an important impact, the 4 and 6 Personal Years have an above average impact, and the 2, 3 and 7 Personal Years have an average impact. Remember that these ratings are only for the purpose of determining the precedence of the various cycles in order to proceed with the delineation.

The following chart summarizes the impacts of the Personal Year, Essence and Transits:

Relative impact chart

RELATIVE IMPACT	PERSONAL YEAR	ESSENCE	TRANSITS
Very important	—	19/1,13/4, 14/5,16/7	—
Important	1,5,8,9,11,22	1,5,9,11,22	Multiple or double A,J,S; E,N,W; I,R
Above average	4,6	4,6,8	Multiple or double 1,5,9 modifier numbers; Below average Transits repeated more than twice; A
Average	2,3,7	—	Below average Transits repeated twice; J,S; E,N,W; I,R
Below average	—	2,3,7	The rest of the Transits

Look at Hal's progressed chart (Figure 33-1) on page 561 along with the relative impact chart.

In 1964, the important 1 Personal Year is likely to take precedence over the above average 8 Essence, the average N and I Transits and the below average L Transit.

In 1966, the very important 19/1 Essence is likely to take precedence over the average 3 Personal Year and average N, I, E Transits.

In 1968, the very important 19/1 Essence, the important 22 Essence and the important 5 Personal Year are all likely to influence the year strongly.

All the years aren't equal in intensity or meaning for the life, but all years may make important contributions to the experiences necessary for the subject's development.

WHEN THE PERSONAL YEAR AND THE ESSENCE ARE THE SAME NUMBER, THERE'S AN OVERBALANCE OF ENERGY LEADING TO OBSTACLES AND PROBLEMS.

When Personal Year and Essence are the same number

On Hal Allen's chart (Figure 33-2 on page 564), we've drawn a circle around the doubled number periods. It's the single digits we're concerned with, not the number behind the digit. In 1947, the 11/2 Personal Year is opposed by the 20/2 Essence. It's the 2·2 that creates problems. Similarly, a 22/4 Personal Year and a 13/4 Essence would indicate 4·4 difficulties. Infrequently, an 11/2 Personal Year combines with an 11/2 Essence, describing 11·11 and 2·2 problems. Or, just as infrequently, a 22/4 Personal Year and 22/4 Essence indicates 22·22 and 4·4 obstacles.

Because the Personal Year extends from January 1 to December 31 and the Essence from birthday to birthday, the problem period is usually only from January 1 to the birthday or from the birthday to December 31. In Hal's chart, the latter case is shown in 1941, 1950, 1958, and 1971. Sometimes, the conflict extends for the entire year as in 1943 and 1947.

Turn to CHART 17: THE ESSENCE, page 738. The bottom row of the chart describes the potential problem period with repeated numbers as well as some approaches to alleviate the difficulties. These periods, though usually short, require a substantial effort to work through.

WHEN THE PERSONAL YEAR HAS ENERGIES SIMILAR TO THE ESSENCE AND/OR TRANSITS, THE PERIOD IS LIKELY TO HAVE A POSITIVE DIRECTION. WHEN

When Personal Year has energies similar to or conflicting with Essence and/or Transits

THERE'S A CONFLICT BETWEEN THE ENERGIES OF THE PERSONAL YEAR AND THE ENERGIES OF THE ESSENCE AND/OR TRANSITS, THE PERIOD IS LIKELY TO HAVE A DIFFICULT OR CONFUSING DIRECTION.

A 1 Personal Year approach probably can help with events described by an 8 Essence or an A Transit. A 6 Personal Year and a 2 Essence or F Transit are usually compatible as is a 3 Personal Year, a 5 Essence and an E or N Transit.

But a 6 Personal Year with a 5 Essence or W Transit or a 7

HARLAN WILLIAM ALLEN
MAY 12, 1941

Age	Medium Term						Year	Long Term	
	Transits			Essence	Personal Year	Universal Year		Period	Pinnacle
0	H	W	A	14/5	5		1941		
1	H	W	L	16/7	6		1942		
2	H	W	L	16/7	7		1943		
3	H	W	L	16/7	8		1944		
4	H	W	L	16/7	9		1945		
5	H	I	L	20/2	1		1946		
6	H	I	L	20/2	11/2		1947		
7	H	I	E	22/4	3		1948		
8	A	I	E	15/6	4		1949		
9	R	I	E	23/5	5		1950		
10	R	I	E	23/5	6		1951		
11	R	I	E	23/5	7		1952		
12	R	I	N	23/5	8		1953		
13	R	I	N	23/5	9		1954		
14	R	L	N	17/8	1		1955		
15	R	L	N	17/8	11/2		1956		
16	R	L	N	17/8	3		1957		
17	R	L	A	13/4	4		1958		
18	L	L	L	9	5		1959		
19	L	L	L	9	6		1960		
20	L	I	L	15/6	7		1961		
21	A	I	L	13/4	8		1962		
22	N	I	L	17/8	9		1963		
23	N	I	L	17/8	1		1964		
24	N	I	E	19/1	11/2		1965		
25	N	I	E	19/1	3		1966		
26	N	I	E	19/1	4		1967		
27	H	I	E	22/4	5		1968		
28	H	I	E	22/4	6		1969		
29	H	A	N	14/5	7		1970		
30	H	M	N	17/8	8		1971		
31	H	M	N	17/8	9		1972		
32	H	M	N	17/8	1		1973		
33	H	M	N	17/8	11/2		1974		
34	H	W	A	14/5	3		1975		
35	A	W	L	9	4		1976		

Figure 33-2
Progressed Chart
with Same Essence and Personal Year Noted:
Hal Allen

Personal Year with an 8 Essence or H Transit—these often spell problems and conflicts. The individual is likely to be pulled from one energy to the other, struggling to find a comfortable balance. Sometimes, the attempt is made to avoid one energy completely; the negated potential usually continues to surface no matter what attempts are made to suppress it. Occasionally, balance can be reached by using the energies alternately. This presents difficulties, too, but it is sometimes the best that can be managed under trying circumstances.

In Hal's chart (Figure 33-2 on page 564) the 1 Personal Year and the 17/8 Essence of 1964 and 1973 present favorable possibilities. The N Transit, although not as strong, can help in both years, but the I Transit in 1964 may be a nuisance.

1965, on the other hand, presents a conflicting potential. In the first part of the year, the 11/2 Personal Year emphasizes illumination, waiting and cooperation, while the 17/8 Essence emphasizes advancement in the business community. (The N, I, L Transits are weaker than the Personal Year and the Essence and are ignored for this discussion.) Even omitting the 11 stress on potential illumination doesn't seem to alleviate the difficulties. Hal's chart indicates that he must work at waiting and cooperating to take advantage of business opportunities. Surprisingly enough, there usually *is* some combination of events and approach which *does* fit the description for the year and, as unusual as it may be, holds out the best potential. Hal, for instance, might find a business venture requiring his skill in dealing with a number of difficult employees. His ability to wait and cooperate in this situation may lead to advancement in the business.

The last part of 1965, with its 2 Personal Year (we're ignoring the 11) and the 19/1 Essence (we're also ignoring the weaker Transits), presents other complications. Hal must wait and cooperate in order to break down old conditions to achieve more independence for himself. It seems strange that waiting and cooperating will bring more independence, but if Hal can identify the opportunity and use the approach he will undoubtedly benefit. Conflicting energies usually *can* be resolved into positive potentials, but they take significantly more energy, of course, than the favorable configurations.

THE SUBJECT'S POTENTIALS MAY BE IMPORTANT MODIFIERS OF THE MEDIUM TERM CYCLES.

Relating subject's potentials and medium term cycles

The potentials from the birthdate, birthname and current name(s)—the core elements, Karmic Debts, Karmic Lessons, Challenge and other strong modifiers—define the subject's ability to enhance, deflect or mute the approach described by the Personal Year, as was mentioned in Chapter 31. The potentials *don't* modify the events or trend of events described by the Essence and Transits. But the potentials *do* modify the subject's ability to deal with the events, so the modifying effect is important in the synthesis.

If a significant energy has the same modifier number as the Personal Year, the Essence or any of the Transits, it's especially likely to make its effect felt. Be sure the delineation reflects these as well as any other strong applicable modifiers.

Calculation short cut for progressed chart

If you're doing a reading for a person who is twenty or thirty years old, it's relatively easy to complete the progressed chart. If, instead, the subject is fifty or sixty, there's a lot of work to calculate the Essence and Transits, and most of the calculation won't even be used for the reading. We can use a short cut instead.

As an example, we're planning to do a delineation for Hal Allen for 1993, the year when he turns 52. We need the data for the Epicycle which includes 1993. No matter where the year is in the Epicycle, we always want to be able to see the data for at least four or five years before and four or five years after so the flow is apparent. We need, then, a progressed chart from about age 47 (five years before age 52) to about 1998 (five years after age 52). We'll extend it to the year 2000 because, as we'll see, that will be required to complete the Epicycle.

We know, from the calculation for the Expression, that the first name Harlan has a 27 year Transit, which means it lasts from Harlan's birth (age 0) to his 26th year. The second Transit of Harlan ends at his 53rd year. (First Transit + second Transit = 26 + 27 = 53.) This means that the last N of Harlan's second Transit is opposite the 53 in the age column. We can then start at age 53, figure the Transits of Harlan to age 58. We can also go *backwards* from age 53 to age 47—five years of N from the end of Harlan, then one year of A, then the L Transit.

The progressed chart and the calculation would now look like Figure 33-3 on page 567.

We calculate the middle name in a similar manner. The first Transit of William lasts 34 years, to age 33. The second Transit ends at age 67 (33 + 34). That's way past age 58 which is as far as we have to go for the Epicycle in which we're interested.

Instead of adding the first and second Transits, we'll add the Transits of the individual letters to the first Transit of William until we're up to or past age 47 to get our starting point. The first Transit of William plus W and I gets us precisely up to age 47. We then go forward up to age 58.

HARLAN WILLIAM ALLEN
MAY 12, 1941

Age	Medium Term					Year	Long Term	
	Transits				Essence	Personal Year	Universal Year		Period	Pinnacle
								1941		
0										
47	L							1989		
48	A							1990		
49	N							1991		
50	N							1992		
51	N							1993		
52	N							1994		
53	N							1995		
54	H							1996		
55	H							1997		
56	H							1998		
57	H							1999		
58	H							2000		

Starting Point → 53

Harlan, first Transit: 27 – 1 =   26
Harlan, second Transit: + 27
                                     ——
                                     53

Figure 33–3
Progressed Chart
with Short Cut for Transit of First Name:
Hal Allen

The progressed chart and the calculation for William would look like Figure 33-4 on page 569.

The progressed chart and the calculations for the last name Allen would look like Figure 33-5 on page 570.

We complete the data we need by filling in the Periods, Pinnacles, Universal Year, Personal Year and Essence for the period from age 47 to 58 (Figure 33-6 on page 571). I always shade in the year of the reading, to more easily distinguish it from the other years. Here, 1993 is shaded. The shaded area for 1993 includes the last half of age 51 and the first half of age 52.

Now, we're ready to do the delineations.

Delineation description of medium term cycles

A delineation synthesizing the medium term cycles includes the following:

A. An awareness of the long term cycles.
B. An awareness of the Epicycle.
C. A description of the desirable approach (Personal Year and, to a small extent, the Universal Year) to the probable events or trend of events (Essence and Transits), modified as necessary by the subject's potentials (core elements and strong modifiers).
D. Preparation for any of the next three or four years which are likely to present difficulties.

Since some of the medium term cycles run from January 1 to December 31 and others from birthday to birthday, be sure the dates of the various periods under discussion are clearly indicated in the reading.

Hal Allen's delineation of medium term cycles: 1993

Here's Hal Allen's delineation for 1993 based on the steps just outlined. The delineation is written in the present tense. We're assuming here that Hal's birthname is also his current name—that there are no additional energies from new names.

THE DATA:

A. *Long term cycles*
    3 Second Period on a 5 Life Path
    11/2 Fourth Pinnacle
B. *Epicycles*
    Third and last Epicycle of the 3 Second Cycle
    First Epicycle of the 11/2 Fourth Pinnacle

HARLAN WILLIAM ALLEN
MAY 12, 1941

Age	Medium Term					Year	Long Term	
	Transits			Essence	Personal Year	Universal Year		Period	Pinnacle
0							1941		
47	I								
48	L						1989		
49	L						1990		
50	L						1991		
51	L						1992		
52	L						1993		
53	L						1994		
54	I						1995		
55	I						1996		
56	I						1997		
57	I						1998		
58	I						1999		
							2000		

Starting Point → (at age 47)

William, first Transit: $34 - 1 =$ 33
William, second Transit: $+ 34$
   $\overline{67}$

William, first Transit: $34 - 1 =$ 33
William, second Transit: $W = + 5$
   $\overline{38}$

   $I = + 9$
   $\overline{47}$

Figure 33–4
Progressed Chart
with Short Cut for Transit of Middle Name:
Hal Allen

HARLAN WILLIAM ALLEN
MAY 12, 1941

Age	Medium Term						Year	Long Term	
	Transits				Essence	Personal Year	Universal Year		Period	Pinnacle
0								1941		
47			N					1989		
48			N					1990		
49			N					1991		
50			N					1992		
51			A					1993		
52			L					1994		
53			L					1995		
54			L					1996		
55			L					1997		
56			L					1998		
57			L					1999		
58			E					2000		

Starting Point (→ points to age 50, N)

Allen, first Transit: 17 − 1 =   16
Allen, second Transit: + 17
                                         ———
                                          33

Allen, third Transit: + 17
                                         ———
                                          50

Figure 33–5
Progressed Chart
with Short Cut for Transit of Last Name:
Hal Allen

HARLAN WILLIAM ALLEN
MAY 12, 1941

Age	Medium Term			Essence	Personal Year	Universal Year	Year	Long Term	
	Transits							Period	Pinnacle
0							1941		
47	L	I	N	17/8	8	9	1989	3	8
48	A	L	N	9	9	1	1990	3	8
49	N	L	N	13/4	1	2	1991	3	11/2
50	N	L	N	13/4	11/2	3	1992	3	11/2
51	N	L	A	9	3	22/4	1993	3	11/2
52	N	L	L	11/2	4	5	1994	3	11/2
53	N	L	L	11/2	5	6	1995	3	11/2
54	H	I	L	20/2	6	7	1996	3	11/2
55	H	I	L	20/2	7	8	1997	3_6	11/2
56	H	I	L	20/2	8	9	1998	3_6	11/2
57	H	I	L	20/2	9	1	1999	3_6	11/2
58	H	I	E	22/4	1	2	2000	6_3	11/2

Figure 33-6
Partial Progressed Chart:
Hal Allen

C. *Medium term cycles*

Essence and Transits, in order of impact, with applicable potentials:

January 1
to
May 11
{
Important: 9 Essence
(9 Soul Urge, 9 Growth Number)
Above average: A Transit
(four 1's Intensity Point, 1 Challenge)
Average: N Transit
(5 Life Path, 14/5 Karmic Debt, 5·5 energy)
Below average: L Transit
(3 Birthday, five 3's Intensity Point, 3 Prime Intensifier)

May 12
to
December 31
{
Important: 11/2 Essence
(11/2 Maturity Number, 2 Karmic Lesson)
Average: L·L Transit
(3 Birthday, five 3's Intensity Point, 3 Prime Intensifier)
Average: N Transit
(5 Life Path, 14/5 Karmic Debt, 5·5 energy)

Personal Year, with applicable potentials:

Average: 3 Personal Year
(3 Birthday, five 3's Intensity Point, 3 Prime Intensifier)

22/4 Universal Year

D. *Preparation*

11/2 Essence continues to 54th birthday in 1995.

1993

THE DELINEATION:

LONG TERM CYCLES

You're likely to be in an environment where sensitivity and receptivity are highly regarded. You'll probably prefer to work with others rather than alone but you may have to get used to a comparative lack of recognition. A harmonious working environment is possible (2 *Fourth Pinnacle*). You may retire or partially retire at a comparatively young age. (*11/2 Fourth Pinnacle. The Fourth Pinnacle starts at age 49, therefore the comment about the comparatively young age.*)

There's apt to be emphasis on friendship, much activity, social life, possibly travel. Be careful not to scatter your energy or to act capriciously or self-indulgently (*3 Second Period on the 5 Life Path*). At more serious times, you may be seeking illumination through philosophic, religious or metaphysical studies. (*11 Fourth Pinnacle. This Pinnacle is only briefly mentioned because Hal has little energy to invest in this potential.*) Perhaps with your earlier restlessness tamed, a flowering of your loving responsible side now may provide much beauty in life (*A comparison of the current long term cycles with earlier ones*).

EPICYCLE

You're in a period of your life now—from 1991 through 1999—where there can be much pleasure and beauty (*last Epicycle of the 3 Second Period*) along with the development of your sensitivity and spiritual awareness (*first Epicycle of the 11/2 Fourth Pinnacle*). The first few years of this period may have presented difficulties. You may have been working on combining your free-wheeling energy with your loving, giving potential in a balanced manner without feeling repressed and limited (*13/4 Essence at age 49 and 50 conflicting with the strong 5 and 6 energy*). At age 51, there's the potential for completion, possibly in some dramatic fashion. This could be the ending of a job or relation, the ending of some feelings about work, restriction or freedom. We'll discuss this year in more detail shortly (*9 Essence at age 51*). There's the possibility of a turning point, perhaps some spiritual illumination at ages 52 and 53 (*11/2 Essence*). These years are followed by four years with the likelihood of cooperation and patient work, four years possibly used to assimilate the drama and awareness of the prior years (*20/2 Essence from age 54 through 57*). There's probably a renewed emphasis on work as the period ends, possibly a new, significant venture or a new way of looking at the work to be accomplished (*22/4 Essence at age 58 and beyond*). The period from 1991 through 1999, as you can see, holds much potential promise. 1993 may prove to be one of the more dramatic years of the period.

JANUARY 1, 1993 TO MAY 11, 1993
ESSENCE, TRANSITS AND PERSONAL YEAR

GENERAL

The beginning of 1993, to about the middle of May, is likely to be more dramatic and emotional than the rest of the year (*9 Essence to May 11; 11/2 Essence after*). Your ability to act with tolerance and compassion as you deal with significant events will be important—the more you can give of affection, love, understanding and sympathy, the more you can grow (*9 Essence with 9 Soul Urge, 9 Growth Number*). There may be important changes to deal with—possibly a change of residence or job—and an important decision to make with implications for the future (*A Transit*). Don't let self-centeredness or lack of flexibility impede your progress (*four 1's Intensity Point*). I expect your willpower can help now, as long as you don't use it to dominate others (*1 Challenge*). You may encounter sudden, unexpected, unusual or exciting events this year—if you're adaptable and enthusiastic rather than restless and impatient, there's likely to be forward progress (*N Transit with 5 Life Path, 14/5 Karmic Debt, 5·5 energy*).

The beginning of the year may mark some completions in your life. This usually means that a close personal relation moves or interests change; only occasionally does completion mean death. The ending will usually give you more freedom, but that's not likely to be apparent at the time the ending occurs. The unexpectedness of the completion is liable to be unsettling (*9 Essence*). In these situations and other emotional situations in which you're involved, try to handle your feelings constructively (*3 Personal Year*). You're likely to be brimming with feeling and very sensitive (*12/3 Birthday*). Try not to scatter your energies (*3 Personal Year with five 3's Intensity Point*). When appropriate, enjoy the satisfaction and accomplishments of bringing objects to a satisfactory conclusion (*3 Personal Year*).

FRIENDSHIP

This is likely to be a good time to make new friends and renew relations with old friends. A desire for freedom, though, may bring breaks in old relationships (*A, N, L Transits*). The positive experiences with friends may be one of the avenues for experiencing happiness and expressing the joy of living. Approach your experiences this year, as much as possible, with joy, cheer and enthusiasm. Entertain, socialize, delight in those times when you can enjoy yourself, but don't indulge only in superficial or capricious activities. Avoid self-indulgence or extravagance (*3 Personal Year*). At times when you want to play and enjoy yourself, don't be surprised to find others bogged down in work and responsibility (*conflict between 3 Personal Year and 22/4 Universal Year*).

ROMANCE, MARRIAGE

At the beginning of the year, romances are apt to be far more difficult than friendships. They're likely to be highly emotional and confusing. You may have to learn the usually painful lesson that ultimate love doesn't restrict, but rather supports freedom (*9 Essence*). Love affairs may prove to be sudden, unusual and short lived. Marriage probably has its rough spots. Unbalanced emotions are likely to cause problems (*N Transit*).

PROFESSIONAL

There may be some involvement with business ventures related to humanitarian or philanthropic endeavors. These may be opportunities to use your creative abilities (*9 Essence*). Concentrate on opportunities for self-improvement, particularly along the line of your strong artistic talents. Use your ideas, intuition, strong imagination, inspiration and vitality. Advancement and some recognition is possible. Emphasize particularly your superior verbal ability—use it in acting, singing or writing (*3 Personal Year with 3 Birthday, five 3's Intensity Point and 3 Prime Intensifier*). New business contacts may help with your creative advance (*A Transit, 3 Personal Year*).

MISCELLANEOUS

There's a good possibility of some travel (*A, N, L Transits*), although your finances may be subject to fluctuation (*N Transit*). There should be some pleasure and happiness to be found in the home life, although this may be difficult to maintain with all the high emotions (*L Transit, 9 Essence*).

MAY 12, 1993 TO DECEMBER 31, 1993
ESSENCE, TRANSITS AND PERSONAL YEAR
GENERAL

The last part of 1993, from about the middle of May to the end of December, will probably feel somewhat different than the first part of the year. There's probably less drama now, and while the emotions may still be running high, you're apt to be somewhat more sensitive and able to handle the feelings better (*9 Essence to May 11; 11/2 Essence after*). From this time up to your 54th birthday, you may receive some new awareness of great importance which will support the development of faith and inner peace. This new understanding may have a profound effect on the entire life, although it's likely to take time for the changes to develop (*11 Essence and preparation for coming years*). You're probably more understanding now of the kind of spiritual or non-material awareness I'm talking about, but, unless you've developed this side of yourself, you may not be aware of the new possibilities (*11 Maturity Number, no other 11 energy*). That heightened sensitivity, as I mentioned, may be helpful in dealing with emotions and may attract new friends who are appreciative of the sensitivity. Be careful that this sensitiveness doesn't cause problems and misunderstandings. When faced with an emotional situation, deal with it directly rather than sidestepping it (*11/2 Essence with 6 Expression, 9 Soul Urge*). There's apt to be some nervous tension which may affect your ability to express your feelings with clarity (*11 Essence with 11 Maturity Number*).

Starting at this time and extending until your 58th birthday, is a period in which there's likely to be an emphasis on patience and cooperation. You may be working as part of a group to satisfy mutual needs or you may be helping others with their needs. There's likely to be some details that must be carefully completed. I expect, at this age, that you've developed the ability to be patient, tactful and concerned with details (*2 Essence with 2 Karmic Lesson*). The loving, giving, responsible side of your character can be of much help working with others (*6 Expression, 9 Soul Urge*).

PROFESSIONAL

These same years—to your 58th birthday—may be involved with the development of associations. Developments of almost any kind are likely to take longer than first expected. Delays and temporary stoppages are apt to prove frustrating, but they may actually improve the ultimate timing needed for reaching your goals (*2 Essence*). You may be able to advance by developing your talents in some creative enterprise. You are strong in creative ability and imagination and this is a time to use these talents, possibly achieve recognition. By all means, use your fine verbal capabilities (*3 Personal Year, L Transit with 3 Birthday, five 3's Intensity Point, 3 Prime Intensifier*). If, particularly in the next two years, you tend to be indolent or selfish, these characteristics are likely to interfere with advancement possibilities (*L·L Transit*).

FRIENDSHIP, ROMANCE, MARRIAGE, HOME, FAMILY

Friendships are likely to be important just as they were in the first part of the year (*L, N Transits*). Romances may still tend to be sudden, unusual and short lived, but they are likely to be considerably more pleasurable than at the beginning of the year (*L, N Transits; ending of difficult 9 Essence*). Marriage may still have its difficulties unless the emotions are well-balanced (*N Transit*). There can be much pleasure at home and with the family. Honestly expressed feelings will probably bring added understandings (*L Transit*). Your personal life, in the last half of the year, may be a source of pleasure and happiness, a place to particularly express the joy of living. An active social life and entertainment may prove sources of pleasure. Be sure not to indulge only in superficial or capricious activities. Be there for others, particularly with your vibrance and vitality (*3 Personal Year*).

MISCELLANEOUS

There's still possibilities for travel (*N, L Transit*) although your finances may still be fluctuating (*N Transit*). You may experience lowered energy and vitality the last half of the year, so be sure to take care of your health (*2 Essence*).

I think you can see how important it is to indicate the relative priorities of the many events and approaches described. The subject's abilities and traits play a large part in the delineation, too, more, I think, than was apparent in the partial readings in the previous chapters. I used Hal's organization sheet for reference during the preparation of this reading to remind myself of his various applicable capabilities.

Many years, like Hal's 1993, have two distinct parts. Others, like Hal's 1994, 1996, 1997 and 1998 will be all of a piece, with the same Personal Year, Essence and Transits applying for the entire year. When the year is divided, distinguish which events carry through for the whole year, which occur only a portion of the time.

Often, events continue past the end of the year under consideration. In the delineation we've been studying, the 11/2

Essence and the N and L·L Transits all continue another year and a half past the end of 1993.

Events described by a given Essence or Transit can occur at any time while it's in effect. The special awareness of the 11/2 Essence, for example, can occur anytime within a two year period. Even though we're reading for 1993, that awareness may not occur until 1995. The period of the Essence or Transit must be given so that the time when certain events may occur is understood.

Be sure that the time span of each Essence and Transit is clear, particularly the starting and ending dates within the year under investigation.

With some practice in this format, you'll be able to produce your own progressed medium term delineations. They should be of great value in helping a subject marshal the energies to make the most of the available opportunities.

CHAPTER 34

SHORT TERM CYCLES, PART 1:
THE PERSONAL MONTH

The short term cycles, the Personal Month and the Personal
Day, are described in this and the following chapters. Although
the energy of these cycles is expressed in a concentrated period
of time, sometimes with striking impact, the medium term
cycles discussed in the last three chapters carry a greater
significance in the life. The Personal Month and Personal Day,
like the Personal Year, describe approaches to events. There are
no short term cycles describing probable events comparable to
the Essence and Transits.

THE PERSONAL MONTH DESCRIBES THE APPROACH **Definition**
TO EVENTS FOR A GIVEN MONTH LIKELY TO PRO-
DUCE GROWTH AND DEVELOPMENT. The Personal
Month should be visualized as a sub-approach or modifier of
the Personal Year approach. By using the described monthly
approach, the subject is in the best posture at that time of year
to take advantage of the events and opportunities presented, as
well as to avoid or alleviate the confusions and difficulties attendant on the experiences encountered. The Personal Month is
an important cycle.

THE PERSONAL MONTH IS THE SUM OF THE CALEN- **Calculation**
DAR MONTH, REDUCED TO A SINGLE DIGIT OR
MASTER NUMBER, AND THE PERSONAL YEAR. THE
SUM IS LIKEWISE REDUCED TO A SINGLE DIGIT OR
MASTER NUMBER.

Example:

Naomi is in a 3 Personal Year. What's her Personal Month in February, August, October and November?

	Calendar Month	+	Personal Year		
February	2	+	3	=	5 Personal Month
August	8	+	3	=	11/2 Personal Month
October	1	+	3	=	4 Personal Month
November	11	+	3	=	14/5 Personal Month

Time span and transitions

The Personal Month lasts one month, from the first to the last day of the calendar month. It may be felt to some degree about the 25th or 26th of the preceding month. Its fading influence can be felt until about the 4th or 5th of the succeeding month. The pure vibrations, then, are only in effect from about the 5th to the 25th, the middle three weeks of each month.

Chart 19: Personal Month/ Personal Day

If you turn to CHART 19: THE PERSONAL MONTH/THE PERSONAL DAY, page 766, you'll find the general description of the Personal Months in the top row. When there's an 11 Personal Month, the approach of both the 11 and 2 would be desirable. Similarly, in a 22 Personal Month, both 22 and 4 would be desirable approaches.

The karmic Personal Months are described in the top row below the general descriptions. When there's a karmic number behind the month's digit—a 19 behind the 1, a 13 behind the 4, a 14 behind the 5, a 16 behind the 7—there's a probability of difficulties in that month. The description of these potential problems would be included in a delineation of that particular Personal Month.

The bottom row of the chart describes character traits likely to produce positive results and other character traits likely to contribute to a disappointing month. These traits should be compared to the subject's characteristics. Matching characteristics and their potential effect should be included as part of the delineation.

Commentary

The Personal Months are *not* used for forecasting. Rather, they're used to channel the approach for the month, focus the monthly energies in the larger framework of the approach described by the Personal Year.

Let's say you're in a 4 Personal Year. September, then, will be a 13/4 Personal Month (9 + 4 = 13/4). If it's possible to schedule the difficult tasks for the year, you should schedule at least some of them for September with its emphasis on hard work. You should be aware, though, that, with the 13/4, you're likely to feel limited and restricted that month, so you should prepare for that, too.

In that same 4 Personal Year, how about a vacation or some light social life in August, a 3 Personal Month (8 + 4 = 12; 1 + 2 = 3), as a foil for the hard work in September? And is a vacation or trip possible in October, a 5 Personal Month (1 + 4 = 5) as a welcome respite from the struggles and strains of September?

I know it's not always possible to schedule work or other events just the way you'd like. I also know, from my own experience, that, in a 4 Personal Year, it's generally a lot easier to do the hard work in September rather than in August or October. Work with your own Personal Months for a while. If you get into the flow, you'll see that work and vacations (and most everything else) often—very often—naturally fall where they are easiest to deal with. You may be surprised to see how you can adjust your life so that the "right" activities occur in the "right" months. And, be assured, if you're in, say, a 5 Personal Month, you are really going to want to expand, enjoy, adventure, have fun. If there's some hard task that's been scheduled, you'll feel painfully restricted and discontent to work hard when your whole being wants to play instead.

Like everyone else, I can't schedule all the activities in my life completely. I *can* schedule a substantial part of them, though, and I *can* prepare myself to use the monthly energies that *are* present for maximum benefit for my various endeavors.

Universal Month

Some numerologists use the Universal Month in addition to the Personal Month in determining the short term approach. The Universal Month, a short term cycle describing the general monthly trend of world influences, is the sum of the calendar month, reduced to a single digit or master number, and the Universal Year, with the sum likewise reduced to a single digit or master number. Although the trend of the influence of the Universal Month can be indicated, I find that the influence is so strongly diffused by the energy put forth by the earth's population as to be of little consequence in determining an individual's desirable approach for a given month.

Monthly epicycle

There's a monthly epicycle similar to the nine year Epicycle. Here's a diagram of the 108 months which constitute a nine year Epicycle. The months are shown in vertical columns, arranged by the number of their Personal Months:

Personal Month ↓ \ Personal Year →	1	2 or 11/2	3	4 or 22/4	5	6	7	8	9
1	SEP	AUG	JUL	JUN	MAY	APR	MAR DEC	FEB NOV	JAN OCT
2 or 11/2	JAN OCT	SEP	AUG	JUL	JUN	MAY	APR	MAR DEC	FEB NOV
3	FEB NOV	JAN OCT	SEP	AUG	JUL	JUN	MAY	APR	MAR DEC
4 or 22/4	MAR DEC	FEB NOV	JAN OCT	SEP	AUG	JUL	JUN	MAY	APR
5	APR	MAR DEC	FEB NOV	JAN OCT	SEP	AUG	JUL	JUN	MAY
6	MAY	APR	MAR DEC	FEB NOV	JAN OCT	SEP	AUG	JUL	JUN
7	JUNE	MAY	APR	MAR DEC	FEB NOV	JAN OCT	SEP	AUG	JULY
8	JULY	JUN	MAY	APR	MAR DEC	FEB NOV	JAN OCT	SEP	AUG
9	AUG	JUL	JUN	MAY	APR	MAR DEC	FEB NOV	JAN OCT	SEP

Since there are twelve months in a calendar year and only nine different Personal Months (think of the 11 Personal Year as a variant of the 2, the 22 as a variant of the 4), the monthly epicycle has some interesting complexities.

Some of the Personal Years contain a complete nine month epicycle:

> In the 6 Personal Year, there's a complete monthly epicycle from April through December.
>
> In the 7 Personal Year, there's a complete monthly epicycle from March through November.
>
> In the 8 Personal Year, there's a complete monthly epicycle from February through October.
>
> In the 9 Personal Year, there's a complete monthly epicycle from January through September.

In Personal Years 1 through 5, there is *not* a complete monthly epicycle in each calendar year. The monthly epicycle, instead, starts in one year, ends in the next and has a funny little hiccup in the middle of the epicycle. The 1 Personal Year, for example, has a 1 Personal Month in September, a 2 Personal Month in October, a 3 Personal Month in November, a 4 Personal Month in December. The 2 Personal Year starts with a 3 Personal Month in January (rather than the 5 Personal Month you might expect to follow December's 4 Personal Month) and a 4 Personal Month in February, followed by the rest of the months in order. This monthly epicycle, then, runs in the following order of Personal Months, 1, 2, 3, 4, 3, 4, 5, 6, 7, 8, 9. The months are consecutive with the exception of the 3, 4, 3, 4 hiccup. There's a similar hiccup in the monthly epicycle in Personal Years 2 through 5.

Even though Personal Years 6 through 9 have a complete monthly epicycle, there's a similar two month overlap of Personal Months at the end of each year and the beginning of the next. In the 6 Personal Year, for instance, November is an 8 Personal Month, December a 9 Personal Month. At the beginning of the 7 Personal Year, January is an 8 Personal Month and February a 9 Personal Month. The sequence of Personal Months runs: 1, 2, 3, 4, 5, 6, 7, 8, 9, 8, 9—a hiccup here, too.

Remember our discussion of the detours and diversions in the nine year Epicycle? The monthly epicycle adds its own additional circumlocutions.

Let's look at a whole year in some detail. The 1 Personal Year emphasizes beginnings, change, moving forward, but the emphasis, looked at monthly, is often meandering. There's only one month—September, a 1 Personal Month—dedicated to beginning and moving forward. (September, the ninth month, always has a Personal Month number the same as the Personal Year number. This double emphasis usually focuses strong attention on the desirable approach every September, sometimes making September the culminating month in the year in terms of significant activity.) September, then, is probably the best time to begin in a 1 Personal Year. If that's the case, the partial monthly epicycle from January to August could be considered a preparatory phase leading to September's strong beginning emphasis.

Having reached this starting point, though, the monthly Epicycle moves into a waiting phase—October, a 2 Personal Month, certainly a meandering follow-up to the beginning focus. (October, the tenth month, always is a Personal Month with the same number as the subsequent Personal Year.) The waiting October is followed by a potentially creative phase in November, a 3 Personal Month and a hard working phase in December, a 4 Personal Month. January, a 3 Personal Month in a 2 Personal Year, repeats the creative phase followed by a repetition of the working phase in February, a 4 Personal Month, and an expansive phase in March, a 5 Personal Month.

You might think of hiccups as giving you a second chance at

a portion of the monthly epicycle. It's not, of course, a pure second chance, because the November 3 Personal Month is in a 1 Personal Year and emphasizes creative forward movement while the January 3 Personal Month, in a 2 Personal Year, stresses creative cooperation and waiting.

Within each Personal Year, there's a repetition of three Personal Months. January and October always have the same Personal Month number. So do February and November as well as March and December. Even with the *same* number Personal Month in the *same* Personal Year, the months reflect somewhat different approaches. January, February and March, with the year just getting under way, generally emphasize preparatory aspects of the approach while October, November and December usually reflect the probability of a more developed approach. Sometimes, one of these repeated Personal Months is a karmic number or a master number and the other is not, making for very different approaches in the two months.

Two of the three repeated Personal Months are also involved in the hiccup. For instance:

> February and March of the 1 Personal Year are 3 and 4 Personal Months.
> So are November and December of the 1 Personal Year.
> So are January and February of the 2 Personal Year.
> And October and November of the 2 Personal Year.

There'll be a lot of emphasis then on creativity (from the 3 Personal Month) and hard work (from the 4 Personal Month) in these two Personal Years, more so than in other years. Other combinations of Personal Years will stress different approaches because of their repeated monthly patterns.

Chart 20: Epicycle

CHART 20: THE EPICYCLE, page 780, like the diagram on page 584, displays a complete nine year Epicycle and its Personal Months. Here, the diagram has been expanded to include a description of each month, the description being a synthesis of the descriptions of the appropriate Personal Year and Personal Month. The description for each of the months is short, due to space limitations. Although the description is accurate, it covers only one or two of the *many* possible approaches for each month. January and February of each year also show the fading influence of the previous year and October, November and December show the evolving influence of the succeeding year.

Read the complete Epicycle from the beginning 2 Personal

Month of the 1 Personal Year to the concluding 3 Personal Month of the 9 Personal Year to get a detailed awareness of the monthly flow along with the considerable detours and meanderings. Read the months of the 11 and 22 Personal Years, too, to get acquainted with the effect of the master numbers on the flow.

A delineation of any Personal Month includes the following:

Delineation description

A. An awareness of the Personal Year. The Personal Month is always expressed as a sub-approach of the Personal Year approach.

B. A description of the Personal Month (from Chart 19). If the Personal Month is a karmic month, include the karmic description. For an 11 Personal Month, read both the 11 and 2 descriptions. For a 22 Personal Month, read both the 22 and 4 descriptions. I don't usually read the 11 or 22 approach unless the subject is over twenty, except to note the nervous tension.

C. An awareness of the place in the Epicycle (from Chart 20). Consult Chart 20 for some possible syntheses, but use your own syntheses if they are more appropriate to the trend of events described by the current Essence and Transits. Include the influence of the previous year in readings for January and February. Include the influence of the approaching year for October, November and December.

D. The subject's potentials—from the birthname and current name(s) as well as the birthdate. The subject's energies define the ability to enhance, deflect or mute the approach described by the Personal Month. The core elements, Karmic Debts, and Karmic Lessons may be of importance, along with any other strong modifiers which either flow or conflict with the approach. Usually, the elements or modifiers with a number matching the Personal Month number are of particular concern.

On occasion, a subject with a Karmic Debt has a Personal Month with the same karmic number. This usually indicates substantial difficulties unless the problems represented by the Karmic Debt have already been faced and overcome. Generally, if the subject is under thirty, the Karmic Debt and the matching karmic Personal Month describe significant obstacles which can benefit by appropriate preparation.

Note particularly the character traits described in the bottom row of Chart 19. Include in the delineation the subject's characteristics matching the traits in the chart and their probable effect on the month.

E. Preparation for the next Personal Month. A short note on the approach of the subsequent month provides some understanding of the ongoing flow. When a delineation presents an entire year of Personal Months or a series of Personal Months, it isn't necessary to discuss preparation for the coming month.

Keep the delineation of the Personal Month relatively brief. We're dealing with a sub-influence of the Personal Year rather than a strong separate cycle, and this should be reflected in the reading. The description of each Personal Month would be considerably shorter than the Personal Year description.

Example: Hal Allen's calculation

We'll delineate all the months of 1993 for Hal Allen.

We can read the number of the Personal Months in Chart 20, or we can calculate them. We should also calculate the Personal Month for January, 1994, so we can indicate some preparation for the beginning of the subsequent year.

	Calendar Month	+	Personal Year	=	Personal Month
1993					
January	1	+	3	=	4
February	2	+	3	=	5
March	3	+	3	=	6
April	4	+	3	=	7
May	5	+	3	=	8
June	6	+	3	=	9
July	7	+	3	=	$10 = 1 + 0 = 1$
August	8	+	3	=	11/2
September	9	+	3	=	$12 = 1 + 2 = 3$
October	1	+	3	=	4
($10 = 1 + 0 = 1$)					
November	11	+	3	=	14/5
December	3	+	3	=	6
($12 = 1 + 2 = 3$)					
1994					
January	1	+	4	=	5

Here's Hal's monthly delineation for 1993 based on the steps previously outlined. You may want to read the delineation for the year in Chapter 33 to refresh your memory on the salient points.

The delineation is written in the present tense. We're assuming here that Hal Allen's birthname is also his current name— that there are no additional energies from new names.

Hal Allen's Personal Month delineation for 1993

1993

JANUARY: 4 Personal Month

Although the year is likely to be one with emphasis on social life, travel and good times, January isn't likely to start the year out like that (*contrast of 3 Personal Year with 4 Personal Month*). This seems, instead, to be a month to work hard, firm up foundations and take care of the details (*4 Personal Month*). Some of the work may require your imagination and creative ability (*3 Personal Year with 6 Expression, 9 Soul Urge, 3 Birthday*) and friends may even be there to help with the work as long as you are tactful and show consideration (*waning energy of previous 2 Personal Year*). The work situation is likely to make you feel limited and restricted— you tend to a somewhat restless nature and the heavy load may not be much to your liking (*4 Personal Month with 5 Life Path, 14/5 Karmic Debt, 5·5 energy*). Health matters may need your attention (*4 Personal Month*).

FEBRUARY: 5 Personal Month

February is apt to be more to your liking—a month with new people, places, opportunities, a time to expand, to delight in friends and adventure (*3 Personal Year, 5 Personal Month*). You're likely to feel freer now than you did all of last year (*Expansion of 5 Personal Month in contrast to waiting of 2 Personal Year*) but be sure to proceed with some caution at least to the end of the month (*waning energy of previous 2 Personal Year*). Don't be surprised if there are sudden, unexpected or unusual events (*5 Personal Month, N Transit*). There may, for instance, be sudden endings or completion of experiences or relations. Be sure to handle them with tolerance and compassion (5 *Personal Month*, 9 *Essence*). You may experience a change of residence or job or be involved in some short-lived but exciting romance (*N Transit*). There may be opportunities to enjoy yourself (3 *Personal Year*) and to put your adventurous, flexible and imaginative capabilities to work (5 *Personal Month positive characteristics with 5 Life Path*, 6 *Expression*, 9 *Soul Urge*, 3 *Birthday*).

MARCH: 6 Personal Month

March is a good time to express the joy of living with family and close friends (3 *Personal Year*, 6 *Personal Month*). Enjoy the pleasures of friendship and love—romances, as in February, may be exciting but short-lived (9 *Essence*, *N Transit*). Marriage, if emotions are balanced, can be beautiful (*N Transit*), children can be sources of much gratification (6 *Personal Month*). Your friendly, understanding side may add to your pleasure at this time (6 *Personal Month positive characteristics with 6 Expression*). You may want to work around the house or take care of some domestic duties or responsibilities (6 *Personal Month with 6 Expression*, 6 *Modified Karmic Lesson*). Your creative imagination may prove helpful (3 *Personal Year with 6 Expression*, 9 *Soul Urge*, 3 *Birthday*).

APRIL: 7 Personal Month

April presents a good time to meditate, reflect, analyze (7 *Personal Month*) or to spend time working alone exploring your artistic talents (7 *Personal Month*, 3 *Personal Year with 6 Expression*, 9 *Soul Urge*, 3 *Birthday*). I suspect that you would prefer more outgoing activities (5 *Life Path*) but you may benefit by developing your inner power and spiritual awareness or by studying and researching on some of your ventures (7 *Personal Month*), possibly putting some of your creative abilities to use (3 *Personal Year with 5 Life Path*, 6 *Expression*, 9 *Soul Urge*, 3 *Birthday*). You may have time to reflect on your plans for the rest of the year (7 *Personal Month*). Take care of health matters that need attention (7 *Personal Month*).

MAY: 8 Personal Month

You may feel a good deal more dynamic in May than in April (8 *Personal Month compared to* 7). This power may be helpful in taking advantage of opportunities, possibly sudden or unusual, to expand business affairs or to improve your financial standing (8 *Personal Month, N Transit*). Friends and social skills may unlock doors (3 *Personal Year*). There may be business opportunities (8 *Personal Month*) involving partnerships or associations, but they are likely to need much patience on your part to develop completely (*start of 2 Essence this month*). Be businesslike and practical in your dealings (8 *Personal Month*), but don't be surprised if your creative abilities and your joie de vivre play a part, too (3 *Personal Year with 6 Expression, 9 Soul Urge, 3 Birthday*).

JUNE: 9 Personal Month

An experience or a relationship may end in June, needing much in the way of tolerance and compassion from you (9 *Personal Month*). There may be much feeling here which is likely to interfere with the general optimism and cheerfulness you've probably been feeling (3 *Personal Year,* 9 *Personal Month*). Developments are likely to take longer than is comfortable (2 *Essence*). You may find some pleasure in artistic or imaginative expression (9 *Personal Month with 6 Expression, 9 Soul Urge, 3 Birthday*), or in helping others in humanistic or philanthropic ventures (6 *Personal Month with 9 Soul Urge*).

JULY: 1 Personal Month

Advance enthusiastically in July with your joyous and lively approach. Exploit your creative imagination and verbal skills to break up old conditions, to begin something new, to make a change (3 *Personal Year,* 1 *Personal Month with 3 Birthday*). It may be a good time to expand the business opportunities started in May or to explore possibilities related to viable partnerships (1 *Personal Month,* 2 *Essence*). Express your originality and individuality in developing opportunities involving friends (*3 Personal Year, 1 Personal Month*).

AUGUST: 11/2 Personal Month

August is apt to seem quiet after the exhilaration of July (*11/2 Personal Month compared to 1 Personal Month*). This is a month to be sensitive and receptive while awaiting developments (*2 Personal Month, 2 Essence*). Enjoy your friends in quiet social situations or cooperate with others on their projects, possibly giving them the benefit of your creative input (*3 Personal Year, 2 Personal Month, 2 Essence with 6 Expression, 9 Soul Urge, 3 Birthday*). You may become aware of some new awarenesses, but this inner growth is probably in a very early formative stage. (*11 Personal Month with 11 Maturity Number. A weak influence, but should be mentioned.*) You're likely to feel some nervous tension this month (*11 Personal Month*). Be careful that this tension along with your current high level of sensitivity is kept under control so as not to precipitate emotional difficulties (*3 Personal Year, 11/2 Personal Month*).

SEPTEMBER: 3 Personal Month

September is a month to enjoy yourself, so move as much responsibility to next month as you can. There's probably been the usual quota of ups and downs this year, but now's the time to express happiness and delight so enthusiastically that it's contagious. Express artistically using your imaginative capability. Enjoy a lively social life. Entertain or be entertained. Travel or vacation (*3 Personal Year, 3 Personal Month with 5 Life Path*).

OCTOBER: 4 Personal Month

October is a month to work hard, to build foundations for ventures started in previous months, to strengthen weak areas, to start to take care of the details (*4 Personal Month*). Use your imagination and creativity. Get help from friends when possible to lighten the work load (*3 Personal Year with 5 Life Path, 3 Birthday*). Exercise patience and cooperation. Don't be surprised if everything takes a little longer than expected (*2 Essence*). You probably won't be that happy with this month's workload, going as it does against your free-wheeling nature. You may feel uncomfortable with the limitations and restrictions imposed (*4 Personal Month with 5 Life Path*). Begin to prepare for next year with its predominant emphasis on hard work (*Approaching 4 Personal Year*).

(*Note similarities and differences between the descriptions for January and October, both 4 Personal Months.*).

NOVEMBER: 14/5 Personal Month

Although November is probably a month with much excitement—new people, new activities—you may have trouble taking advantage of the opportunities presented. Although the tone of this adventurous month seems to go with your basic nature, you may find that your restlessness, erratic actions and excessive appetite for physical stimulation may hamper developments (*14/5 Personal Month with 5 Life Path, 14/5 Karmic Debt, 5·5 energy*). You'll probably enjoy your friends and the excitement of the month's social activities (*3 Personal Year, 14/5 Personal Month*), but there's likely to be work to be done, possibly left from last month, as well as additional work on the horizon. You're apt to be uncomfortable getting the work done now, but your tendency to avoid it may cause added difficulties (*14/5 Personal Month, approaching 4 Personal Year*).

(*Note the strong differences between February, a 5 Personal Month and November, a 14/5 Personal Month*).

DECEMBER: 6 Personal Month

December's merriment, enthusiasm and joy are likely to center around the family and close friends. There can be much friendship, love and pleasure from lover, spouse or children and artistic or creative endeavors related to them or to the home (*3 Personal Year, 6 Personal Month*). There are likely to be domestic duties which feel restrictive, at this time, although you'd be well advised to take care of them (*6 Personal Month with 6 Expression, 6 Modified Karmic Lesson*). You can probably see the additional work coming next year and it's likely to feel like it will be limiting (*approaching 4 Personal Year conflicting with 5 Life Path, 14/5 Karmic Debt, 5·5 energy*). You'll probably find fun and adventure next month, though, along with the beginnings of some substantial work (*preparation for next January, a 5 Personal Month*).

(*Note the similarities and differences between the descriptions for March and December, both 6 Personal Months*).

The change in May, 1933 from the 9 Essence to the 11/2 Essence is apparent in the monthly readings. Hal's character traits play an important part, too. His 5 energies are particularly apparent in the 3 and 5 months and the probable conflict in the 4 months. His creative 3, 6 and 9 energies are also in constant focus in the 3 Personal Year.

The monthly readings should be given as broadly as possible to delineate the general tone of each month as modified by the subject's personality and special abilities.

CHAPTER 35

SHORT TERM CYCLES, PART 2:
THE PERSONAL DAY

THE PERSONAL DAY DESCRIBES THE APPROACH TO **Definition**
EVENTS FOR A GIVEN DAY LIKELY TO PRODUCE
GROWTH AND DEVELOPMENT. The Personal Day should
be visualized as a sub-approach or modifier of the Personal
Month approach. The Personal Day is important in pinpointing a precise day to schedule an action to take advantage
of the events and opportunities presented, as well as to avoid or
alleviate the confusions and difficulties encountered with poor
timing. The Personal Day is an important cycle.

THE PERSONAL DAY IS THE SUM OF THE CALEN- **Calculation**
DAR MONTH AND CALENDAR DAY, BOTH REDUCED
TO A SINGLE DIGIT OR MASTER NUMBER, AND THE
PERSONAL YEAR. THE SUM IS REDUCED TO A SINGLE
DIGIT OR MASTER NUMBER.

Examples:

What's Arthur's Personal Day on March 8 in a 6 Personal
Year?

Calendar		Calendar		Personal		
Month	+	Day	+	Year	=	Personal Day
3	+	8	+	6	=	17
					=	1 + 7
					=	8 Personal Day

What's Anne's Personal Day on November 22 in a 22 Personal Year?

Calendar Month	+	Calendar Day	+	Personal Year	= Personal Day
11	+	22	+	22	= 55
					= 5 + 5
					= 10
					= 1 + 0
					= 1 Personal Day

Don't calculate the Personal Day by adding the calendar day, reduced to a single digit or master digit, and the Personal Month, with the sum then reduced to a single digit or master number. This may seem like a short cut, but you may pick up or lose a karmic day or a master number day.

Example:

What's Eunice's Personal Day on May 9 in an 8 Personal Year?

Calendar Month	+	Calendar Day	+	Personal Year	= Personal Day
5	+	9	+	8	= 22/4 Personal Day

If you incorrectly added the calendar day and the Personal Month, you'd have ended up with a 13/4 Personal Day instead. Quite a difference!

Time span and transitions

The Personal Day lasts one day, from midnight to midnight. There may be some slight overlap of influences, but since the time period is so short, transitions are of little consequence.

Chart 19: Personal Month/ Personal Day

If you turn to CHART 19: THE PERSONAL MONTH/THE PERSONAL DAY, page 766, you'll find the general description of the Personal Day in the second row.

The 11 Personal Day is described for a subject only if there's an 11 core element, and the 2 Personal Day description is also included. If there's no 11 element, the 11 is reduced to a 2 Personal Day with the addition of the likelihood of nervous tension.

The 22 Personal Day, similarly, is described only if there's a 22 core element and the 4 Personal Day description is also included. If there's no 22 core element, the 22 is reduced to a 4 Personal Day with the addition of the likelihood of nervous tension.

The karmic Personal Days are described in the second row

below the general description. When there's a karmic number behind the day's digit—a 19 behind the 1, a 13 behind the 4, a 14 behind the 5, a 16 behind the 7—there's a probability of difficulties that day. The description of these potential problems would be included in a delineation of that particular Personal Day.

The bottom row of the chart describes character traits likely to produce positive results and other character traits likely to contribute to a disappointing day. These traits should be compared to the subject's characteristics. Matching characteristics and their potential effect should be included as part of the delineation.

Commentary

The Personal Day, as I indicated, is especially important for timing. If there's an important event in your life which lasts a day or less, schedule it for the appropriate Personal Day if possible. Sign a business contract on an 8 Personal Day, visit your crotchety uncle on a 6 Personal Day. Help a friend move into a new apartment on a 4 Personal Day—it'll still be a lot of work, but it's apt to feel better than on a 5 Personal Day.

Since many activities last more than a day, use the appropriate Personal Day for the beginning of the activity. For instance, if you're going on vacation, start on a 3 or 5 Personal day and you'll be off to a good beginning. Or, there's a family responsibility which will take a month or two to work out. Get going on it on a 6 (or 2 or 9) Personal Day if possible.

The Personal Day is of less importance than the Personal Month. It's of considerable significance to schedule activities in the appropriate month, less significant to choose the correct day. If you can do both, so much the better; if you can schedule only one, concentrate on the month. Because of the limited time involved, the Personal Day with a karmic number or a master number rarely indicates a strong impact.

Universal Day

Some numerologists use the Universal Day in addition to the Personal Day in determining the short term approach. The Universal Day, a short term cycle describing the general daily trend of world influences, is the sum of the calendar day and calendar month, reduced to a single digit or master number, and the Universal Month, with the sum likewise reduced to a single digit or master number. The influence of the Universal Day is even more diffuse than the influence of the Universal Month and is of little consequence.

Daily epicycle

Like the monthly epicycle that structures the Personal Months, there's a daily epicycle that structures the Personal Days. A month contains two or three complete daily epicycles along with one or two partial epicycles. You may find three or four days a month with the same Personal Day number—there are, then, three or four 1 Personal Days, good days to start important activities, and three or four 3 Personal Days, good days to schedule social events or entertainments.

There's usually a hiccup at the end of each month and the beginning of the next, similar to the Personal Month hiccup. If a month has thirty days, two Personal Days are repeated as the months change; if a month has thirty-one days, three Personal Days are repeated. February, when it has twenty-eight days, has no hiccup, but continues the daily cycle in consecutive order. When February has twenty-nine days, there's a repeat of one Personal Day as February ends and March begins.

Keep the daily epicycle in mind as a month proceeds. You'll quickly begin to feel the difference, say, between a 4 and 5 Personal Day or between a 9 and 1 Personal Day. The flow here, while of less importance than the flow of the monthly epicycle, still provides a guide to the meanderings and detours, the ups and downs in your activities and relationships.

Delineation description

A delineation of any Personal Day includes the following:

A.   An awareness of the Personal Month. The Personal Day is always expressed as a sub-approach of the Personal Month approach.

B.   A description of the Personal Day (from Chart 19). If the Personal Day is a karmic day, include the karmic description. Use the 11 or 22 Personal Day descriptions only if the subject has the master number as a core element and always include the description of the 2 or 4 Personal Day. Even if the 11 or 22 description isn't used, the nervous tension of the master number should be added to the 2 or 4 description.

C.   The subject's potentials—both from the birthname and the current name(s) as well as the birthdate. The subject's energies define the ability to enhance, deflect or mute the approach described by the Personal Day. Use only the core elements or Karmic Debts here, when they either flow or conflict with the approach. Usually the elements or Karmic Debt with a number matching the Personal Day number are of particular concern.

On occasion, a subject with a Karmic Debt has a Personal Day with the same karmic number. This usually indicates some difficulties unless the problems represented by the Karmic Debt have already been faced and resolved. Generally, if the subject is under thirty, the Personal Day matching a Karmic Debt describes a day with the possibility of disturbing impediments.

Note particularly the character traits described in the bottom row of Chart 19. Include in the delineation the subject's characteristics matching the traits in the chart and their probable effect on the day.

Keep the Personal Day delineation deliberately brief. Give the subject the description of a week or two at a time if the particular time span is of importance. The epicycle flow is not usually accentuated in the delineation, although the epicycles later in the month tend to be slightly more developed than the earlier ones. A 1 Personal Day later in the month, for instance, may be somewhat stronger for starting activities than the first 1 Personal Day of the month, but this is of consequence only when the subject has a choice of those two days for the start of an activity. Because of the short time span of the Personal Day, no description for the next day need be included.

We'll delineate the last six days of October, 1993 and the first six days of November, 1993 for Hal Allen. 1993 is, for Hal Allen, a 3 Personal Year. Here are the calculations for the Personal Days:

Example: Hal Allen's calculation

		Calendar Month	+	Calendar Day	+	Personal Year	=	Personal Day
October	26	1	+	8	+	3 = 12	=	3
	27	1	+	9	+	3	=	13/4
	28	1	+	1	+	3	=	5
	29	1	+	11	+	3 = 15	=	6
	30	1	+	3	+	3	=	7
	31	1	+	4	+	3	=	8
November	1	11	+	1	+	3 = 15	=	6
	2	11	+	2	+	3	=	16/7
	3	11	+	3	+	3 = 17	=	8
	4	11	+	4	+	3 = 18	=	9
	5	11	+	5	+	3	=	19/1
	6	11	+	6	+	3 = 20	=	2

Here's the daily delineation based on the steps previously outlined. I've included the Personal Month delineations from Chapter 34.

Hal Allen's Personal Day delineation

The delineation is written in the present tense. We're assuming here that Hal's birthname is also his current name—that there are no additional energies from new names.

OCTOBER: 4 Personal Month

October is a month to work hard, to build foundations for ventures started in previous months, to strengthen weak areas, to start to take care of the details. Use your imagination and creativity. Get help from friends when possible to lighten the work load. Exercise patience and cooperation. Don't be surprised if everything takes a little longer than expected. You probably won't be that happy with this month's workload, going as it does against your free-wheeling nature. You may feel uncomfortable with the limitations and restrictions imposed. Begin to prepare for next year with its predominant emphasis on hard work.

OCTOBER 26: 3 Personal Day

If you can, take a break from the heavy work load (*3 Personal Day in a 4 Personal Month*). Visit with friends, express your pleasure and delight in the day. Use your imaginative or creative talents in some artistic venture. Have a good time (*3 Personal Day with 3 Birthday*).

(*The Personal Month usually fits into the flow of the monthly epicycle so that the monthly approach meshes with the activities and experiences of the year. On the other hand, the Personal Day, because of its short duration, can provide a needed break, as in the above 3 Personal Day, rather than be adjusted to fit into the flow.*)

OCTOBER 27: 13/4 Personal Day

A good day to complete routine tasks, keep your nose to the grindstone. Get as much of the monthly work as possible out of the way today. You're likely to feel uncomfortably limited or restricted, but try to get some satisfaction from completing the job at hand (*13/4 Personal Day conflicts with 5 Life Path, 14/5 Karmic Debt*).

OCTOBER 28: 5 Personal Day

You've probably been struggling all month with a lot of work. This may be the day to take a chance, make an important change that will affect the work load. If you're afraid of taking risks, the opportunity may pass you by. (*14/5 Karmic Debt may make Hal restless or afraid of taking risks.*)

(*Since this is the last 5 Personal Day in the month, and since a 5 Personal Month is coming next, this is a good day to make a much needed change. I wouldn't have recommended the change on a 5 Personal Day earlier in the month because of Hal's probable restlessness.*)

OCTOBER 29: 6 Personal Day

There's likely to be some physical work to be completed around the house or some special service or assistance to be given there. Work or help others but give friendly and loving feelings. You'll probably get similar feelings returned (6 *Expression stresses positive results*).

OCTOBER 30: 7 Personal Day

With so much work, you probably haven't had much time by yourself for a while. Today would be a good day to spend some time alone. Review what you've accomplished this month and plan for some expansion in the coming month. Don't make any changes today.

(*This last 7 Personal Day in the month is a good time to take stock and plan for the 5 Personal Month that's coming. Remember that the influences of the new month can be felt toward the end of the preceding month and should be mentioned in the daily reading where appropriate. Hal, of course, has no 7 energy to help or hinder the day's prospects.*)

OCTOBER 31: 8 Personal Day

You have a lot of ability to make things happen today. Use that ability decisively to get some task completed. This accomplishment may register a maximum impact in business or financial matters.

The work you do today may prove significant relative to your advancement. (*Hal has no 8 energy to help or hinder the day's prospects.*)

NOVEMBER: 14/5 Personal *Month*

Although November is probably a month with much excitement—new people, new activities—you may have trouble taking advantage of the opportunities presented. Although the tone of this adventurous month seems to go with your basic nature, you may find that your restlessness, erratic actions and excessive appetite for physical stimulation may hamper developments. You'll probably enjoy your friends and the excitement of the month's social activities, but there's likely to be work to be done, possibly left from last month, as well as additional work on the horizon. You're apt to be uncomfortable getting the work done now, but your tendency to avoid it may cause added difficulties.

NOVEMBER 1: 6 Personal Day

There may be some domestic duties to finish up, but this is apt to be a good day to enjoy the pleasures of domestic life with your wife or children. You may be involved in some exciting social activities with friends or new acquaintances (*6 Expression stresses positive results.*)

NOVEMBER 2: 16/7 Personal Day

Spend some time today in quiet contemplation, planning the changes you may be making during the rest of the month. Give some thought to next year's work load, too. Try not to disconcert or confuse others by being self-centered, argumentative or withdrawn. Explain yourself as clearly as possible to alleviate difficulties even though you may find that your communication tends to be clouded with emotion. (*No 7 energy to help or hinder the day's prospects.*)

NOVEMBER 3: 8 Personal Day

Use your ability today to expand your activities, possibly in some business venture. If you can apply your power with creativity and imagination, you may help make a desired change or help advance your position. (*No 8 energy to help or hinder the day's prospects but the 5 Life Path could be helpful here.*) For maximum benefit, control your tendency to be erratic or irresponsible. (*14/5 Karmic Debt can be a problem if it hasn't been overcome—remember this is a 14/5 Personal Month.*)

NOVEMBER 4: 9 Personal Day

A good day to complete relations, experiences or activities which may hamper the possibility of fun and excitement for the rest of the month. Act with sensitivity and compassion. Be prepared to deal with strong feelings, even some sudden or unusual dramatic situation. (*Hal's 9 Soul Urge should help produce positive results.*)

NOVEMBER 5: 19/1 Personal Day

If you're feeling self-centered, overaggressive, fearful or indecisive today, it may interfere with the exciting activities in which you may want to engage. Take time out to work on any of these uncomfortable characteristics which may be bothering you. Postpone putting any new plans into action today relating to changes you've been contemplating—you may get off on the wrong foot. (*The 19/1 should be heeded although Hal's 5 Life Path and 14/5 Karmic Debt may make him impatient.*)

NOVEMBER 6: 2 Personal Day

Try to be aware of subtle nuances about you—you may learn something of significance for the future. This is a fine day for pleasant, but quiet, social activities. Don't look for adventure or excitement today, but, rather, help routine affairs move forward smoothly. (*2 Karmic Lesson and 2 Maturity Number energies may prove helpful.*)

As you can see, the last days of October, like any other month, reflect the end of the approach used that month—in October's example, the end of the work accomplished that month. The first days of November, like any other month, reflect the planning and beginning stages of the approach to events used in November. The middle days of a month reflect the ongoing activities rather than the start or finish.

A knowledge of your own Personal Days will probably increase your effectiveness and provide added help over the rough spots.

CHAPTER 36

ADVANCED PROGRESSED DELINEATION: AN EXAMPLE

We'll imagine it's toward the end of 1990. A client, Hope Edythe Lynch, has asked for a reading. She was born on March 28, 1962, so she's now twenty-eight years old. Hope has had a rather busy and confusing time in the last few years, she says, and she'd appreciate having some idea of what to expect in the coming year. Several important areas of her life seem to be changing and she would especially like to know about them.

A client with some questions

She's been engaged for a little over six months. She wants to schedule the wedding for a Sunday in February, March or April of 1991. What Sunday would I recommend?

What can she expect of marriage at this time? Is the confusion she's been experiencing going to continue unabated? (A complete analysis of the possibilities of marriage would also include a discussion of Hope's new name [see Chapter 24] and a comparison of her energies with the energies of her husband-to-be [see Chapter 39]. Since our primary interest here is the progressed delineation, we'll ignore these other discussions at this time.)

Hope says she's had a fine job for several years. She's recently received several new job offers, two of which are particularly attractive. She could start either of these jobs at the beginning of the year at her own convenience. Should she take either of them or remain at her current job? If she decides to take a new job, when is the best time to start?

Hope, like Hal Allen, is a fictitious character. If she was a real person, I'd start by being sure she understood that numerologists are *not* fortune tellers. I *can't* tell how the marriage will work out, I *can't* tell if she is going to continue to feel confused and I *can't* tell which job is going to work out better. I *can* indicate Hope's current energies, the probable obstacles in her life and probable events to come, but I have no way of knowing precisely what Hope will do with her energies, how she will choose to face the obstacles, how she will react to the unfolding events.

Having completed this preamble, we can get down to work.

Procedure to answer the client's questions

First, we'll calculate and organize the basic data.

Second, we'll do a progressed delineation for 1990 and 1991, including

> a short summary of Hope's character traits,
> the background influences for both years,
> the probable events or trend of events and the desirable approach for growth and development for both years,
> the influence of the beginning months of 1991, the months with which Hope is particularly concerned, and
> the influence prevailing on all the Sundays in the month or months appropriate for her wedding.

Third, we'll discuss each of Hope's questions. The answers to her questions will be related to the progressed delineation.

Hope Edythe Lynch: calculation sheet, organization sheet and progressed chart

To begin, we'll perform the standard calculations (Figure 36-1 on page 608). For simplicity, we'll assume that Hope's birthname is also her current name—that there are no additional energies from new names.

Then we'll group Hope's energies on the organization sheet (Figure 36-2 on page 609).

We'll prepare the progressed chart with the Epicycle including 1990 and 1991, the years under discussion (Figure 36-3 on page 610). The rows representing 1990 and 1991 are shaded on the chart for easy reference.

Finally, we'll calculate the Personal Months for the beginning of 1991.

Calendar Month	+	Personal Year	=		Personal Month
January	1	+	6	=	7
February	2	+	6	=	8
March	3	+	6	=	9
April	4	+	6	= 10 =	1
May	5	+	6	=	11/2

Hope Edythe Lynch: Personal Month calculation

PROGRESSED DELINEATION: 1990, 1991
FOR
HOPE EDYTHE LYNCH
BORN MARCH 28, 1962

Progressed delineation for Hope Edythe Lynch

SUMMARY OF CHARACTER TRAITS

Your main lesson in life is to learn the advantage of order and system as well as learning to live with the limitations you find (*4 Life Path*).

There are a lot of strong positive potentials here. You're likely to be quite practical, good at systematizing and managing and good at handling groups (*4 Life Path, 2 Expression*). You are probably honest, sincere and responsible (*4 Life Path*). I expect that you have innate business capability (*8 Soul Urge, three 8's*), that you use your executive ability, fine analytic mind, technical ability, energy and ambition to make your way (*8 Soul Urge, three 7's*). You're apt to have an independent attitude with original or out-of-the-ordinary ideas or an unusual viewpoint (*28/1 Birthday, three 7's*).

I suspect there are some impediments which, until resolved, may get in the way of making the most of the above potentials. I can't determine which of these problem areas have already been taken care of, but I expect that at least some of them still need considerable effort. You probably have to work hard, far harder than your fair share to get most jobs done. This may make you feel restricted (*13/4 Karmic Debt*). You seem to have a tendency to be rigid, obstinate or dogmatic (*13/4 Karmic Debt, 8·8 energy*) as well as self-centered (*4 Life Path, 8 Soul Urge, 9 Karmic Lesson*). Some of the limitations you feel may be produced or reinforced by your own unbending views and lack of

4 FIRST PINNACLE   (0–32)
1 SECOND PINNACLE (33–41)
5 THIRD PINNACLE   (42–50)
3 FOURTH PINNACLE (51 on)

March   28,   1962

$$3 \; + \; \underset{\smile}{1} \; + \; 9 \; = \; \boxed{13/4}$$

(0–23)   (24–59)   (60 on)

$$3 - 1 = 2$$
$$9 - 1 = 8$$
$$8 - 2 = 6 \text{ CHALLENGE}$$

$$\frac{11}{6 \; 5} \; + \; \frac{(17) \; 8}{5 \; 7 \quad 5} \; + \; \frac{7}{7} \; = 26 = \boxed{8}$$

HOPE   EDYTHE   LYNCH

$$\frac{8 \; 7}{(15) \; 6} + \frac{4 \; \; 28}{(14) \; 5} + \frac{3 \; \; 538}{(19) \; 1} = 12 = 3 \text{ SECRET SELF}$$

$$\frac{8675}{(26) \; 8} + \frac{547285}{(31) \; 4} + \frac{37538}{(26) \; 8} = 20 = \boxed{2}$$

no 1 ←
one 2
two 3's
one 4
four 5's
one 6
three 7's
three 8's
nc 9 ←

PHYSICAL	EEDE	4–Strong
MENTAL	HPHLNH	6–Strong
EMOTIONAL	OT	2–Average
INTUITIVE	YYC	3–Average

MATURITY NUMBER = 4 + 2 = 6

Figure 36–1
Calculation Sheet:
Hope Edythe Lynch

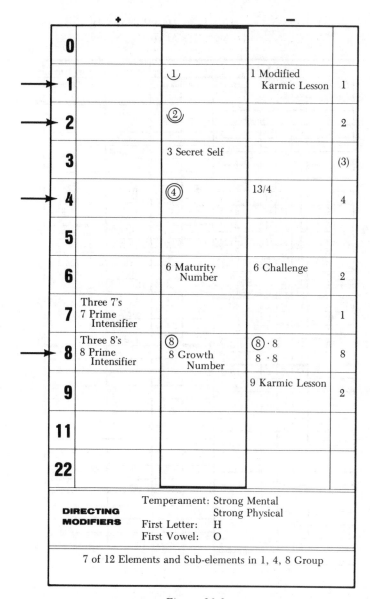

	+		−	
0				
1		①̣	1 Modified Karmic Lesson	1
2		②̣		2
3		3 Secret Self		(3)
4		④	13/4	4
5				
6		6 Maturity Number	6 Challenge	2
7	Three 7's 7 Prime Intensifier			1
8	Three 8's 8 Prime Intensifier	⑧ 8 Growth Number	⑧ · 8 8 · 8	8
9			9 Karmic Lesson	2
11				
22				

DIRECTING MODIFIERS	Temperament: Strong Mental Strong Physical First Letter: H First Vowel: O

7 of 12 Elements and Sub-elements in 1, 4, 8 Group

Figure 36-2
Organization Sheet:
Hope Edythe Lynch

constructive adaptability (*13/4 Karmic Debt*). You may also tend to be dominating and too exacting (*8 Soul Urge*). You're likely to be materialistic, possibly obsessed with goals and achievements (*8·8 energy, three 8's, 8 Prime Intensifier*). There may be a lack of confidence which makes it difficult to promote yourself at times (*1 Modified Karmic Lesson*).

HOPE EDYTHE LYNCH
MARCH 28, 1962

Age	Medium Term				Personal Year	Universal Year	Year	Long Term	
	Transits			Essence				Period	Pinnacle
0							1962		
21	E	H	H	21/3	7	3	1983	3_1	4
22	E	H	H	21/3	8	22/4	1984	3_1	4
23	E	H	H	21/3	9	5	1985	3_1	4
24	E	H	H	21/3	1	6	1986	1_3	4
25	E	H	H	21/3	11/2	7	1987	1_3	4
26	H	E	L	16/7	3	8	1988	1_3	4
27	H	E	L	16/7	4	9	1989	1	4
28	H	E	L	16/7	5	1	1990	1	4
29	H	E	Y	20/2	6	2	1991	1	4
30	H	E	Y	20/2	7	3	1992	1	4
31	H	E	Y	20/2	8	22/4	1993	1	4
32	H	E	Y	20/2	9	5	1994	1	4
33	H	E	Y	20/2	1	6	1995	1	1
34	O	E	Y	18/9	11/2	7	1996	1	1

Figure 36–3
Partial Progressed Chart:
Hope Edythe Lynch

There are some additional strong potentials here, but your business orientation and the obstacles mentioned in the last paragraph may make it difficult for these potentials to develop easily. You could be or become exceedingly sensitive to others' feelings. You can develop into a diplomatic, considerate, courteous and cooperative person (2 *Expression*). You'll have to learn not to repress your feelings, a very strong tendency (*9 Karmic Lesson, three 8's*), and not to succumb to timidity or uncertainty (*2 Expression*). You may be subject to many emotional upsets until you learn concern for others along with a clear expression of your feelngs and a clear response to others' feelings (*9 Karmic Lesson*).

BACKGROUND INFLUENCES

(The 4 First Pinnacle, with the related 4 Life Path and 13/4 Karmic Debt, is likely to be more important than the 1 Second Period, with its related 1 Birthday and 1 Modified Karmic Lesson.)

At this time in your life, you're likely to be in a practical environment with down-to-earth activities and experiences (*4 First Pinnacle*). Your capability at systematizing and organizing is likely to be useful in this environment as are your conscientious, dependable and responsible attitudes. There's probably a need for hard work, determined effort and constant application, and you're certainly capable of that (*4 First Pinnacle with 4 Life Path, 8 Soul Urge*). The opportunities and activities are likely to develop more slowly than you'd like (*4 First Pinnacle*).

Although practicality and hard work are stressed, there's also likely to be an emphasis on the ability to act independently using your own resources. Individuality and originality are apt to be encouraged (*1 Second Period on the 4 Life Path*). You have the potential to be independent (*28/1 Birthday*) and your original ideas and unusual viewpoint (*28/1 Birthday, three 7's*) are likely to be appreciated, but I suspect that your shyness, uncertainty (*2 Expression*) and lack of confidence (*1 Modified Karmic Lesson*) must be overcome to maximize the potential of these characteristics. Achievements based on your independent outlook are likely to be rewarded with recognition and financial gain (*1 Second Period on the 4 Life Path*).

I discussed your probable feelings of limitation before, but I suspect that these feelings are felt strongly at this time in your life. You may have had to work hard from an early age, you may have had to live with economic limitations and had little time for youthful activities. These experiences, along with your rigidity, exacting approach and materialistic needs all contribute to your current feeling of restriction (*4 First Pinnacle with 13/4 Karmic Debt, 8 Soul Urge, 8·8 energy*). I doubt that you have had much time to develop the sensitive, adaptable side of your personality (*2 Expression*).

From age 33 to 41, you're likely to find less restrictive circumstances. You're apt to find it easier to express your independence while continuing to develop your superior business abilities (*preparation for 1 Second Pinnacle with 1 Birthday, 4 Life Path, 8 Soul Urge*). From age 42 to 50, you may well find yourself in a period with few restrictions and much in the way of change, variety and freedom. By that time, the more flexibility you've developed, the more advantage you'll be able to take of the opportunities (*preparation for 5 Third Pinnacle with no related energy*).

CURRENT EPICYCLE

In the current period of your life, from 1986 to 1994 (age 24 to 32) there's the possiblity of a development from a sociable interest in friends to a considerably more sensitive concern for others which could lead to very close and beautiful relationships. (*The Epicycle starts with several years of a 21/3 Essence, ends with several years of a 20/2 Essence.*) This period may mark an ending or at least a substantial lessening of the feelings of limitation and restriction (*end of 4 First Pinnacle*) as well as the beginning of a stronger, more independent approach (*start of 1 Second Period*).

26TH TO 29TH BIRTHDAY

A difficult and important transition runs for three

years, from your 26th to your 29th birthday. This transition, then, will be ending at the end of March in 1991. This time is likely to mark important changes in your life. At your 29th birthday, you'll probably be in a better position than at your 26th birthday, but the period between the birthdays provides little in the way of signposts. It is difficult to clearly comprehend the direction to take. The apparent direction must often be accepted on instinct. Confusion, negativity and frustration may be felt until a final understanding is reached. Much of your energy is likely to be devoted to clarifying experiences, searching for the stages leading to a final breakthrough. Some substantial development of your spiritual faith may occur during this period (*16/7 Essence*).

The period may have opportunities for study and introspection, withdrawing for reflection and meditation, searching for inner peace, but the turmoil of the transition search will probably make it difficult to concentrate on any of these quiet activities (*7 Essence present but secondary to 16/7 Essence*).

1990

GENERAL

1990 may be especially confusing. There are likely to be new people, new places, new opportunities, the possibility of adventure and excitement. You'll probably be involved with a variety of experiences (*5 Personal Year*). You're likely to feel a sense of beginning and expansion in the air (*1 Universal Year*). There may be some times of absolute delight, but, with the confusions of the transition period I previously described along with your own inflexibility, I suspect you may be somewhat overwhelmed by all the possibilities (*5 Personal Year, 16/7 Essence with 13/4 Karmic Debt and 8·8 energy*).

Some of the changes related to the transition period may well occur this year, possibly a change of residence or a change in your family situation (*5 Personal Year, E Transit*).

PROFESSIONAL

This change might relate to work. With your strong potential in this area (*4 Life Path, 8 Soul Urge, three 8's*) there may be more authority for you here or recognition of your practical, hard working contribution (*H Transit*).

If you're involved in research or educational pursuits, this may be a good time to move ahead by studying, writing or teaching, possibly in relation to fundamental concepts. You might find yourself pursuing some completely new area—possibly scientific, religious or metaphysical—an area different than any in which you've had previous experience (*7 Essence*). Your excellent analytical mind, technical ability and unusual viewpoint may prove extremely helpful (*three 7's, 7 Prime Intensifier*).

FINANCIAL

Your financial affairs may fluctuate (*E Transit*) but, overall, there may be some financial gain (*H Transit*). Be careful not to block possibilities here by straining too hard or by being selfish (*1 Modified Karmic Lesson, 8·8 energy*).

PERSONAL

There may be new friends. There could be exciting love affairs but they may prove to be short-lived. Although impulsiveness at this time may precipitate marriage, I would advise strongly against it (*5 Personal Year, E Transit*).

TRAVEL

Vacation trips or travel on business matters may prove sources of fun and pleasure (*5 Personal Year, E, H Transits*).

JANUARY THROUGH MARCH, 1991

GENERAL

The first few months of 1991, until the end of

March, conclude the potentially important transition. During these months, there may well be the final changes or consolidation of changes culminating the three year period (*16/7 Essence*). The hectic activities of 1991 are likely to subside into a far quieter pattern (*5 Personal Year changes to 6 Personal Year*).

HOME, FAMILY

In these first few months, and in the rest of the year, too, there's likely to be strong emphasis on home life and responsibilities related to family matters. The whole year is a time to work for harmony and balance in the family, to enjoy the deep quiet pleasures of romance, love, marriage. This can be a fine year to get married if the emotions are balanced and clearly and openly expressed (*6 Personal Year*). Your tendency to repress feelings may cause problems in close relations. You may have to work on improving your communication (*9 Karmic Lesson*).

MISCELLANEOUS

Business affairs may continue to advance through 1991 with financial fluctuations similar to those in 1990. Friends are likely to be as important as last year and there are probably additional opportunities for travel (*continuation of E, H Transits*).

APRIL THROUGH DECEMBER, 1991

HOME, FAMILY

With the beginning of April, 1991, the transition period, with its attendant confusions, fades into the past (*end of the 16/7 Essence*). The emphasis on home and family matters continues to the end of the year (*continuation of the 6 Personal Year*).

GENERAL

Events and opportunities through the end of 1991 are likely to emphasize cooperation and patience. This is probably a good time to develop relations or associations, to work to satisfy mutual needs, to show interest in helping others with their needs (2 *Essence*). Partners may develop problems precipitated by new interests or a desire to be alone. Lack of clear communication may present difficulties (Y *Transit*).

Developments may take a little longer than you may expect, so don't be surprised if there are delays from time to time. There's a likelihood of high emotions and increased sensitivity now. There may be some health matters needing attention (2 *Essence*).

There may be a new interest, possibly a desire for continuing study, research or meditation. If you tend to withdraw or if you're difficult for others to understand, there may be some problems (Y *Transit*).

1992 THROUGH 1996

Until your 34th birthday in 1996, there's likely to be emphasis on the growth of relations and associations, new interests, study, meditation, advancing business affairs (*continuation of 2 Essence, H, E, Y Transits*). There will be some different emphases added each year (*different Personal Years*), but the stress on cooperation, patience and sensitivity will continue (*continuation of 2 Essence*).

You were particularly concerned with the beginning months of 1991. Let's look at them in more detail.

JANUARY, 1991: 7 Personal Month

Spend time alone in January, reviewing the past and present and contemplating the future, particularly in regard to home and family matters (*6 Personal Year, 7 Personal Month*). Review the important changes made in the last few years and, if possible, plan the conclusion of the transition which will end in the next few months (*16/7*

Essence). You may want to draw on your unusual viewpoint to help with the plans (*three 7's*). There may be much excitement and activity around you similar to last year's, but this will probably be a more growing month if you spend your time primarily in introspective activity (*waning of the 5 Personal Year, 7 Personal Month*). Inflexibility may cause difficulties (*7 Personal Month with 13/4 Karmic Debt, 8·8 energy*).

FEBRUARY, 1991: 8 Personal Month

In February, you may make a strong impact with your ability to make things happen. Take advantage of the opportunities, possibly unusual or exciting ones, to advance, find recognition or expand in the business world (*8 Personal Month, waning of 5 Personal Year*). Your innate business ability and your organized, realistic approach should prove helpful (*4 Life Path, 8 Soul Urge, three 8's*). Be sure that your progress in business doesn't conflict with home or family matters (*6 Personal Year, 9 Personal Month*).

MARCH, 1991: 9 Personal Month

March may be a month full of drama and strong emotions. There may be endings here, completions of experiences, activities, or close relations, particularly relations having to do with domestic matters (*6 Personal Year, 9 Personal Month, end of 16/7 Essence*). Be prepared to help others this month. Be as generous as possible (*9 Personal Month*). Clear expression of your feelings and clear responses to others' feelings may still be difficult for you and may add to the problems at this time (*9 Karmic Lesson*).

APRIL, 1991: 1 Personal Month

April heralds a time for change, breaking up old conditions, the start of new activities — all probably related to home and family matters. This is a fine month to make the move you've been thinking about for some time. As you approach your new endeavors, be aware of and express your individuality, but keep a balanced approach so as not to irritate or alienate others (*6 Personal Year, 1 Personal Month*). April is a fine time to start developing relations and associations. Be as adaptable and sensitive as possible (*2 Essence, 1 Personal Month*). May will allow for further development of your sensitivity, possibly along with new awarenesses (*preparation for May, an 11/2 month*).

Of the four months we've just delineated, I think it's clear that April would be the perfect time for your planned wedding. We'll look at all the Sundays in April.

	Calendar Month	+	Calendar Day	+	Personal Year	=	Personal Day
April 7	4	+	7	+	6	=	17 = 8
April 14	4	+	5	+	6	=	15 = 6
April 21	4	+	3	+	6	=	13/4
April 28	4	+	1	+	6	=	11/2

APRIL 7: 8 Personal Day

This is a day to use your power and your organized, practical approach in business and financial matters. You'll probably register a strong impact (*8 Personal Day with 4 Life Path, 8 Soul Urge, three 8's*). Make sure to explore ventures diplomatically with an understanding of others' needs and desires (*8 Personal Day with 2 Expression*).

APRIL 14: 6 Personal Day

A day to enjoy home and family, the pleasures of domestic life, possibly a day to start something new related to domestic matters (*1 Personal Month, 6 Personal Day*). Selfishness may cause problems (*6 Personal Day with 13/4 Karmic Debt*).

APRIL 21: 13/4 Personal Day

Complete routine tasks related to home and family, keep your nose to the grindstone. This isn't a day for starting new ventures or looking for new opportunities. Feelings of limitation or restriction may be present. They're likely to impede your work so try to change or overcome those tendencies (*13/4 Personal Day*). Your serious, methodical approach can be helpful in getting the job accomplished (*4 Life Path*).

APRIL 28: 11/2 Personal Day

A day for a pleasant, probably quiet social time at home. Cooperate with others in their work and enjoy your own routine. Move routine matters forward smoothly but don't attempt to change direction (*2 Personal Day*). Your responsiveness and support may be important (*2 Expression*). Nervous tension may be present. (*11 Personal Day. The tension is the only manifestation of the 11 Personal Day since there's no 11 core element.*)

Hope, let's discuss your specific questions now.

What can you expect of marriage at this time? Is the confusion you've been experiencing going to continue unabated?

Discussion of Hope Edyth Lynch's questions

As discussed in the delineation, you're just completing a three year transition period with much probable confusion (*16/7 Essence from 26th to 29th birthday*), augmented by the variety of experiences in 1990 (*5 Personal Year*). With the transition ending at your birthday in March, 1991, the confusion should, to a great extent, disappear (*end of 16/7 Essence*). 1991 is a fine year to get married (*6 Personal Year, 2 Essence from April to December*). The following several years may provide a good environment for mutual growth for you and your husband (*2 Essence continues until 34th birthday*). Much will depend on overcoming your self-centeredness (*4 Life Path, 8 Soul Urge, 8·8 energy, 9 Karmic Lesson*) and your repression of feelings (*13/4 Karmic Debt, 9 Karmic Lesson, three 8's*). The growth of your sensitivity and adaptability will be extremely helpful (*2 Essence with 2 Expression*).

You met your husband-to-be in a year with much emphasis on expanding your life (*5 Personal Year*) so I would expect that marriage represents a step toward significant growth. I'm glad that you waited until 1991 (*6 Personal Year*) to marry because 1990, with its emphasis on change and variety, is not especially propitious for marriage (*5 Personal Year*).

Is February, March or April in 1991 good for the wedding? Which Sunday is best?

April is the best month at the beginning of 1991 for your wedding. February is heavily business-oriented and wouldn't be a good month for marriage (*8 Personal Month*). March, a month of completions, wouldn't be a good time either (*9 Personal Month*). April, a month for beginnings in a year with emphasis on home and family (*1 Personal Month, 6 Personal Year*), is as good a time (*in the whole Epicycle*) for marriage as you can find.

Of the Sundays in April, April 14 is a fine day, perfectly suited for the beauty of a wedding (*6 Personal Day*). The other Sundays are considerably less satisfactory.

Should you take either of the two new jobs? If you decide to take a new job, when is the best time to start?

Your two job offers come, again, in a year with emphasis on expanding your life (*5 Personal Year*). I'd suggest that you take the position with the most long term potential using your specific abilities—your capability at organization and system especially (*4 Life Path, 8 Soul Urge, three 8's*), along with your fine analytical mind and your unusual ideas (*three 7's*).

February, 1991 would be a fine time to change jobs (*8 Personal Month*) as long as it doesn't interfere in matters involving your future husband (*8 Personal Month may conflict with 6 Personal Year*). April, 1991 (*1 Personal Month*) would be good, too. If your wedding is scheduled in April, though, it might be easier to shift employment in February. There's likely to be much opportunity for professional advancement through the beginning of 1996 (*H Transit extends to 34th birthday in 1996*).

The outcome of Hope's marriage and new job will ultimately depend on how she decides to use her energies—her actual approach to events and opportunities as they occur in her life. The information provided by the progressed delineation should prove helpful in assessing desirable directions in which to move. Progressed delineations can never, of course, provide all the answers about the future, but they certainly provide many useful insights.

PART VI:
SPECIAL AREAS

CHAPTER 37

HELPING PARENTS NAME THEIR BABIES; HELPING PEOPLE CHANGE THEIR NAMES

Numerology assumes the existence of reincarnation. The soul, in a physical body, comes back to the earth plane many times to learn the varied lessons which can only be learned on this plane. When all of the lessons are learned, the soul no longer returns to earth, ascends instead to a higher level for advanced tutelage.

Each time the soul makes the decision to return, it chooses what lessons it wants to learn. It may sometimes decide what abilities it would like to bring with it and what inner desires it will work to satisfy. These decisions are coded into the birthdate and birthname and decoded by the use of numerology—the Life Path, Expression and Soul Urge describe respectively the lessons, the capabilities and the inner needs. With each new incarnation, the soul also brings the Karmic Debts, the vestiges of misused energies from previous lives which have not been "made up" in subsequent lives, as well as the Karmic Lessons or Modified Karmic Lessons, areas of potential which have been ignored or virtually unexplored in past existences.

I don't think that a soul purposely chooses a difficult life here on earth, but sometimes the numerology reading shows much in the way of difficulty. Why does this happen?

In order to receive the Life Path the soul desires and, at the same time accommodate the Karmic Debts and Karmic Lessons related to the soul, it may be necessary to adjust the Expression,

Numerology and reincarnation

Soul Urge and other areas of the energy. Because of these adjustments, the resultant chart may sometimes indicate more problem areas than the soul had originally expected.

Naming the baby

The core elements and modifiers are directly related to the needs and debts of the soul. The birthdate and birthname are, as we've discussed, directly related to the elements and modifiers, and, therefore, far from arbitrary matters. In some unexplained manner, the parents of a baby about to be born (that is, a soul about to be reincarnated) tune in on some universal wavelength so that the baby's birthdate confirms the soul's desired lesson. The baby's name is likewise related to the soul's requirements, even though the parents have no awareness of the correlation. Although the parents may spend hours poring over lists of names, conferring with friends and relatives, thinking about and discussing the possibilities, the baby's name (or several possible names) is determined by the universe and broadcast to the earth plane in some inexplicable subconscious process.

The baby will always receive the name the soul needs, but the most direct path to that name is through the baby's parents. The name should be chosen by the parents (or by the adoptive parents when the baby is adopted shortly after birth). If a numerologist is consulted, it should be in an advisory capacity only. If the parents have several names under discussion, the numerologist can be helpful in distinguishing the characteristics and impediments related to each name.

The numerologist *should not* suggest names; he should only advise on names suggested by the parents. If the parents are dissatisfied with the characteristics or impediments of names they have chosen or if they are having difficulty agreeing on a satisfactory name, they should meditate and listen to their inner voices for guidance.

The name, of course, is always linked to the date of birth. If the parents consult with the numerologist prior to the birth, the numerologist will have to advise on several names since both the sex and birthdate are not yet known. I've occasionally advised parents on names covering a period of a week or two—the period during which the baby's birth is expected.

I always express, as clearly as I can, the characteristics involved, both positive and negative. All names have their share of strengths and weaknesses and the parents should have correct information to weigh in making their choice. Withholding knowledge about such negative matters as Karmic Debts or repeated elements is doing a disservice to all concerned.

Although the birthname is so important, most of us use other names at least some of the time: nicknames, professional names or middle initials instead of middle names. In Chapter 24, we discussed these other names and the way to evaluate the energy they bring.

Changing the name

When a person decides to change the name he or she commonly uses, that individual is symbolically announcing that different energies are about to be used in the life. In our society, as the most obvious example, when a woman marries, she usually drops her last name and substitutes her husband's last name—symbolically attesting to the dramatic change in her life. (Since men in our society don't usually change their names in marriage, I would suggest that (a) there may be less of a change of energy for most men, or (b) there may be a difference in the emphasis on existing energy—a latent 2, 6, 9 might, for instance, be activated.)

The change of name is usually a carefully planned demonstration of an individual's evolving nature. Like a drastic change in hair style or dress, the individual is announcing that he or she feels differently about himself or herself.

For the purposes of numerology, it doesn't matter if the name is changed legally or not—if the person believes that he *is* the person with the new name, that's the key. Acceptance of the new name begins to make the new energy operative. Sometimes, a person chooses to change his name only in the business world or only in the personal life. The new energy operates when the new name is being used. If it's not being used all the time, it's not as strong an energy change as a name that is actually being used constantly.

The new name should come from the individual desiring the change. The numerologist can advise on the traits and obstacles of the new name relative to the old, but he shouldn't suggest names or indicate preferences on names selected by a subject.

When helping with a name change, the numerologist must be aware of the purpose of the change so that he can confirm the probable availability of the specific energy desired. Here are a few illustrations from my files:

Confirming the purpose of the name change

Martin had been a writer for many years but was dissatisfied with his lack of professional progress. At his request, we discussed a number of variants of his birthname—using the middle name, using the middle initial, using an initial for his first name. He chose to use the name which best expressed energy devoted to creativity and financial success. Within a few months, he had become associate editor of a west coast magazine and was selling articles to this magazine and other leading periodicals.

Did the name change really account for this dramatic advance in his writing career? Martin's new name announced symbolically that he wanted more recognition and reward for his creative endeavors. When he started using the new name, I expect he had gained added skill and confidence, heightened awareness of markets and a stronger ability to sell himself. The name change was a public affirmation of the new state of affairs.

Betty had a 14/5 Life Path and a 3 Expression. Less than thirty years old, she had been married and divorced twice and had an inconsistent employment record. In a dream one night, she visualized a new name—a very unusual first name and a last name with no relation to her birthname or either of her married names. She asked me what she might expect if she adopted the new name. Since this name had a 6 Expression, I indicated that the 6 energy was likely to be in direct conflict with the 14/5 energy. As we discussed the potential for conflict, Betty began to focus on the fact that the 6 energy, because of the conflict, could well slow the frantic pace of the 14/5 energy as well as adding energy to attract love and affection, energy that had not been present previously. I indicated the probable difficulty in assimilating a brand new energy, but Betty felt she would like to make the effort.

She adopted the new name on the spot and, within six months, there was an appreciable difference in the pace of her life. It had slowed considerably so she had more time to appreciate herself and others. She had applied herself with continued diligence and a clear understanding of her goals so that her efforts were amply rewarded.

With Martin and Betty, the new names proved especially effective. Both had well-understood ends in view and both applied themselves to assimilating the new energies while continuing to use the positive potential of their birth energies. With this kind of motivation, a name change can prove to be a dramatic turning point in an individual's life.

CHAPTER 38

VOCATIONAL GUIDANCE

Numerology is useful in determining the vocations which would be most satisfying and most growth producing. The determination of the one best job isn't possible—the determination of a desirable direction and the subject's talents and adaptability for specific vocational areas is comparatively easy.

Some numerology charts indicate a direction by virtue of the large number of core elements and sub-elements which belong in one of the groups described in Chapter 20:

Groups of elements and sub-elements

1, 4, 8: business, order, system
2, 6, 9: helping, caring
3, 6, 9: artistic, creative
11, 22: special potential

If forty percent of the total of elements and sub-elements in a subject's chart are in one group *or* if at least two of the four core elements are in one group, that particular group would be an especially fitting area in which to invest the talents.

Six of Hal Allen's twelve sub-elements, for example, belong in the 3, 6, 9 group *and* three of his four elements are in the same category (Figure 28-2 on page 493). Hal would be admirably suited for an artistic or creative vocation.

The grouping, when present, defines the general vocational area, but the Life Path and the Expression are the major determinants of the desirable career. Between them, they define seventy percent of an individual's total core energies. The Life Path defines the major lesson to be learned in the life, the cen-

Life Path and Expression as major career determinants

tral focus of a subject's existence, while the Expression describes the natural talents and capabilities. If an individual can find a livelihood combining these energies, he's in a position with significant growth potential.

Hal, with his 5 Life Path and 6 Expression, might look for employment, for example, as a set designer (combining the potential creativity of the 5 with the potential artistic ability of the 6), as an author of books about travel (combining the probable travel of the 5 with the potential writing skills of the 6), or as a music composer working in a progressive style (combining the forward-looking approach of the 5 with the potential musical aptitude of the 6).

Marlene has a 9 Life Path and an 8 Expression. She might find satisfaction as an administrator (8 energy) of a social welfare agency (9 energy), a psychologist (9 energy) researching projects related to wealth and status (8 energy), or a fund-raiser (8 energy) for a philanthropic association (9 energy).

As you can see, there's a wide variety of desirable employment available to Hal or Marlene—or anybody. In discussing a subject's career plans, don't narrow the field by presenting specific jobs but, rather, define wide areas of probable expertise to make the choice as broad as possible.

An ideal vocation would include many facets of the available energies. A 6 Life Path or Expression might relate to creative endeavors, responsibility, balancing situations, domestic relations, working with the old, young and infirm, bettering the community. An architect involved with the design of housing developments or hospitals, for instance, could be using many of these 6 potentials.

Many people, on the other hand, use only one or two aspects of their energy in their work. Often, an individual selects a job in a field which doesn't seem to necessarily relate to his energies, then adapts the job to fit the available potential. A bookkeeper could be a balanced expression of 4 or 8 energy, a more limited expression of the responsibility and adjusting found in 6 energy. A nursery school teacher could be a strong expression of 6 or 9 energy, or, if the individual chooses, the work might reflect the service and hard work of 4 potential.

The energy, then, will often define the *specific* emphasis placed in a broad field of endeavor. If, for instance, Emma had a 4 Life Path, she might choose to be an engineer. If she had a 1 Expression, she might prefer to initiate the work with broad strokes. If, instead, she had a 2 Expression, she might prefer to be the administrator coordinating a team of other engineers. With an 8 Expression, on the other hand, she might be involved in negotiating and writing the contracts for engineering projects. Or, with a 22 Expression, she might do advance planning on large projects like hydroelectric dams or major port facilities.

Although it's preferable to make use of both the Life Path and Expression, you'll find many people emphasizing one over the other in choosing their vocation. The Expression is more commonly the potential expressed on a day-to-day basis with the Life Path used only as a broad general focus. Some individuals choose to use only one energy in their work and completely ignore the other. A woman with a 2 Life Path and an 8 Expression may prefer the 2 background quality over the 8 hustle-bustle while another woman with the same elements may, conversely, aspire to the status and activity of the 8 rather than deal with the quiet receptivity of the 2. Sometimes, one energy is ignored in favor of the other because of the seeming difficulty of combining both energies in a single vocation—a 7 Life Path/22 Expression or an 11 Life Path/ 5 Expression, for instance. The individual is, of course, limiting the potential growth by omitting development of one of the strong energies.

Repeated numbers

If the Life Path and Expression are the same number, or if the Soul Urge or Birthday repeat the number of the Life Path or Expression, or if one of the sub-elements repeats the Life Path or Expression number, we then have a negative cast to the vocation potential. (See Chapter 9, page 87, and Chapter 13, page 143.) The individual should choose a career befitting the repeated number, but is likely to experience difficulties until he's converted the negative to positive energy. His development is likely to proceed more quickly if he uses the remedy outlined in parentheses with the repeated numbers on CHART 6: THE ASPECTS, page 292).

If, for instance, Roger has a 1 Life Path and a 1 Expression, he would do well to choose a livelihood which will use his leadership, his executive and administrative ability, his good mind—and also provide opportunities for him to learn to be comfortable in group situations (from the 1·1 aspect on Chart 6).

Soul Urge, Birthday, Intensity Points, Prime Intensifier

If possible, the vocation should satisfy the Soul Urge needs, too, but if that energy seems headed in a different direction, it is often neglected. Strong positive traits described by the Birthday, strongly divergent positive Intensity Points or a strongly divergent Prime Intensifier may well describe significant talents which can be put to good use. The more capabilities in process of development, the greater the possibilities for growth and satisfaction.

**First Letter,
First Vowel**

There are several other vocational determinants which are not as important as the Life Path and Expression, but are about on a par with the elements and modifiers mentioned in the last paragraph. Confirm the individual's natural approach to experience, as described by the First Letter and First Vowel. (See Chapter 20, page 185.) With the long A starting her name, Amy, for instance, would probably enjoy an assertive leadership role while Julian, with his long First Vowel U, is likely to prefer a job related to idealistic ends of a relatively conservative bent.

Temperament

When it indicates significant strengths and weaknesses, the Temperament should be taken into account. (See Chapter 19, page 173). A strong Mental component, for example, with its interest in reason, logic and facts would indicate one type of career position while a strong Intuitive component, with its concern with spiritual and philosophical matters would indicate a very different calling. On the other hand, a subject with a weak Emotional component should not be placed in employment requiring substantial emotional interaction or he is likely to feel uncomfortable and insecure.

**Names other
than
birthnames**

If the subject uses a name (or names) in business other than his birthname, that name, of course, adds its own energy, though it's generally considerably weaker than the birthname energy. If the new name contributes a different Expression, Soul Urge, First Letter, First Vowel, or strongly divergent positive Intensity Points or Prime Intensifier, the potentials of these elements and modifiers should be considered.

**Periods and
Pinnacles**

The Periods and Pinnacles can be useful determinants of the vocational direction. (See Chapter 28, page 485 and Chapter 29, page 499). Although the First Period and First Pinnacle may play an especially significant part in the life, they usually play less of a role in relation to the career than you might expect. Particularly when the subject has become a young adult, these formative influences should be important, but immaturity and inability to successfully focus the energies at a young age often dilute their effect. On the other hand, the Second Period and the Second and Third Pinnacles, the productive cycles, are vitally connected with the working life during what is often its most significant period. If the livelihood expresses the influences of the middle Period and Pinnacles, the life is likely to be fulfilling and pleasurable. The role of the Third Period and the Fourth Pinnacle in career matters is apt to be important too. With developed maturity, the individual is probably far more capable of adapting his energies to the influences of the integrative cycles. You can see that a given career potential may express in remarkably different manners, say, in a 2 Period as compared to an 8 Period, or in a 4 Pinnacle as compared to a 5 Pinnacle.

Epicycle

The Epicycle often gives some general insights into the vocation and should be taken into consideration when appropriate. Read the Epicycle broadly for some awareness of future vocational direction.

Personal Year, Essence, Transits

The Personal Year, Essence and Transits don't usually define the vocational energy, but rather indicate emphases within the chosen field of endeavor and aid in the timing of specific actions. Knowing the best time to begin, expand or conclude ventures, the best time to work hard or take a break can be of considerable importance. These and many lesser matters can be determined as functions of the medium term cycles.

Example of vocational guidance: John Melville Jenkins

We'll assume it's the beginning of 1990. Enter John Melville Jenkins, born July 2, 1970. "I'd like some idea," says John, "of what careers hold the most promise for me." John is, of course, another fictitious character. But we'll give him some help as an example of vocational guidance.

Let's first perform the standard calculations. I'll assume, for the purposes of the delineation, that John uses his birthname in business. See Figure 38-1, page 634, for John's calculation sheet.

The progressed chart showing the Epicycle which includes 1990, the year under discussion, is shown on Figure 38-2, page 635.

CURRENT VOCATIONAL POTENTIAL
FOR
JOHN MELVILLE JENKINS
BORN JULY 2, 1970

INTRODUCTION

In your life, you'll probably find a lot of career opportunities in the business world, possibly in some creative capacity (8 *Life Path*, 3 *Expression*). The influences during your youth and young adulthood, though, may interfere with your taking full advantage of your vocational capabilities at this time (*Conflict between 8 Life Path, 3 Expression with 7 First*

9 FIRST PINNACLE   (0–28)
1 SECOND PINNACLE (29–37)
1 THIRD PINNACLE   (38–46)
6 FOURTH PINNACLE (47 on)

July   2,   1970

7   + $\widetilde{2}$ +   8   = 17 = $\textcircled{8}$

(0–28)   (29–55)   (56 on)

7 – 2 = 5
8 – 2 = 6
6 – 5 = 1 CHALLENGE

$$\frac{6}{6} \; + \; \frac{(19)\;1}{5\quad 9\quad 5} \; + \; \frac{(14)\;5}{5\quad 9} \; = 12 = \textcircled{3}$$

J OHN   MELVILLE   JENKINS

$$\frac{1\;\;85}{(14)\;5} + \quad \frac{4\;\;34\;\;33}{(17)\;8} \quad + \quad \frac{1\;\;52\;\;51}{(14)\;5} \quad = 18$$
$$= 9 \text{ SECRET SELF}$$

$$\frac{1685}{(20)\;2} + \quad \frac{45349335}{(36)\;9} \quad + \quad \frac{1552951}{(28)\;(10)\;1} \quad = 12 = \widetilde{\textcircled{3}}$$

three 1's
one 2
three 3's
two 4's
  six 5's
one 6
no 7 ←
one 8
two 9's

PHYSICAL	MEEE	4–Average
MENTAL	JHNLLLJNN	9–Strong
EMOTIONAL	OIIS	4–Average
INTUITIVE	VK	2–Weak

MATURITY NUMBER = 8 + 3 = 11/2

Figure 38–1
Calculation Sheet:
John Melville Jenkins

JOHN MELVILLE JENKINS
JULY 2, 1970

Age	Medium Term				Personal Year	Universal Year	Year	Long Term	
	Transits			Essence				Period	Pinnacle
0							1970		
18	N	I	I	23/5	9	9	1989	7	9
19	N	I	I	23/5	D	1	1990	7	9
20	J	I	I	19Q			1991	7	9
21	O	I	I	24/6	11/2	2	1991	7	9
22	O	I	N	20/2	3	3	1992	7	9
23	O	I	N	20/2	4	22/4	1993	7	9
24	O	I	N	20/2	5	5	1994	7	9
25	O	L	N	14/5	6	6	1995	7	9
26	O	L	N	14/5	7	7	1996	7	9
27	H	L	S	12/3	8	8	1997	7	9
28	H	L	J	12/3	9	9	1998	7	9
29	H	L	E	16/7	1	1	1999	2	1
30	H	L	E	16/7	11/2	2	2000	2	1

Figure 38-2
Partial Progressed Chart:
John Melville Jenkins

Period, 9 First Pinnacle). I'll first discuss your
substantial potential, then clarify the impediments
which may be interfering with development of that
energy. (A discussion of the core and modifiers will be
followed by a discussion of the progressed cycles).

GROUPS

(With a 3 Expression, a 3 Soul Urge and four out of twelve elements and sub-elements in the 3, 6, 9 group, John is likely to be involved with creative or artistic work. His abilities in this area are discussed below relative to his Expression.)

8 LIFE PATH, 3 EXPRESSION

You have the potential to deal with money and material matters in commercial endeavors with an efficient, energetic and dependable approach. You can be a good organizer and administrator using a realistic, practical manner. When you're using your potential fully, you're not likely to waste time with daydreams. Your ability to judge character along with your ambition and self-confidence can prove helpful (*8 Life Path*).

You may have some artistic or creative capabilities which will be useful in business. You're likely to be extremely verbal—you can easily learn to present almost any material in an imaginative manner. When you express your friendly, gracious manner, your sociability and your enthusiasm, you can open many doors (*3 Expression*).

If you tend to be a bit frivolous and scatter your forces, you may appear too easy going and not make the right impression. If you are a little timid or afraid to stand up and say what's on your mind, you may not be able to develop some of the creative or social opportunities that come your way (*negative potential of 3 Expression/3 Soul Urge*). You probably have to learn to accept your responsibilities (*one of the approaches to alleviate the difficulties of the 3·3 aspect, shown in* CHART 6: THE ASPECTS).

Learn to keep a sense of proportion in the business world. It's sometimes easy to get so immersed in the attainment of money, possessions, status or power that you miss out on some deeper satisfactions. If you are very materialistic, obsessed with goals or extremely rigid, you're likely to hold yourself back (*negative potential of 8 Life path/8 sub-*

element). Try to see and appreciate the inherent values in life, not only the purely material values. Study and meditation on the inner satisfactions as well as the material satisfactions may prove helpful (*one of the approaches to alleviate the difficulties of the 8·8 aspect, shown in* CHART 6: THE ASPECTS).

3 SOUL URGE, 2 BIRTHDAY. NO STRONG POSITIVE INTENSITY POINTS OR PRIME INTENSIFIERS.

(*Attributes of 3 Soul Urge are similar to 3 Expression and need not be repeated.*) You're likely to develop considerable skill working with others. Your potential to develop as a diplomatic, considerate and cooperative person may make a place for you as an arbitrator or negotiator in the business world. Your sensitivity to others is likely to prove helpful, too (*2 Birthday*).

FIRST LETTER J, FIRST VOWEL O

You have a good mind and excellent ideas which can help you to be a leader. Although you probably have deep feelings, you can learn to keep those feelings in balance in business dealings so that they don't interfere with seeing all sides of an issue. I expect you'd tend to a relatively conservative or traditional mold (*First Letter J, First Vowel O*).

TEMPERAMENT: STRONG MENTAL COMPONENT, WEAK INTUITIVE COMPONENT

I expect you'll rely heavily on reasoning and facts in reaching your conclusions. These logical deductions are likely to be a strong motivating force in your life. Added to your will and determination, this rational disposition can help promote your leadership potential in business or politics (*strong Mental component*). You aren't likely to display much interest in spiritual or metaphysical matters (*weak Intuitive component*).

7 FIRST PERIOD, 9 FIRST PINNACLE

As I mentioned at the beginning of the reading, I don't expect that your childhood and young adulthood have allowed you to develop the abilities we've discussed to anywhere near the possible potential. In your youth, you may have had few friends, often felt alone and lonely. The forces around you probably felt repressive. You may have withdrawn, appeared cool and detached. I expect you haven't felt particularly comfortable in a business environment (7 *First Period on the 8 Life Path*). Your business talents, your creative abilities and your social skills may have had little chance to blossom (*conflict between 7 First Period and 8 Life Path/3 Expression*).

There's apt to be some time yet before you can feel comfortably free of the forces that have hindered your development, but it's important that you keep working to free yourself and to move forward to use the generous potential you possess. (*John has to struggle with his 7 First Period and 9 First Pinnacle until 1999. His 2 Second Period, starting at that time, will be more amenable to development of the talents related to his 3 Expression and 2 Birthday. His 1 Second Pinnacle, starting at the same time, will allow a freer development of his independence and business abilities*). There's probably been a lot of drama and emotion in your life so far and there's likely to be more in the next few years (9 *First Pinnacle*). Give of yourself selflessly when possible, but don't lose sight of your interest in business and your healthy desire for money and possessions (*conflict between the 9 First Pinnacle and the 8 Life Path*).

EPICYCLE

In the next decade or so, although there's apt to be much struggle, I suspect you'll develop some of your social skills and some of your artistic talents. (*Epicycle moves through three years with a 20/2 Essence and two years with a 12/3 Essence.*) You should feel a sense of more freedom and creativity as you near the end of your twenties. (*Epicycle moves from 20/2 to 14/5 to 12/3 Essences.*)

1990

1 PERSONAL YEAR, 23/5 AND 19/1 ESSENCES, N, J, AND I·I TRANSITS

The year 1990 can be an important one in your career development. You may be able to capitalize on the feelings of freedom you've experienced over the last few years (*continuing 23/5 Essence*), and possibly find a job allowing you to break from existing limiting conditions. There are probably some obstacles to the achievement of complete independence, but the right job may teach you important lessons in this area. There may be much activity and some false starts, so it may be difficult to clearly perceive the best direction (*positive and negative of 1 Personal Year and 19/1 Essence*).

Vocationally, this is a good year to develop new ideas or interests or possibly turn an avocation into a livelihood (*1 Essence*). Clarify your goals and start working toward their achievement. Emphasize your individuality. An important change (or changes) or events of significance can occur this year, primarily due to your own efforts (*1 Personal Year, I Transit*). Be prepared for conflicts at work stemming from strong emotions and high sensitivity. Don't be surprised if business developments take longer than anticipated. (*I·I Transit. There are so many relatively important cycles present that the average N and J Transits are not discussed at all*).

As you may have gathered, I purposely constructed John's birth data to indicate just about all the problems that may surface in choosing a vocation. Although John has good potential—and I certainly stressed that—the potential has its share of obstacles: the 8·8 and the 3·3 will most likely impede the growth of the strong 8 and 3 energy. The beginning Period and Pinnacle, in addition, give little support to John's inherent potential. Note that the delineation addresses all the problem areas squarely. (Don't do the subject a disservice by sugarcoating the reading.) The reading, though, also indicates directions to take to overcome the obstacles. Since the influence of the future productive Period and Pinnacle are likely to be considerably more helpful to John's growth, they are also mentioned.

John's difficult delineation is not that common. Most people can get a real boost from a vocational reading and, occasionally, get in touch with potentials of which they were uncertain or completely unaware.

CHAPTER 39

COMPARISON DELINEATIONS:
BUSINESS RELATIONS
SOCIAL RELATIONS
FAMILY RELATIONS

We've seen how you can use numerology to describe a person's potential strengths, areas of conflict and general approach. With a little practice, you can compare two people in a business, social or family situation and see why they'll get along well or why they'll have difficulty with each other. Or, you can look at a group—three, four or more people interacting—and develop the patterns which describe the probable person in charge, the responsibilities handled by each person, the individuals who contribute to maintaining harmony and balance.

In looking at these relations, you're simply comparing the numerology charts of the people involved. By comparing the elements, modifiers and progressed cycles, you can not only see why people are close or far apart, but you can also have an understanding of their probable present and future interest in each other.

A comparison reading, like a delineation for an individual, is based on an analysis of the potentials. As a numerologist, you *can't* determine if two people should get married. You *can*, though, tell them the ways they're likely to interact and probable pleasures and obstacles with which they'll be dealing as their lives progress. Don't make the mistake of assuming that people with similar numbers always go together while others with dissimilar numbers never do. It's true that many marriages and close relations are based on significant similarities

Introduction

between the parties. That is, of course, the easiest way, but you'll find many close relationships where the individuals involved learn to grow and develop just because of the inharmonious or conflicting energies present. Using numerology, it's easy to spot the harmonious energies and the discordant energies. In comparison readings, I describe the potential harmony or discord (there's usually some of each present) and let the individuals involved decide if and how they care to deal with the situations likely to develop.

For important relationships like mariage, complete chart comparisons are desirable. For other relations, it's usually necessary to compare only certain areas of the chart. If a subject uses a name other than the birthname, be sure to take the energy associated with that name into account.

Let's examine a number of common situations to determine the key comparisons involved.

BUSINESS RELATIONS

Employer's relation with employee

We'll begin with the simplest of situations: an employer in search of an employee. The employer is probably concerned with two areas: (1) the employee's abilities and any impediments to the use of those abilities, and (2) the employee's ability to get along with his immediate supervisor and the other personnel with whom he's directly involved.

The employee's abiities are, of course, a function of the individual chart as discussed in Chapter 38. The Life Path and the Expression are the key elements here, but doubled elements and important modifiers are also likely to play a part.

The employee's relation to his supervisor and other personnel is related to the directing modifiers of all concerned. Comparisons of everyone's Temperament, First Letter and First Vowel are apt to show whether or not there's a compatible general approach among the individuals. You can't expect a precise match of the directing modifiers, but a person with a strong Physical component, for instance, is likely to get on better with another with a strong, or, at least, average Physical component than with an individual with a weak Physical component. If you try to match, say, a person with a strong Mental component and a weak Intuitive component with a person who has a weak Mental component and a strong Intuitive component, you'll probably have two people with difficulty understanding and trusting each other's basic approach.

If you have Ada, Amy and Ava trying to work together, you're likely, with the long A as First Vowel, to have three co-workers struggling for leadership. Burt, Tom and Lucy, with less forceful First Letters and First Vowels, are more likely to get along.

It's not usually possible to get the data to completely check your relation with your employer or supervisor. Usually, you can, at least, compare your First Letter and First Vowel with those of the boss. If your supervisor's birth information should happen to be available, the calculation of his Life Path and Expression will give you a good idea of his general abilities and opportunities and, when compared to your own, a good idea of your relative compatibility. An awareness of any doubled or multiple elements or any significant modifiers should be helpful in indicating significant problem areas to avoid.

Employee's relation with employer

If you're going into business with someone, the relation is usually considerably more complex than an employer/employee relation. Compare your Soul Urges to determine what you're both looking for in life. A comparison of your Soul Urges and Life Path should tell you much about the nature of your compatibility. Neither of the elements have to be the same or even similar for a good relation. The comparative elements, instead, should make for a comfortable relation between the two of you as well as indicating the potential to make a significant contribution to your mutual business affairs. Each Expression should be compatible with the specific parts of the work with which you'll each be involved. If you have the same or similar Expressions, you're probably going to be stumbling over each other a good deal of the time and constantly invading each other's territory. Temperaments, First Letters and First Vowels may be similar or opposite, depending on the approach necessary to accomplish each person's workload.

Business partners

Compare the Periods and the Pinnacles, too. If either or both will be changing in the near future, particularly from compatible to relatively inharmonious cycles, recognize and discuss the potential problems that may need attention. For the immediate future, be sure that the Personal Years, Essences and Transits relate well to the work in progress. If, for instance, a period of hard work is at hand for both of you, several years of a 5 Essence for either of you isn't likely to bode well. In a numerological analysis of a partnership, clarify how you get on with each other personally as well as your respective abilities to carry your individual share of the load.

SOCIAL RELATIONS

Comparisons of social relations are somewhat different than comparisons of business relations. Often, the areas of com-

Friends

patibility may be only a small part of the make-up, but may be enough to sustain an ongoing relation.

Two people with the same or compatible Life Paths may delight in developing similar opportunities together or on parallel paths. With the same or compatible Expressions, friends may be involved in the same vocation or avocation, with both contributing in a harmonious manner to the ongoing work. With the same or compatible Soul Urges, two people may view the world similarly and form a friendship.

The compatibility of just one core element in two individuals' charts may be enough to sustain a relation, particularly if the Temperaments, First Letters and First Vowels are likewise harmonious. Occasionally, if only the directing modifiers are compatible, that link by itself may be enough to lead to friendship.

If the same or similar numbers appear as different core elements in two individuals' charts, an attraction may result. Ivan, with a 7 Life Path, may be attracted to Peter, with a 7 Expression, because Peter has the ability to express the very abilities and attitudes which Ivan is in the process of developing. Peter may enjoy his role as teacher here, too, although if this is the only basis of attraction, that attraction may eventually wane. Edna, with her 8 Soul Urge and Francine, with her 8 Expression, may likewise enjoy a friendship. Here, Edna is likely to appreciate Francine's ability to use her abilities to give herself the very things which Edna would like. Here, Francine fulfills the roll of teacher. If there are no other areas of compatibility, this friendship, too, is probably going to fade.

Although a friendship can develop from just one compatible element or energy, the more similarities present, the greater the possibility of a deep and ongoing interaction. If the similarities are limited, the shift of a Period, Pinnacle, Essence or Transit may be enough to end the friendship or, at least, considerably dampen the mutual enthusiasm.

Lovers

When a friendship deepens into an affectionate or loving relation, there's likely to be strong emotional energy present in addition to the similarities which support friendships. For lovers, compare the affectionate energy of both partners—how much positive 2, 3, 6 or 9 potential, in particular, is available, and how much negative 2, 3, 6 or 9 energy which can be converted to positive. Check the elements, of course, but check the strong modifiers also, especially the significantly divergent Intensity Points and Prime Intensifiers. You may be able to clearly discern how much love or affection is being shared.

A comparison reading may determine who has difficulty

keeping the emotions in balance as well as who is repressing feelings. An analysis like this, based primarily on the quantity and quality of the "friendly, affectionate, loving" energy (see the discussion of this energy on page 390 of Chapter 23) can be useful in helping a couple understand and enlarge their ability to respond to each other.

A comparison delineation of two people contemplating marriage is merely an extension of the analyses above of friends and lovers. When preparing this kind of reading, I compare virtually all the elements, modifiers and progressed cycles so that the couple is fully cognizant of their basic character compatibility as well as the prospects for this year and, probably, something of the next. I don't read too far ahead—there's always enough interest and development in the immediate future to hold anyone's attention.

In a comparison delineation, I compare the characteristics of both subjects in the following general order:

> The Life Path
> The Expression
> The Soul Urge
> The Birthday
> The Mind
> The Emotions
> The Directing Modifiers
> The Periods and Pinnacles
> The Current Year(s)

When comparing, say, the traits of the Life Paths, compare other related traits—both *positive and negative*—at the same time. For example, if Betty has a 7 Life Path and Charles has a 3 Life Path, a comparison would include:

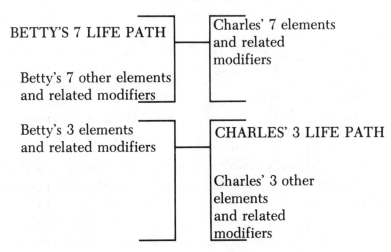

BETTY'S 7 LIFE PATH — Charles' 7 elements and related modifiers

Betty's 7 other elements and related modifiers

Betty's 3 elements and related modifiers — CHARLES' 3 LIFE PATH

Charles' 3 other elements and related modifiers

Marriage partners

Example of
comparison
delineation

We'll look in detail at a couple contemplating marriage. Georgine Fletcher, born September 5, 1950 and Blaine Evan Carolina, born June 22, 1949, are a couple of fictitious subjects who, at the beginning of 1980, have asked for a numerological comparison of their potential.

We'll do a complete comparison delineation, looking at various elements, modifiers and progressed cycles in turn.

First, we'll prepare the basic calculations and the organization sheet for Georgine (Figures 39-1 on page 648 and 39-2 on page 649) and Blaine (Figures 39-3 on page 650 and 39-4 on page 651). We'll assume that both use only their birthnames. We'll also assume that both plan to continue using their birthnames after marriage.

Why did I pick Georgine and Blaine for this comparison example?

With her 2 Life Path and his 6 Life Path, there's likely to be some strong potential related to affection and love, and Blaine's 2 Soul Urge is harmoniously related to Georgine's 2 Life Path, too. Of course, Blaine's 6·6 energy is likely to throw a negative emphasis on some of that affectionate energy and Georgine's 13/4 Expression is likely to be in conflict with Blaine's 14/5 Expression, too. I felt that a delineation with these strong harmonies and discords would prove a good example.

COMPARISON DELINEATION
FOR
GEORGINE FLETCHER
BORN SEPTEMBER 5, 1950
AND
BLAINE EVAN CAROLINA
BORN JUNE 22, 1949

COMPARISON OF LIFE PATHS
AND RELATED TRAITS

Georgine with:
    2 Life Path
    3 Challenge
    9 Prime Intensifier
    (6 Maturity Number omitted because Georgine, at the beginning of 1980, is not yet thirty years old.)

Blaine with:
    6 Life Path

6·6 energy
2 Soul Urge
three 3's Intensity Point
3 Secret Self
6 of 12 elements and sub-elements in 2, 6, 9 group
(11 Maturity Number omitted because Blaine, at the beginning of 1980, is just thirty years old.)

Both Georgine and Blaine are sensitive people (*all
that 2, 3, 6 and 9 energy*). She's probably emotional,
tactful and cooperative. Her patience, care and
consideration are appreciated. She's likely to be a
good friend, expressing and receiving friendship
and love (*2 Life Path*).

Blaine is apt to be an emotional person, too. He's
probably ready to help others, capable of rectifying and balancing situations, capable of being loving and appreciative. Family and friends are likely
to be one of the focuses of his life (*6 Life Path, 2
Soul Urge*). Blaine and Georgine should be able to
give much love to each other with much sensitivity
(*2 Life Path/6 Life Path very harmonious*).

Georgine may, at times, tend to be too sensitive,
even shy and uncertain (*negative of 2 Life Path*).
Blaine is probably responsible, but there's a possibility that he's *too* responsible and doesn't take care
of his own needs because of his extreme concern
with others (*6·6 energy*). He may still be working to
balance his responsible side with his desire to be a
free spirit (*6 Life Path and 6·6 energy conflict with
14/5 Expression*).

I wouldn't expect that Blaine is too concerned
with material needs (*6 Life Path*). Georgine is probably somewhat more interested in material matters (*8 Soul Urge*), but not to any large extent (*2 Life
Path*). Both are likely to have interests in artistic or
imaginative activities (*Georgine's 9 Prime Intensifier,
Blaine's three 3's Intensity Point*).

(*Note that some of the less important modifiers,
Georgine's 3 Challenge and Blaine's 3 Secret Self, are
not included. Note also the inclusion of Georgine's 8
Soul Urge and Blaine's 14/5 Expression when appropriate*).

14/5 FIRST PINNACLE   (0–34)
11/2 SECOND PINNACLE (35–43)
16/7 THIRD PINNACLE   (44–52)
  6 FOURTH PINNACLE (53 on)

September   5,   1950

$$9 \quad + \quad 5 \quad + \quad 6 \quad = 20 = \boxed{2}$$

(0–25)   (26–52)   (53 on)

$$9 - 5 = 4$$
$$6 - 5 = 1$$
$$4 - 1 = 3 \text{ CHALLENGE}$$

$$\frac{(25)\ 7}{5\ 6\ \ \ 9\ \ 5} + \frac{(10)\ 1}{5\ \ \ \ 5} = \boxed{8}$$

GEORGINE   FLETCHER

$$\frac{7 \quad 97\ 5}{(28)\ (10)\ 1} + \frac{63\quad 238\quad 9}{(31)\ 4} = 5 \text{ SECRET SELF}$$

$$\frac{7\,5\,6\,9\,7\,9\,5\,5}{(53)\ 8} + \frac{6\,3\,5\,2\,3\,8\,5\,9}{(41)\ 5} = \boxed{13/4}$$

no 1 ←
one 2
two 3's
no 4 ←
five 5's
two 6's
two 7's
one 8
three 9's

PHYSICAL	EEEE	4–Strong
MENTAL	GGNLH	5–Strong
EMOTIONAL	ORITR	5–Strong
INTUITIVE	FC	2–Average

MATURITY NUMBER = 2 + 4 = 6

EFFECTIVENESS:

$$\boxed{4} - \boxed{2} = 2$$
$$\boxed{8} - \boxed{2} = 6$$
$$\boxed{8} - \boxed{4} = \frac{4}{12}$$

Figure 39–1
Calculation Sheet:
Georgine Fletcher

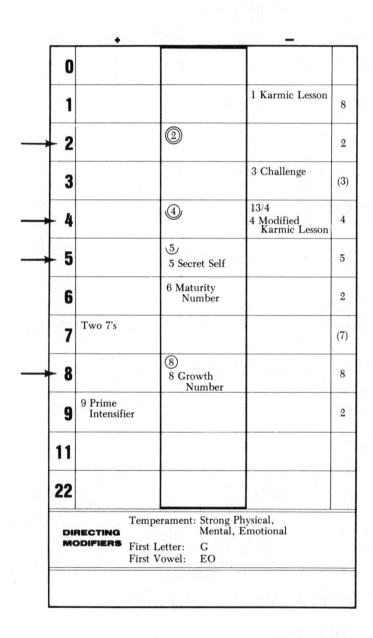

	+		−	
0				
1			1 Karmic Lesson	8
2		②		2
3			3 Challenge	(3)
4		④	13/4 4 Modified Karmic Lesson	4
5		⑤ 5 Secret Self		5
6		6 Maturity Number		2
7	Two 7's			(7)
8		⑧ 8 Growth Number		8
9	9 Prime Intensifier			2
11				
22				

DIRECTING MODIFIERS	Temperament: Strong Physical, Mental, Emotional First Letter: G First Vowel: EO

Figure 39–2
Organization Sheet:
Georgine Fletcher

1 FIRST PINNACLE   (0–30)
9 SECOND PINNACLE (31–39)
1 THIRD PINNACLE   (40–48)
11/2 FOURTH PINNACLE (49 on)

June   22,   1949
6   + 22 +   5   = 33 = ⑥

(0–30)   (31–57)   (58 on)

6 – 4 = 2
5 – 4 = 1
2 – 1 = 1 CHALLENGE

$$\frac{(15)\ 6}{19\ \ 5} + \frac{6}{5\ \ 1} + \frac{(17)\ 8}{1\ \ 6\ \ 9\ \ 1} = 20 = ②$$

BLAINE   EVAN   CAROLINA

$$\frac{2\ 3\ \ \ \ 5}{(10)\ 1} + \frac{4\ \ 5}{9} + \frac{3\ \ 9\ \ 3\ \ 5}{(20)\ 2} = 12$$
= 3 SECRET SELF

$$\frac{2\ 3\ 1\ 9\ 5\ 5}{(25)\ 7} + \frac{5\ 4\ 1\ 5}{(15)\ 6} + \frac{3\ 1\ 9\ 6\ 3\ 9\ 5\ 1}{(37)\ (10)\ 1} = ⑭⁄5$$

four 1's
one 2
three 3's
one 4
five 5's
one 6
no 7 ←
no 8 ←
three 9's

PHYSICAL	EE	2–Weak
MENTAL	LANANALNA	9–Strong
EMOTIONAL	BIROI	5–Average
INTUITIVE	VC	2–Weak

MATURITY NUMBER = 6 + 5 = 11/2

EFFECTIVENESS:

⑥ – ⑤ =   1

⑥ – ② =   4

⑤ – ② =   3
                    ――
                     8

Figure 39–3
Calculation Sheet:
Blaine Evan Carolina

	+		**−**	
0				
1	Four 1's 1 Prime Intensifier		1 Challenge	5
2		②		2
3	Three 3's	3 Secret Self		6
4				
5		⑤	14/5	5
6		⑥	⑥ 6 6·6	6
7		7 Growth Number	7 Karmic Lesson	(7)
8			8 Karmic Lesson	22
9				
11		11 Maturity Number		2
22		⑳		22

DIRECTING MODIFIERS	Temperament: Strong Mental, Weak Physical, Intuitive First Letter: B First Vowel: AI

50% (6 of 12) Elements and Sub-elements in 2, 6, 9 Group

Figure 39–4
Organization Sheet:
Blaine Evan Carolina

COMPARISON OF EXPRESSION
AND RELATED TRAITS

Georgine with
 4 Expression
 13/4 Karmic Debt
 4 Modified Karmic Lesson
 5 Birthday
 5 Secret Self

Blaine with
 5 Expression
 14/5 Karmic Debt
 four 1's Intensity Point
 1 Prime Intensifier
 1 Challenge

> Georgine and Blaine have very different ways of working. There's likely to be much to resolve between them in these areas. (*Conflict between Georgine's 4 energy and Blaine's 5 energy. Although Georgine has some 5 energy, it's nowhere near as strong as her 4 energy*).
>
> Georgine tends to be organized and systematic, practical and down to earth (*4 Expression*). She tends to work patiently and accurately with details in a persevering and dertermined manner (*4 Modified Karmic Lesson*).
>
> Blaine, on the other hand, is likely to be restless, impatient, erratic. He tends to scatter himself and his energy and often chafes at routine (*5 Expression, 14/5 Karmic Debt*). He sometimes has an unrealistic or unclear view of his talents. He may be vague, dreamy or impractical in approaching work to be accomplished (*14/5 Karmic Debt*).
>
> Blaine is enthusiastic and adaptable, loves to move in progressive directions, delights in change, travel and the unusual (*5 Expression*). Georgine tends to be conservative (*4 Expression*), often stubborn or dogmatic with strong likes and dislikes (*13/4 Karmic Debt*). Although Georgine enjoys new experiences, travel and social activity, she deals with these areas in a relatively controlled manner. (*Georgine's 5 energy is considerably dampened by her stronger 4 energy.*) Blaine is probably uncomfortable some of the time due to the "rolling stone"

nature of his commitment (*14/5 Karmic Debt*), while Georgine is apt to feel restricted by the type and amount of work at hand (*13/4 Karmic Debt*).

Georgine sometimes misses the larger picture because of her involvement with details and her occasional dogged pursuit of interests in a rigid, one-track direction (*13/4 Karmic Debt*). Blaine, on the other hand, may miss the big picture in the excitement generated by a new interest (*5 Life Path*).

Both can be bossy and dominating, Georgine because of her rigidity (*13/4 Karmic Debt*), Blaine because of his self-centeredness and strong needs (*four 1's Intensity Point, 1 Prime Intensifier*). In his early years, Blaine may have felt that his needs weren't met. By now, he's probably better able to use the courage of his convictions to get more satisfaction for himself (*1 Challenge*).

Georgine could learn about freedom from Blaine while she could teach him how to better apply himself. These are difficult areas for both of them.

COMPARISON OF SOUL URGES AND RELATED TRAITS

Georgine with:
    8 Soul Urge
    8 Growth Number
    1 Karmic Lesson

Blaine with:
    2 Soul Urge
    8 Karmic Lesson
    22 Birthday
    (11 Maturity Number omitted because Blaine, at the beginning of 1980, is just thirty years old.)

When Georgine learns to achieve a balanced success in the business world, it will be helpful in her growth (*8 Soul Urge, 8 Growth Number*). I expect that this type of success, while important to her, can be kept in reasonable proportion (*8 energy considerably dampened by stronger 2 energy*). Georgine is probably still learning not to look to others for direction and not to be pressured by others' decisions because of her difficulty or fear in making her own decisions (*1 Karmic Lesson*).

Blaine's sensitivity (*6 Life Path, 2 Soul Urge*) may be helpful, but when he works to meet his own needs, he's likely to dominate Georgine (*14/5 Karmic Debt, four 1's Intensity Point, 1 Prime Intensifier*). Blaine, though, is probably still learning to use and understand money, to handle his material affairs with reasonable practical judgment (*8 Karmic Lesson*), but he may function reasonably well in the business world (*22 Birthday*). Georgine, far more capable at financial matters (*8 Soul Urge*), could be helpful to Blaine here, but her lack of faith in her own ability (*1 Karmic Lesson*) may limit her helpfulness.

COMPARISON OF BIRTHDAYS AND RELATED TRAITS

Georgine with:
  5 Birthday
  5 Secret Self

Blaine with:
  22 Birthday
  5 Expression
  14/5 Karmic Debt

Blaine's nervous tension may, at times, make for problems with Georgine (*Blaine's 22 Birthday*).

(*Blaine's positive 22 energy as well as Blaine's and Georgine's 5 energy have been covered in previous paragraphs and need no repetition.*)

COMPARISON OF MISCELLANEOUS ENERGIES

Georgine with:
  two 7's Intensity Point

Blaine with:
  7 Growth Number
  7 Karmic Lesson

There are a few other areas worth noting.

Georgine has a good analytical mind, may well have an unusual viewpoint or out of the ordinary ideas (*two 7's Intensity Point*). When she expresses this side of her personality, it may cause conflicts with Blaine.

Blaine probably has some interest in studying and

meditating (7 *Growth Number*). He may need time alone to clarify for himself the difference between the material and the non-material (spiritual) world (7 *Karmic Lesson*). When he's engaged in these solitary pursuits, Georgine may feel left out.

COMPARISON OF EMOTIONS

Georgine with:
  2 Life Path

  Repressed feelings with:
  4 Expression
  8 Soul Urge
  two 7's Intensity Point

Blaine with:
  6 Life Path
  2 Soul Urge
  6·6 energy
  three 3's Intensity Point

> As I mentioned at the beginning of the reading, Georgine and Blaine are a sensitive emotional couple (*Georgine's 2 Life Path, Blaine's 6 Life Path, 2 Soul Urge*). Blaine usually expresses himself well (*three 3's Intensity Point*), although when he feels overwhelmed with responsibility (*6·6 energy*) his emotions aren't likely to be expressed too clearly. At times when he's taking care of his own needs (*14/5 Karmic Debt, four 1's Intensity Point*), his feelings may also not be well communicated.
>
> Although Georgine also feels deeply (*2 Life Path*), she is probably still learning to be clear about her feelings. Often, it's likely to be easier for her to repress the emotions or not state them with complete clarity (*4 Expression, 8 Soul Urge, two 7's Intensity Point*). Both Georgine and Blaine have to learn to express more clearly to alleviate difficulties in communication.

COMPARISON OF MINDS

Georgine with:
  two 7's Intensity Point

Blaine with:
  no elements or modifiers here

(No material here. Georgine's two 7's Intensity Point has been previously covered.)

COMPARISON OF DIRECTING MODIFIERS

Georgine with:
  Strong Physical, Mental, Emotional components
  First Letter G
  First Vowel EO

Blaine with:
  Strong Mental component
  Weak Physical, Intuitive components
  First Letter B
  First Vowel AI

> In their general approach to their experiences, both Georgine and Blaine will respond well to reason, logic and facts (*both strong Mental components*). Both will approach situations with emotion, but Georgine, in general, tends to be more nervous and high-strung (*Georgine with strong Emotional component, Blaine with average Emotional component*). Georgine is more apt to move ahead in a practical, common sense manner (*strong Physical component*), while Blaine's approach often is little concerned with practicality, sometimes concerned with avoiding work (*weak Physical component*).
>
> At times, Georgine's uncertainty expresses itself as reserve or self-containment (*First Letter G, First Vowel O*), and the distance created may cause difficulties with Blaine. At these times, she probably doesn't give much affection or respond readily to Blaine's affection (*First Letter G*). Even when she's acting distant, Georgine still has deep feelings (*First Vowel O*) and is still aware of the logical side of matters (*First Vowel E*).
>
> Blaine is, at times, a self-starter (*First Vowel A*), although he'll tend to be, like Georgine, relatively conservative (*Blaine's First Vowel I, Georgine's First Vowel O*). Because of his sensitivity, he may appear indecisive, sometimes critical (*First Letter B*). He may provoke conflicts with Georgine because of these traits.

Now, we'll prepare the progressed charts for the couple (Figure 39-5 below and Figure 39-6 on page 658). (If we wanted to save time, we could just prepare partial Progressed Charts covering the Epicycle which includes 1980.)

We'll continue the delineation:

GEORGINE FLETCHER
SEPTEMBER 5, 1950

Age	Medium Term			Essence	Personal Year	Universal Year	Year	Long Term	
	Transits							Period	Pinnacle
0	G	F		13/4	2	6	1950	9	14/5
1	G	F		13/4	3	7	1951	9	14/5
2	G	F		13/4	4	8	1952	9	14/5
3	G	F		13/4	5	9	1953	9	14/5
4	G	F		13/4	6	1	1954	9	14/5
5	G	F		13/4	7	2	1955	9	14/5
6	G	L		10/1	8	3	1956	9	14/5
7	E	L		8	9	22/4	1957	9	14/5
8	E	L		8	1	5	1958	9	14/5
9	E	E		10/1	2	6	1959	9	14/5
10	E	E		10/1	3	7	1960	9	14/5
11	E	E		10/1	4	8	1961	9	14/5
12	O	E		11/2	5	9	1962	9	14/5
13	O	E		11/2	6	1	1963	9	14/5
14	O	T		8	7	2	1964	9	14/5
15	O	T		8	8	3	1965	9	14/5
16	O	C		9	9	22/4	1966	9	14/5
17	O	C		9	1	5	1967	9	14/5
18	R	C		12/3	2	6	1968	9	14/5
19	R	H		17/8	3	7	1969	9	14/5
20	R	H		17/8	4	8	1970	9	14/5
21	R	H		17/8	5	9	1971	9	14/5
22	R	H		17/8	6	1	1972	9	14/5
23	R	H		17/8	7	2	1973	9s	14/5
24	R	H		17/8	8	3	1974	9s	14/5
25	R	H		17/8	9	22/4	1975	9s	14/5
26	R	H		17/8	1	5	1976	5s	14/5
27	G	E		12/3	2	6	1977	5s	14/5
28	G	E		12/3	3	7	1978	5s	14/5
29	G	E		12/3	4	8	1979	5	14/5
30	G	E		12/3	5	9	1980	5	14/5
31	G	E		12/3	6	1	1981	5	14/5
32	G	R		16/7	7	2	1982	5	14/5
33	G	R		16/7	8	3	1983	5	14/5
34	I	R		18/9	9	22/4	1984	5	14/5
35	I	R		18/9	1	5	1985	5	11/2

Figure 39–5
Progressed Chart:
Georgine Fletcher

COMPARISON OF LONG TERM CYCLES OPERATING IN 1980:

Georgine with:
5 Second Period
14/5 First Pinnacle

Blaine with:
Start of 22/4 Second Period
Start of 9 Second Pinnacle

BLAINE EVAN CAROLINA
JUNE 22, 1949

Age	Medium Term						Year	Long Term	
	Transits			Essence	Personal Year	Universal Year		Period	Pinnacle
0	B	E	C	10/1	6	5	1949	6	1
1	B	E	C	10/1	7	6	1950	6	1
2	L	E	C	11/2	8	7	1951	6	1
3	L	E	A	9	9	8	1952	6	1
4	L	E	R	17/8	1	9	1953	6	1
5	A	V	R	14/5	11/2	1	1954	6	1
6	I	V	R	22/4	3	2	1955	6	1
7	I	V	R	22/4	4	3	1956	6	1
8	I	V	R	22/4	5	22/4	1957	6	1
9	I	A	R	19/1	6	5	1958	6	1
10	I	N	R	23/5	7	6	1959	6	1
11	I	N	R	23/5	8	7	1960	6	1
12	I	N	R	23/5	9	8	1961	6	1
13	I	N	O	20/2	1	9	1962	6	1
14	I	N	O	20/2	11/2	1	1963	6	1
15	N	E	O	16/7	3	2	1964	6	1
16	N	E	O	16/7	4	3	1965	6	1
17	N	E	O	16/7	5	22/4	1966	6	1
18	N	E	O	16/7	6	5	1967	6	1
19	N	E	L	13/4	7	6	1968	6	1
20	E	V	L	12/3	8	7	1969	6	1
21	E	V	L	12/3	9	8	1970	6	1
22	E	V	I	18/9	1	9	1971	6	1
23	E	V	I	18/9	11/2	1	1972	6	1
24	E	A	I	15/6	3	2	1973	6	1
25	B	N	I	16/7	4	3	1974	6	1
26	B	N	I	16/7	5	22/4	1975	6	1
27	L	N	I	17/8	6	5	1976	6	1
28	L	N	I	17/8	7	6	1977	6	1
29	L	N	I	17/8	8	7	1978	6	1
30	A	E	I	15/6	9	8	1979	6	1
31	I	E	N	19/1	1	9	1980	22/4	9
32	I	E	N	19/1	11/2	1	1981	22/4	9
33	I	E	N	19/1	3	2	1982	22/4	9
34	I	E	N	19/1	4	3	1983	22/4	9
35	I	V	N	18/9	5	22/4	1984	22/4	9

Figure 39-6
Progressed Chart:
Blaine Evan Carolina

This is likely to be a very active time for Georgine. Since about the middle of her 25th year, she's probably been in an environment stressing freedom, variety and uncertainty. There're apt to be a lot of different opportunities coming her way (5 *Second Period*, 5 *First Pinnacle*). This environment may not be that easy for her to handle. This could be a fine time to expand and develop, a good time to break through the rigidity or obstinacy we previously mentioned (*13/4 Karmic Debt*). It's apt to take a lot of work, but Georgine does have energy that could help in that direction (5 *Birthday*).

Georgine should be aware that now, and for many years to come, a good deal of her life will be in constant flux. If she gets married, she would do well to be prepared for much change and activity in the family life, many adjustments to be made by both husband and wife (*continuing 5 Second Period*). At this time, Georgine probably feels the excitement of her strong attraction to Blaine (*14/5 First Pinnacle*), but that excitement shouldn't blind Georgine to some of the other realities we've discussed.

This year is likely to feel quite different to Blaine compared to previous years. Some of the energies in his environment have undergone a considerable shift. (*6 First Period has changed to 22/4 Second Period. 1 First Pinnacle has changed to 9 Second Pinnacle.*) There may be an expansion of the loving, giving side of Blaine—he has a lot to give to others, as in the past, but he may now be content with less return than previously (*Current 9 Second Pinnacle compared to previous 6 First Period*). I'm sure Georgine's sensitivity and deep feelings are important to him. (*Georgine's 2 Life Path has energy similar to Blaine's 9 Second Pinnacle.*)

There's some slight possibility of a large scale business venture in Blaine's life. Chances are it won't get fully operational for a while. (*Start of 22/4 Second Period. Although Blaine has a 22 Birthday, he has little other energy with which to develop the 22 potential.*) Whether that venture gets started or not, there's still apt to be a lot of work and routine.

He may feel limited and restricted (*4 energy of the Second Period*). That restricted feeling certainly goes against Blaine's desire for freedom and expansion, and is probably especially uncomfortable for him (*5 Expression*). At this time, he may feel some heightened nervous tension (*22/4 Second Period*).

With that expansion of Blaine's loving, giving side, he probably feels a lot of attraction to Georgine. He must remember that there are other strong energies in his life which need his attention.

COMPARISON OF MEDIUM TERM CYCLES OPERATING IN 1980:

Georgine with:
  5 Personal Year
  12/3 Essence
  G, E, Transits

Blaine with:
  1 Personal Year

  January through June:
  15/6 Essence
  A, E, I Transits

  July through December:
  19/1 Essence
  1 Essence/1 Personal Year
  I, E, N Transits

If ever there's a year in Georgine's life to expand and feel free, 1980 is it (*5 Personal Year, 12/3 Essence, E Transit*). This is a fine time to work on overcoming both shyness and stubbornness (*2 Life Path, 13/4 Karmic Debt*) but a good deal of effort is involved. The more loose and free she feels, the more her horizons can expand. She must be careful not to scatter her energy with little result (*5 Personal Year*). I expect she has a sense of control that won't let that happen (*4 Expression*).

There's the possibility of an important change this year, a change that could affect Georgine's work, residence or family situation. Marrying Blaine may well affect all three areas. If she can take advantage of the change, her whole life may move forward dramatically (*5 Personal Year*).

Some of Georgine's expansive possibilities may relate to friends, social activities or travel. The opportunities have been there since about the middle of 1977, but there probably have been obstacles present which made it difficult to take advantage of the opportunities. (*12/3 Essence, 3 Personal Year in 1978 indicated obstacles. 12/3 Essence, 4 Personal Year in 1979 indicates conflict.*) I think she can make more of the opportunities now and build on those opportunities for the next few years. (*12/3 Essence continues to mid-1982.*)

The same potential which gives Georgine the opportunity for expansion also gives most of her experiences this year a relatively non-permanent character. I expect she feels strongly attracted to Blaine and sees marriage as an exciting expansion of their relation. We've previously discussed a number of areas which need work. Georgine should be aware that the relation with Blaine is likely to undergo substantial changes, even from this year to next (*positive and negative of 5 Personal Year*).

For Blaine, too, change seems to be in the air this year. This would be a good time to clarify his goals, stress independence, and take advantage of any opportunities for new beginnings (*1 Personal Year*). There may be a strong change—it could be marriage—sometime between June, 1980 and July, 1984 which may trigger a sequence of events which produces substantial alterations in almost every facet of his life (*1 Essence*).

At the beginning of this year, there may be enjoyable social activities, a high level of love and romance and the possiblity of marriage (*6 Essence*). From July to the end of the year, Blaine may have difficulty seeing his direction clearly because of the probable increase in activity (*1 Personal Year·1 Essence*).

From his birthday this year to his 35th birthday in 1984, he'll have the opportunity to achieve independence by making changes in existing situations which he finds restrictive. Much effort will be required, but the overcoming of the difficulties may involve important lessons leading to development and growth (*19/1 Essence*). These lessons, relating to Blaine's need to be independent, may strongly affect his feelings about himself and his relation to Georgine. If he marries her, he will have much to work out so that he can relate well and still feel free (*19/1 Essence with four 1's Intensity Point and 1 Prime Intensifier*).

Commentary

Georgine's and Blaine's comparison delineation clearly describes the areas of attraction and harmony as well as the areas likely to provoke conflicts or problems. 1980 is, undoubtedly, a year of strong attraction—it's up to them whether the attraction develops into marriage. Blaine's 19/1 Essence, as described, is apt to place a substantial strain on the mutual relation. In 1981, I'd expect that Georgine's 6 Personal Year, with its loving, giving energy aided by her 2 Life Path, will probably express the desire to work through whatever problems may develop between them. From September, 1982 through September, 1984, her 16/7 Essence may be describing some major upheaval in her life. This could be (1) problems with Blaine or (2) problems of her own which would deflect much of her energy from working out the conflicts which are likely to develop with Blaine. The early years of this marriage are not likely to be easy ones.

In the reading, I delineated only 1980 in detail although I already had information covering the next few years. I find it best to read only one or, at the most, two years ahead. It's difficult for a subject to fully understand and appreciate the complications as well as the positive experiences too far in the future. The response to any experience is dependent on the subject's development up to the beginning of the experience. Describing the influences of a karmic Essence period starting at the fortieth birthday to a twenty year old is of little consequence. Similarly, describing influences even three or four years ahead are of little service.

Don't assume, because there are difficult or conflicting energies, that people won't be able to work through the problems. Georgine will have a 16/7 Essence and Blaine a 19/1 Essence *whether or not they marry*. If they do marry, they will have to deal with each other's problems as well as their own. This could lead to fuller development and awareness for both of them. As you can see, the advice of a numerologist may be extremely useful in preparing Georgine and Blaine to handle the coming problems as well as indicating the direction their energies are likely to take for optimum growth.

FAMILY RELATIONS

A variant of the comparison delineation is a reading for a family (or small group of people) describing the complex relations among them. Here, rather than discussing each person's relation to all the others, it's usually clearer to discuss such matters as:

Comparison delineation of a family

> who seems to run the family;
> whose influence, though behind-the-scenes, has a strong impact on the way the family is run;
> who carries the different responsibilities;
> who tends to run away from responsibilities;
> who works at the maintenance of peace and harmony within the family;
> who takes advantage of others; and
> who, instead, tends to sacrifice for the others.

An analysis like this is usually valuable and revealing for all the family members. Be sure to study everyone's progressed cycles. The readings will be considerably different in different years due to the effect of these cycles.

The readings covered in this chapter required advanced skills in accurately portraying the many possible harmonies and discords. Work on these readings, at first, in relation to yourself and others close to you so you can check your reading against the events as they actually transpire.

Comparison delineations, though they often involve a good deal of work, may be one of the most valuable services the numerologist can render.

CHAPTER 40

ADDRESSES,
PHONE NUMBERS, ETC.

All of us are associated with many names and numbers during our daily lives. You have a home address, a work address, several telephone numbers, an automobile license number, a social security number, etc., etc. You live in a city, in a state, in a country. Let's examine the numerology impact of some of these names and numbers.

Deriving the numbers on place names with which you're associated can be interesting and informative. By using the founding date and the name of the geographic area, you can calculate the equivalent of the Life Path, Expression, Soul Urge and Birthday and then describe the influences and characteristics of that particular area. For instance:

**City,
state,
country**

Founding date: July 4, 1776
7 + 4 + 3 = (14/5)

$$\frac{(17)\ 8}{3\ \ 9\ \ 5} + \frac{6}{1\ \ 5} + \frac{22}{6\ \ 1\ \ 5\ \ 9\ \ 1} = 36 = \underline{9}$$

UNITED   STATES   OF   AMERICA

$$\frac{3\ 5\ 9\ 2\ 5\ 4}{(28)\ (10)\ 1\ +} \quad \frac{1\ 2\ 1\ 2\ 5\ 1}{(12)\ 3\ \ +} \quad \frac{6\ 6}{} \quad \frac{1\ 4\ 5\ 9\ 9\ 3\ 1}{(44)\ 8} = 12 = (3)$$

Founding Date: September   4,   1781
$$9 \ + \ 4 + \ 8 \ = 21 = \textcircled{\textcircled{3}}$$

$$\frac{6 \ + \ \ \ 11}{6 \ \ \ 1 \ \ \ 5 \ \ 5} \ = 17 = \textcircled{8}$$

LOS   ANGELES

$$\frac{3 \ 6 \ 1 \ \ \ 1 \ 5 \ 7 \ 5 \ 3 \ 5 \ 1}{(10) \ 1 + \ \ \ (27) \ 9} \ = 10 = \textcircled{1}$$

What could be a more appropriate Life Path for the United States, with its emphasis on liberty and the struggles for civil rights than the 14/5! The 9 Soul Urge describes the humanistic and philanthropic ideals of the country and the 3 Expression delineates America's concern with the good life.

And, look at the 3 Life Path of Los Angeles. Few cities are as concerned with self-expression, creativity, the joy of life as this one. There's the 1 Expression (with its 1 sub-element)—where else will you find so many people concerned with their individuality and their need to be themselves, and often so unaware of their one-sided needs? And the 8 Soul Urge—Los Angeles thrives on the struggles for status, power, material possessions, ostentation.

These descriptions are undoubtedly accurate in the same sense that the description of the Universal Years are accurate. But although the general configuration of a city, state or country can be delineated, the characteristics are too broad to be applied specifically to any one individual. Although the creative artist with the 3 Life Path may find what he needs in Los Angeles, so, quite possibly, will the religious leader with her 11 Life Path or the contractor with his 4 Life Path. I see little correlation between a person's core elements and the core elements of the geographic area. The potential of the city, state or country is too diffused to react directly on a particular subject.

Similarly, numbers like zip codes and area codes are of little consequence to individual potential.

Home address

The address of a person's home, on the other hand, has the same impact on the individual's characteristics as an important modifier. Let's look at this more closely.

Calculation

STEP 1

Add up the digits in the number of the address and reduce the sum to a single digit or master number. That single digit or master number is the main component of this modifier. Take special note of the karmic numbers.

If the address number has a suffix like 1440 A or 367 ½, the suffix (the A or the ½) would be omitted.

If there's an apartment number or suite number, that number would be omitted.

STEP 2

If the street is expressed in numbers—like 174th Street—add up the numbers and reduce to a single digit or master number to determine the secondary component. Take special note of the karmic numbers.

If the street is expressed in words—like Magnolia Boulevard—add up the number values of the letters in the name of the street and reduce to a single digit or master number to determine the secondary component. Take special note of the karmic numbers.

Disregard the word Street, Avenue, Boulevard or the like.

If the name is hyphenated or more than one word, use the same rules as in Chapter 2, page 16, for complex names.

If both components are the same number, there's a stronger impact of that energy (not a negative potential). In the rare case where a karmic number is repeated, the karmic energy expresses very potently.

Here are a few examples:

8212¾   Main   Street,   Apartment 123

	MAIN		
8 2 1 2	4 1 9 5	—	—
(13) 4	(19) 1		

Main component = 13/4
Secondary component = 19/1

143   12th   Avenue

143	12	—
8	3	

Main component = 8
Secondary component = 3

The home address describes:

An important lesson to be learned by the individuals living in the home and some types of experience they're likely to encounter.

Commentary

The emphasis on the family life in the home, and the general tone to be expected.

The number of the address constitutes about seventy percent of the energy while the street—name or number—makes up about thirty percent. The lesson to be learned is synthesized from the numbers of the two components. The main part of the lesson is read from the top row on CHART 2: THE LIFE PATH under the number of the address component. The secondary part of the lesson is read in the same place using the number of the street component. If either or both is a karmic number, the negative cast described in the top row on CHART 7: THE KARMIC DEBT would be added to the synthesis.

The experiences encountered can be synthesized from CHART 3: THE EXPRESSION using the numbers of the two components. Generally, the experiences will relate to the Positive Attitudes shown in the middle row. If a karmic number is present, the experiences will also relate to the Negative Attitudes shown in the bottom row.

The emphasis on the family life in the home will relate to CHART 3: THE EXPRESSION in a manner similar to the experiences described in the preceding paragraph.

Example

Let's look at a family living at 6233 Page Avenue.

$$6233 \qquad \text{PAGE}$$

$$\frac{6233}{(14) \ 5} \qquad \frac{7 \ 1 \ 7 \ 5}{(20) \quad 2}$$

Main component   =   14/5
Secondary component =   2

The family in this home will be learning the exhilaration of the constructive use of freedom as well as enjoying the satisfactions of group activites (5 *and 2 from top row of* CHART 2: THE LIFE PATH). Life here is likely to be full of enthusiasm, progressive endeavors, change, unusual people, unusual ideas (5 *from middle row of* CHART 3: THE EXPRESSION). There may, at times, be very erratic activity, little sense of accomplishment, possibly an overindulgence in physical pleasures (14/5 *from top row of* CHART 7: THE KARMIC DEBT). There's likely to be a feeling of friendliness and consideration, too (2 *from middle row of* CHART 3: THE EXPRESSION). Although there's an innate desire for harmony in the family, this need isn't likely to be fulfilled because family members are probably off in all directions, involved with their own highly individual ventures (*5·2 conflict. 5 energy likely to overpower 2 energy because more 5 energy present*).

Each member of the family will accept these influences differently depending on his or her own potential. For instance, if the father has an 11/2 Life Path and a 6 Expression, he's likely to work toward the cooperation and association of the 2 energy and find it something of a struggle to take advantage of the potential related to freedom. If he had a 5 Soul Urge, he probably would want to expand his life, but with his other strong energies, that expansion isn't apt to come that easily.

If the mother has a 6 Life Path, a 9 Expression and a 6 Soul Urge, she probably works to keep the family concerned and interested in each other, but she's likely to be disappointed as everyone rushes off to take care of their own concerns. A young daughter with a 22/4 Life Path would probably express the negative 4 energy, feel blocked and intimidated by the 5 influence, uninterested in the 2 potential. If she could feel open enough to use the 5 for expansion, she could develop appreciably, but that isn't likely to be easy. A young son with a 5 Life Path, a 3 Expression and a 5 Soul Urge could, more than anyone else in the family, use the 5 influence to develop his many talents. He may have trouble learning not to scatter his energies and not to overindulge in physical pleasures. There's likely to be much change, activity and excitement at 6233 Page Avenue, but not much feeling of a cohesive family unit.

Office, store or factory address

The address of an individual's office, store or factory is treated similarly to the home address but has considerably less impact. The vocational influence is often strongly controlled by the person or persons in charge so that the address is often of minor concern. If the subject is one of the people in charge, the office address is likely to have more meaning in the life.

Other numbers in the life

Although it's often fun to check out the numbers in your life— the various telephone numbers, the automobile license plate, social security number, etc.—I haven't found any serious correlation between the numbers and an individual's life. Aside from the home address, the other numbers are of little importance.

PART VII:

CONCLUSION

CHAPTER 41

ON BEING A NUMEROLOGIST

Many of you reading this book will undoubtedly enjoy giving readings to relatives and friends. A few of you may be interested enough to become numerologists.

Clients often empower a numerologist with far more power than he actually possesses. No matter how skeptical they may appear, I've found that most people are looking for some understandings and insights from other than a scientific or practical viewpoint. If the numerologist can establish a sense of confidence by mentioning a few characteristics which ring true, the client may assume that everything the numerologist says has validity, that any advice the numerologist gives must be of special value. I mention this, not to puff up the importance of numerology, but rather to raise a red "caution" flag. Be extremely careful how you disseminate the information you receive through the numbers!

Many years ago, a woman for whom I had done a reading called to ask if I "did parties." At first, I didn't understand the phrase, but she explained that she would like me present at her next social affair to entertain her guests with readings. I politely declined.

I don't see numerology as an entertainment, but rather as a very serious and vital endeavor. I think it can be misleading or even harmful to feed people little bits of numerology to titillate them. With a little practice, it's easy to figure, say, a person's Life Path in your head and reel off a list of interesting characteristics, but I feel most uncomfortable with this practice.

Suppose, for instance, you've just met Diane, and, with a quick calculation, have determined that she has a 4 Life Path. You may be able to delight her with all sorts of things about her orderliness, practicality, patience with detail. Suppose that later, when you have more time, you discover that Diane has another 4 element, or some strongly negative 4 modifiers. Or that she's currently in the middle of a 13/4 Period or a 13/4 Essence. The information you've already given her isn't exactly wrong, but, under the circumstances, it's incomplete and may be misleading.

When I give partial information, and I admit I occasionally succumb to the temptation, I try to explain that the information *is* incomplete and that it's necessary to receive a complete reading in order to have a well-rounded picture. I also emphasize the importance of choice—free will—as well as the ability which everyone has to use his or her energies in a variety of ways.

When giving readings, I try to provide a peaceful physical setting. A comfortable study or office, one with quiet, privacy and a lack of interruption is important. Many people who come for readings are uncertain about what they're going to receive, a little uneasy about occult matters in general. I try to set a mood of calmness to put the client at ease. I usually spend a few minutes chatting about numerology in very broad terms in order to give a nervous client time to settle down and be comfortable.

Many subjects try to help make everything the numerologist says come out correctly. I usually indicate, before the reading, that the delineation isn't likely to be 100% accurate. When you start giving readings, though, it may be tempting to say as little as possible on matters with which the client may disagree. If, for instance, Emma's numbers indicate a great deal of adaptability—and Emma has smilingly nodded agreement—you may be reluctant to tell her that, at times, she exhibits considerable inflexibility. You're probably reluctant to tell her because, if you haven't had too much experience, you're likely to worry that the inflexibility doesn't fit very neatly with the adaptability which has already been confirmed. And you know that whether Emma confirms or denies this characteristic, she's not likely to be as happy with this trait as with the previously described adaptability. You have to remember that the object isn't to please the client or to be 100% accurate—the object, rather, is to communicate, as correctly as possible, useful information in the way that it can be best heard and assimilated.

Sometimes, people don't see all of their traits too clearly. If a trait is clearly described by the numerology chart and yet not accepted by the client, invite him to check with people who know him well. These people are likely to recognize the characteristic in question. You'll have an occasional reading where the subject, for some reason, can't see a trait obvious to all around him. The awareness of that trait may be the most important information he receives from the delineation.

Some clients concentrate primarily on the parts of the delineation describing obstacles and problems. I've given what I've considered extremely positive readings with just a smattering of negative energy, only to be told something like, "Boy, I sure have a lot of work to do." With a little experience, you'll see this point of view early in the reading. As in all delineations, emphasize the positive energy and report the negative energy clearly and constructively. Make a point of the client's ability to employ free will to make the best use of the energies present. If there's a substantial amount of negative energy, be well prepared to describe ways of converting that energy to positive potential.

Some people desiring readings are at crossroads in their lives. Occasionally, you'll have a client who is looking for help in many directions—occult, spiritual, religious, psychological—sometimes with a desperate intensity. DON'T—I can't say this too strongly—DON'T do anything beyond transmitting numerology information. DON'T advise on whether a subject should get married or divorced, leave a job or enter a new field, take a trip or stick with some heavy responsibility. Give clients all the information from the charts—the energy available and the current influences—but let them make their own decisions.

I read for a young woman several years ago who was mired in a problem marriage and, because of it, working at a job well below her abilities. Her chart was strikingly clear; she was exceptionally bright, capable of work on a significant level. The chart also indicated the probability of a substantial struggle to throw off her dependent needs and to move forward as an independent woman. When I'd completed the reading, this client confided that the numbers had confirmed information she'd previously received from a palm reading, information she'd readily accepted as a statement of her current position. She could see how she was keeping herself dependent, but she admitted to a great fear of losing her husband and children. She kept asking if this was the right time to strike out on her own, the right time to separate. I could only answer that the numbers indicated that this *was* a good time to learn about independence *if* she was comfortable in doing it. (I tried to clarify the difference between the numbers' description of learning about independence and her own desire to leave her husband.) I told her that if she preferred not to make a move now, that this was certainly within the province of her own free will. She didn't have to change her life now—or ever. She could work toward independence very slowly—or not at all. She could learn about independence later in her life when it might feel more comfortable—or in lives to come. I felt that she was looking for a very specific directive from me. I was satisfied that I'd left the decision-making responsibility with her—where it belonged.

At the end of a reading, I enjoy receiving feedback from my clients. Many of the subtleties they describe increase my awareness and help make subsequent readings more meaningful for others. Sometimes, a discussion with a client gives me a new way to describe a characteristic so it can be more understandable.

Some clients prefer to ask questions during the course of a reading, others save up their questions until the delineation is completed. I've done a few delineations where there are no questions or discussion during or after the reading. I'm disappointed in these readings because I feel that I haven't made contact with the client in a way that I would like.

I always ask my clients to call or write if they have any additional questions after digesting all the information. Like the feedback at the conclusion of the delineation, questions raised by clients, sometimes months after the reading, have often been a source of new understandings for me.

When I started giving readings, I felt comfortable typing the delineation and giving it to the client. The typed reading allowed me to take my time and work over what I wanted to say. Until I felt sufficiently experienced, I continued to use the typed reading.

Most of my readings now are face-to-face with the client. I enjoy the give and take of a personal meeting. (I prefer to have the birth data in advance, if at all possible, so that I can complete my calculations and spend time by myself understanding the different facets of the personality.) I usually tape the reading in progress and give the tape cassette to the client. I've found that there's so much information that it's almost impossible to digest at one sitting and my clients are appreciative of the opportunity to go over the delineation if they find it necessary.

Some of my readings, for people who live too far away to come in, are recorded on a tape cassette and mailed. You might expect these delineations to be more objective—after all, there's no possibility of feedback and, often, no direct contact with the client. With experience, though, I think there's little difference in objectivity whether the client is present or not.

When I read for people I know well, I've had to learn to ignore what I know about them and *just read the numbers*. That's often been very difficult to do.

A close friend, for instance, had a desk job which he'd accomplished superbly, but his chart indicated he'd probably have a lot of trouble with an inside job, that he'd do far better if he could move around. I knew that he'd been working at his present job for well over ten years. It seemed incongruous to tell him that the job didn't seem to fit his nature very well. With considerable effort, I told him what the numbers said. "You're so right," was his answer. "You have no idea how hard it is for me to sit in one place all day. Sometimes, it just about drives me crazy." A little over a year later, he'd managed to restructure his work so that his freedom was no longer impaired. It was another example for me confirming that, when the information derived from the numbers disagreed with my knowledge of the client, the numbers usually proved to be valid.

Numerology has helped me to be of service to others and has immeasurably enriched my own life. The study of the numbers has considerably altered my view of myself and my relation to the universe. I have more of a sense now of the complexity of that universe and a glimmering of awareness of the energies which surround me. I've learned from the numbers that everyone is doing what they're doing in their own good time and in their own special way. I've developed a sense of questioning and belief, of awe and understanding, of tolerance and humility. And I've experienced a great deal of satisfaction and contentment along the way.

I hope this book has helped a little in your own exploration of yourself and the universe. I hope that you find, in your study of the numbers, much understanding and much pleasure.

THE REFERENCE CHARTS

THE REFERENCE CHARTS

CHART **13** THE NUMBERS—ADVANCED SYMBOLISM

OVERBALANCED
ENERGY

The negative potential described by an overbalance of the energy caused by:

The presence of too much of a given energy, as with repeated core elements, or

The exclusive use of a given energy without the offsetting use of other available energies.

BALANCED
ENERGY

The positive potential which can be developed by the balanced use of the energy. See Chapter 22, page 385.

UNDERBALANCED
ENERGY

The negative potential described by an underbalance of the energy caused by:

The lack of a given energy or the relatively limited amount of a given energy, or

The avoidance of the use of a given energy.

CHART **13**		**1**	INDIVIDUATION
NUMBERS–ADVANCED SYMBOLISM			INDEPENDENCE
			ATTAINMENT

OVERBALANCED ENERGY

aggressive	constraining	impulsive	rigid
antagonistic	contrary	insatiable	self-centered
arbitrary	defiant	insolent	self-important
arrogant	demanding	militant	self-indulgent
authoritarian	dictatorial	obsessed	selfish
autocratic	dominating	obstinate	stubborn
bellicose	egocentric	opinionated	subjugating
boastful	egotistic	perverse	swaggering
bombastic	grasping	pompous	unyielding
bossy	greedy	possessive	vain
chauvinist	haughty	pretentious	voracious
coercive	headstrong	prideful	willful
conceited	impatient	quarrelsome	
conflicting	imperious	rash	

BALANCED ENERGY

achieving	compelling	full of spirit	persistent
active	confident	independent	powerful
adventurous	courageous	individualistic	progressive
ambitious	creative	influential	resolute
aspiring	determined	initiative	secure
assertive	dynamic	intrepid	self-sufficient
assured	energetic	inventive	self-reliant
attaining	enterprising	leader	venturesome
authoritative	executive ability	organizer	vigorous
bold	forceful	original	
commanding	forward looking	persevering	

UNDERBALANCED ENERGY

changeable	impotent	lazy	spiritless
compliant	indifferent	lethargic	submissive
cowardly	indolent	malleable	subservient
defeatist	insecure	passive	unaggressive
defenseless	lack of application	powerless	vulnerable
dependent	lack of energy	procrastinator	wavering
fearful	lack of initiative	reluctant	weak
helpless	lack of self-respect	resigned	

CHART 13

NUMBERS–ADVANCED SYMBOLISM

2 RELATION COOPERATION

OVERBALANCED ENERGY			
busybody	disparaging	meddling	sly
condescending	fault-finding	over-sensitive	stand-offish
cool	inhospitable	reproachful	timid
deprecatory	interfering	scheming	unsupportive
devious	intriguing	shy	wily
disapproving			

BALANCED ENERGY			
adaptable	cordial	hospitable	sensitivity to
affable	courteous	humble	people
agreeable	devoted	kindly	sincere
altruistic	diplomatic	loving	soft-hearted
amenable	emotional	loyal	supportive
amiable	feeling	modest	sympathetic
background	flexible	patient	tactful
contributor	friendly	pliant	tender
benevolent	genial	prudent	tolerant
cautious	gentle	receptive	trustworthy
compliant	gracious	responsive	understanding
conciliatory	harmonizing	sensitivity to	unpretentious
considerate	helpful	music, rhythm	
cooperative			

UNDERBALANCED ENERGY			
apathetic	inactive	rude	unconcerned
careless	inconsiderate	self-depreciating	unmoved
cowardly	indecisive	sluggish	unresponsive
discourteous	indifferent	spiritless	vacillating
dininterested	insensitive	stagnant	weak-willed
faint-hearted	lukewarm	tactless	
fearful	negligent	uncaring	
ill-mannered	phlegmatic	uncertain	

CHART **13**	**3** EXPRESSION
NUMBERS–ADVANCED SYMBOLISM	JOY OF LIVING

OVERBALANCED ENERGY

bellicose	extravagant	opinionated	silly
biased	garrulous	ostentatious	snobbish
blatant	gossipy	over-enthusiastic	stuck-up
boastful	haughty	patronizing	supercilious
bombastic	immodest	pompous	superficial
cocky	irresponsible	prejudiced	temperamental
conceited	lacks concentration	pretentious	vain
condescending	lacks direction	prideful	verbose
dabbling	loquacious	quarrelsome	wasteful
dilettante	long-winded	scatters energy	
exaggerating	narcissistic	shallow	

BALANCED ENERGY

aesthetic	discriminating	hearty	popular
affable	eager	hospitable	responsive
amicable	ebullient	imaginative	self-expressive
amusing	effervescent	instinctive	sociable
animated	emotional	intuitive	sparkling
appreciated	enthusiastic	joie de vivre	spirited
appreciative	exhilarated	joyous	stylish
artistic	feeling	kind	sympathetic
blithe	fertile mind	literate	tasteful
chatty	friendly	lively	understanding
comical	full of inspiration	lovable	verbal
compatible	good host, hostess	loving	vivacious
considerate	good taste	merry	welcoming
cordial	gracious	natural	witty
creative	gregarious	optimistic	youthful
cultivated	happy	original	

UNDERBALANCED ENERGY

anxious	doleful	indiscriminate	temperamental
apprehensive	downcast	inhospitable	timid
bored	envious	insensitive	touchy
brusque	evasive	intolerant	unfeeling
callous	fault-finding	jealous	unforgiving
cheerless	fretful	melancholy	unfriendly
complaning	fussy	moody	unkind
critical	gloomy	pessimistic	unmoved
curt	greedy	petty	unresponsive
defeatist	grouchy	reserved	unsociable
dejected	grumpy	reticent	unsympathetic
depressed	hesitating	self-indulgent	vacillating
disapproving	ill-disposed	selfish	whining
disconsolate	inarticulate	shy	withdrawn
discourteous	indecisive	spiteful	worrying
disgruntled	indifferent	sulky	
dispirited	indiscreet	tactless	

CHART **13**

NUMBERS–ADVANCED SYMBOLISM

4 LIMITATION ORDER SERVICE

OVERBALANCED ENERGY

antagonistic	humorless	pedantic	sluggish
argumentative	ill-mannered	pedestrian	stiff
bigoted	immovable	perverse	stodgy
blunt	impassive	pig-headed	strait-laced
boorish	impertinent	ponderous	stubborn
brusque	inflexible	provincial	stuffy
cantankerous	intolerant	pugnacious	tenacious
coarse	intransigent	quarrelsome	thick-skinned
contradictory	insensitive	quibbling	unbending
contrary	limited	recalcitrant	uncompromising
crude	lost in detail	repressive	uncouth
discourteous	narrow-minded	resistant	ungracious
dogmatic	obstinate	restricted	unimaginative
dull	obstructive	rigid	unrefined
fixed	obtuse	rude	unyielding
headstrong	opinionated	slow	vulgar
hidebound			

BALANCED ENERGY

accurate	dependable	industrious	reliable
attentive	determined	integrity	reliant
balanced	devoted	law-abiding	resolute
businesslike	dignified	loyal	responsible
candid	diligent	manager	scrupulous
careful	direct	measured	self-possessed
cautious	disciplinarian	methodical	sensible
competent	disciplined	meticulous	serious
compliant	dutiful	moderate	sober
composed	earnest	obedient	solid
confident	economical	organized	stable
conforming	efficient	orderly	steady
conscientious	endurance	painstaking	straightforward
conservative	exacting	patient	systematic
consistent	experienced	persevering	thorough
constant	faithful	practical	thrifty
constructive	factual	pragmatic	tireless
controlled	firm	precise	trustworthy
conventional	frank	prepared	unwavering
cool-headed	frugal	principled	upright
dedicated	imperturbable	productive	well-behaved
definite	incorruptible	prudent	
deliberate	indefatigable	reasonable	

UNDERBALANCED ENERGY

apathetic	irresponsible	plodding	uncertain
careless	lacking authority	servile	uncommitted
detached	lagging	slavish	undecided
dilatory	lax	slipshod	unemployable
disorganized	lazy	submissive	unfocused
impractical	lethargic	tired	unproductive
incompetent	narrow	unaccountable	weak-kneed
indifferent	negligent	unadaptable	weak-willed
inefficient			

CHART 13
NUMBERS–ADVANCED SYMBOLISM

5 CONSTRUCTIVE FREEDOM

OVERBALANCED ENERGY

agitated	heedless	nervous	thrill-seeking
arbitrary	hysterical	outlandish	unaccountable
audacious	ill-advised	overactive	unbridled
bizarre	impatient	over-indulgent	uncontrollable
capricious	impetuous	over-sexed	unconventional
careless	imprudent	peculiar	unexpected
contrary	impulsive	rash	unpredictable
debauched	inconsistent	reckless	unprepared
dissatisfied	incontinent	regretful	unreliable
drinker	indiscriminate	restless	unrestrained
eccentric	injudicious	scandalizing	unstable
erratic	insatiable	self-indulgent	unsteady
excitable	intemperate	shallow	unusual
extravagant	irresponsible	shocking	wanton
forgetful	licentious	skittish	wasteful
frenzied	loose	spendthrift	wayward
frivolous	mercurial	superficial	wild
gluttonous	negligent	thoughtless	

BALANCED ENERGY

active	energetic	independent	quick
adaptable	enterprising	individual	resourceful
adventurous	entertaining	informal	sales ability
affable	enthusiastic	inquisitive	skillful
agreeable	emancipated	intuitive	sociable
alert	exciting	inventive	spirited
amicable	expansive	lively	spontaneous
animated	exuberant	malleable	stylish
ardent	flair	many-sided	talented
broadminded	flexible	merry	unconventional
changeable	footloose	natural	unconfined
charming	forward-looking	non-conformist	unique
clever	free	opportunist	unprejudiced
convivial	free-thinking	original	up-to-date
creative	friendly	plain-spoken	venturesome
curious	fun-loving	pliant	versatile
daring	gifted	productive	vigorous
dashing	gracious	proficient	warm
delightful	gregarious	progressive	whimsical
demonstrative	go-getting	prolific	willing
dynamic	hospitable	promotor	witty
eager	imaginative	questioning	

UNDERBALANCED ENERGY

apathetic	dull	ineffective	unadaptable
behind the times	fear of freedom	old-fashioned	uncertain
boring	fear of new	out of date	undecided
cautious	fear of progressive	passionless	undemonstrative
colorless	fear of risks	purposeless	unimaginative
conforming	hesitant	spiritless	unresponsive
doubtful	inactive	stagnant	unsure
dubious	indecisive	static	vague

CHART **13**		**6**	BALANCE RESPONSIBILITY LOVE

NUMBERS–ADVANCED SYMBOLISM

OVERBALANCED ENERGY

anxious	discouraged	jittery	over-responsible	smothering
apprehensive	disheartened	loser	over-sensitive	suspicious
argumentative	dismayed	malcontent	overwhelmed	troubled
bitter	dissatisfied	martyr-complex	panicky	uneasy
complaining	drudge	meddlesome	pessimistic	unforgiving
conforming	envious	melancholy	possessive	unhappy
conventional	faint-hearted	negative	quibbling	unkind
critical	fault-finding	nervous	regretful	upset
defeated	fearful	obstructing	resentful	victimized
dependent	hindering	officious	sacrificing	vindictive
despairing	inferior	over-emotional	servile	weak
discontent	interfering	over-involvement	slavish	worried

BALANCED ENERGY

accommodating	conscientious	feeling	loyal	soft-hearted
accountable	concerned with home,	fervent	moral	solid
adjusting	family and children	friendly	obliging	steady
admiring	considerate	generous	pacifying	stable
advising	constant	genial	passionate	supportive
affectionate	content	gracious	patient	sympathetic
altruistic	cordial	happy	peace-making	tasteful
amiable	creative	healing	philanthropic	teaching
appreciative	decent	helpful	protective	temperate
approving	demonstrative	honorable	romantic	tender
ardent	dependable	hospitable	resolute	tolerant
artistic	devoted	humanitarian	resourceful	tranquil
balancing	disarming	idealistic	responsible	trustworthy
benevolent	domestic	imaginative	sacrificing	uncomplaining
careful	dutiful	indulgent	satisfied	understanding
charitable	earnest	kind	sentimental	unselfish
compassionate	emotional	likable	serving	virtuous
complimentary	ethical	lovable	sharing	well-intentioned
conciliatory	faithful	loving	sincere	wise
congenial				

UNDERBALANCED ENERGY

biased	harsh	irresponsible	phlegmatic	unforgiving
bigoted	heedless	lax	prejudiced	unfriendly
callous	hostile	listless	provincial	ungracious
cool	ill-natured	loveless	selfish	unimaginative
cranky	impassive	lukewarm	self-seeking	uninvolved
crotchety	impersonal	nasty	slipshod	unkind
cynical	inattentive	negligent	sullen	unloved
dishonest	inconstant	non-committal	tactless	unloving
disillusioned	indifferent	opinionated	unaccountable	unorganized
disinterested	inhospitable	parochial	uncaring	unreasoning
disloyal	insensitive	passionless	unconcerned	unreliable
distant	insipid	pedantic	uncooperative	unresponsive
greedy	intolerant	petty	unfeeling	unsympathetic

CHART 13
NUMBERS–ADVANCED SYMBOLISM

7 ANALYSIS UNDERSTANDING

OVERBALANCED ENERGY

agnostic	disparaging	indecisive	odd	stubborn
aloof	dissident	indifferent	opinionated	suppresses feelings
antisocial	distant	inferiority complex	out of touch	suppressive
anxious	distrustful	inflexible	over-analytical	suspicious
aprehensive	dogmatic	insecure	pedantic	taciturn
bigoted	eccentric	insensitive	perfectionist	tactless
callous	evasive	intimidated	pessimistic	thick-skinned
caustic	extreme different	intimidating	powerless	timid
contrary	wavelength	intransigent	prudish	unadaptable
controlled	extremist	jealous	puritanical	uncomplimentary
controlling	fanatic	joyless	repressed	uncompromising
cool	fault-finding	malcontent	reserved	undemonstrative
crank	fearful	melancholy	reticent	unfeeling
critical	fussy	misanthropic	retiring	unrealistic
cunning	guarded	monosyllabic	sarcastic	unresponsive
cynical	hesitant	nervous	secretive	unsociable
deceitful	humorless	non-committal	self-conscious	wary
derisive	hypercritical	nonconformist	selfish	weak
despairing	impatient	obsessed	shy	wily
detached	impersonal	obstructive	spineless	withdrawn
devious	impractical	obtuse	stoic	worried

BALANCED ENERGY

accurate	dependable	inquisitive	occult interests	respectable
analytical	devout	inspired	original	responsible
astute	different wavelength	instinctive	patient	rigorous
attentive	diligent	intellectual	peaceful	scholarly
austere	discriminating	introspective	penetrating thinker	scientific
authoritative	dreamer	intuitive	perceptive	searching
bookish	efficient	inventive	philosophical	sincere
broad-minded	enlightened	investigator	poised	skillful
calm	erudite	logical	probing	spiritual
capable	exact	learned	profound	studious
cerebral	expert	mature	psychic	technical
clairaudient	faithful	meditative	pure	telepathic
clairvoyant	fertile mind	mental	rational	theoretical
competent	gifted	metaphysical	reasoning	truth-seeker
conscientious	idealistic	interests	reflective	unworldly
contemplative	imperturbable	meticulous	religious	visionary
creative	individualistic	mystical	researcher	well-read
deep	influential	observant	resourceful	wise
deliberate	ingenious			

UNDERBALANCED ENERGY

amateurish	foolish	illiterate	overlooked	undeveloped
awkward	forgetful	immature	short-sighted	unenlightened
backward	gauche	lack of depth	silly	uninformed
blank	inane	lack of faith	simple	unqualified
dense	incompetent	lack of poise	slow	unthinking
disregarded	ineffectual	muddle-headed	superficial	untrained
dull	inexperienced	mystified	uncertain	vague
empty-headed	ignorant	naive		

CHART 13
NUMBERS–ADVANCED SYMBOLISM

8 MATERIAL SATISFACTION

OVERBALANCED ENERGY

abuses power	combative	ill-bred	opinionated	tactless
abusive	contemptible	ill-mannered	over-ambitious	tense
adamant	contentious	impatient	pedantic	thoughtless
aggressive	contrary	imprudent	possessive	threatening
avaricious	cool	inconsiderate	prejudiced	uncaring
awkward	corrupt	indecent	provincial	uncooperative
bad taste	crude	indifferent	quarrelsome	uncouth
biased	demanding	inflexible	rebellious	undignified
bigoted	dishonest	insensitive	repressive	unfeeling
blatant	disreputable	intolerant	restrictive	ungracious
blunt	egotistical	irresponsible	rigid	unprincipled
boorish	fanatic	lacking trust	scheming	unreasonable
bullying	fascist	lawless	selfish	unreliable
callous	fraudulent	militant	self-indulgent	unresponsive
cantankerous	gaudy	materialistic	shameless	unsociable
chauvinistic	gross	myopic	sneaky	unsympathetic
clumsy	hard	narrow-minded	stiff	unyielding
coarse	hidebound	negligent	strait-laced	vulgar
cold-blooded	hot-headed	one-track mind	stubborn	

BALANCED ENERGY

administrator	courageous	forceful	persevering	self-confident
affirmative	dedicated	frank	planner	self-reliant
ambitious	definite	good judgment	positive	self-possessed
appreciative	dependable	governing	powerful	serious
assertive	dignified	high-powered	practical	shrewd
assured	direct	honest	pragmatic	skillful
astute	director	honorable	preeminent	spirited
authoritative	disciplined	industrious	principled	stamina
businesslike	discriminating	influential	progressive	status
candid	dynamic	initiating	prosperous	straightforward
capable	earnest	integrity	prudent	strong
clear-headed	effective	leadership	realistic	successful
clever	efficient	loyal	reliable	supervising
commanding	energetic	manager	resolute	supportive
compelling	enterprising	material freedom	resourceful	systematic
competent	enthusiastic	money maker	respected	upright
confident	executive ability	opportunist	responsible	venturesome
conscientious	far-sighted	organizer	ruling	vigorous
consistent	financial awareness	persuasive		

UNDERBALANCED ENERGY

apathetic	feeble	lack of perspective	poor judgment	undisciplined
careless	inept	in material matters	procrastinating	uninterested
cheating	illogical	lazy	restricted	unorganized
circumscribed	immature	limited	shameless	unprepared
cowardly	impractical	misdirected	short-sighted	unrealistic
defenseless	inattentive	narrow	slipshod	unreliable
dishonest	incoherent	negligent	slovenly	unresponsive
disorderly	indifferent	nervous	spiritless	unsteady
disreputable	insecure	non-observant	timid	vulnerable
fearful	lack of confidence	oblivious	uncaring	weak
fear of failure				

CHART **13**
NUMBERS–ADVANCED SYMBOLISM

9 SELFLESSNESS HUMANITARIANISM

OVERBALANCED ENERGY

avaricious	discourteous	impractical	over-emotional	temperamental
biased	disloyal	indecisive	pedantic	tiresome
bigoted	dissatisfied	indiscreet	pessimistic	unaccountable
bitter	dogmatic	ineffective	petty	uncertain
capricious	doubtful	inexperienced	possessive	unfaithful
changeable	downcast	injudicious	prejudiced	unimaginative
chauvinist	dreamer	insecure	provincial	uninvolved
confusing	egotistic	intolerant	quarrelsome	unpleasant
cowardly	elusive	irascible	resentful	unreasonable
crank	evasive	irresponsible	selfish	unreliable
cross	faint-hearted	jealous	self-centered	unsmiling
deceiving	fearful	joyless	short-sighted	unstable
defeatist	fickle	meek	shy	unsteady
dejected	forbidding	melancholy	submissive	unsympathetic
demanding	foolish	misanthropic	sullen	vacillating
depressed	gloomy	moody	superficial	vague
despondent	grasping	mournful	sullen	victimized
disapproving	greedy	naive	superficial	wavering
disconsolate	grouchy	narrow-minded	tactless	weak-kneed
discontent	humorless	non-cooperative	tedious	

BALANCED ENERGY

affectionate	cordial	generous	liberal	sensitive
agreeable	creative	genial	loving	sentimental
altruistic	decent	gracious	loyal	soft-hearted
amiable	dedicated	helpful	merciful	staunch
ardent	demonstrative	hospitable	missionary	sympathetic
artistic	devoted	high-minded	modest	tactful
benevolent	discriminating	humane	passionate	tender
broadminded	emotional	humble	philanthropic	tolerant
capable	enlightened	idealistic	prudent	trustworthy
charitable	enthusiastic	impassioned	reasonable	understanding
chivalrous	fair-minded	impressionable	reliable	unprejudiced
compassionate	faithful	indulgent	responsible	warm
compatible	feeling	inspired	responsive	welcoming
compliant	forbearing	intense	selfless	well-intentioned
considerate	forgiving	intuitive	self-sacrificing	willing
cooperative	friendly	kindly		

UNDERBALANCED ENERGY

aloof	harsh	lack of compassion	strait-laced	unemotional
apathetic	headstrong	limited	stubborn	unenthusiastic
biased	hidebound	listless	tactless	unfeeling
bigoted	ill-disposed	narrow	thick-skinned	unforgiving
callous	impassive	obstinate	ultraconservative	unkind
circumscribed	impersonal	oppressive	unbending	unresponsive
detached	indifferent	passionless	uncaring	unsympathetic
discouraged	inflexible	prejudiced	unconcerned	unyielding
disloyal	inhospitable	repressed	uncooperative	vindictive
distant	intolerant	restricted	undemonstrative	willful
half-hearted	insensitive	rigid		

CHART 13		
NUMBERS–ADVANCED SYMBOLISM		**11** ILLUMINATION

OVERBALANCED ENERGY

absolute	fiery	obsessed	undoubting
crusading	hysterical	opinionated	unequivocal
dogmatic	impractical	over-righteous	unquestioning
extreme nervousness	impassioned	overzealous	unrealistic
extreme tension	lack of humanity	overwrought	unreasonable
formalistic	lost in dreams	ritualistic	very high strung
fanatic	misguided	uncontrollable	warped viewpoint
fervent			

BALANCED ENERGY

absent-minded	exhilarating	mystical	religious
aware	faithful	nervous	revealing truth
clairaudient	guiding	occult interests	reverent
clairvoyant	high-strung	oracular	saintly
compelling	idealistic	pensive	sensitive
contemplative	imaginative	perceptive	spiritual
contributing	impressionable	poetic	stimulating
creative	influencing	prayerful	tactful
dedicated	inspired	progressive	telepathic
devout	inspiring	prophetic	tense
discerning	instinctive	psychic	theological
discriminating	intuitive	pure	unworldly
dreamy	inventive	reforming	visionary
encouraging	meditative		

UNDERBALANCED ENERGY

aimless	inactive	obtuse	undirected
aloof	indifferent	pedantic	unenthusiastic
amateurish	indiscreet	provincial	unfeeling
apathetic	indiscriminate	slow	unfocused
biased	inexperienced	spiritless	unimaginative
bumbling	lethargic	submissive	uninformed
detached	lifeless	tactless	unresponsive
dull	lukewarm	torpid	
fearful of occult	myopic	unaffected	(The underbalance of
fearful of psychic	narrow	unaware	both master numbers
feeble	negligent	uncertain	are similar.)
impractical			

CHART **13**
NUMBERS–ADVANCED SYMBOLISM

22 MASTER BUILDER

OVERBALANCED ENERGY

absolute	extreme nervousness	misusing power	pressuring
abusive	extreme tension	obsessed	pretentious
blatant	fanatical	opinionated	self-important
coercive	fiery	oppressing	squandering
conceited	frantic	ostentatious	swaggering
confused	frenzied	overdoing	turbulent
disorganized	hysterical	overwhelmed	uncontrollable
dogmatic	indiscriminate	overwhelming	undisciplined
dominating	manipulative	overwrought	vain
egotistic	mismanaging	perverted	very high-strung
exaggerating	misrepresenting	pompous	

BALANCED ENERGY

achieving	enterprising	inspirational	purposeful
active	enthusiastic	inspired	recognized
altruistic	expert	intense	reforming
authoritative	forceful	inventive	resourceful
benevolent	goal-oriented	liberal	rewarded
bettering	guiding	masterly	successful
compelling	high-strung	nervous	superior
constructive	humane	organizing	stimulating
contributing	humanitarian	planning	strong
creative	idealistic	powerful	tense
dynamic	imaginative	practical	uplifting
effective	impelling	productive	vigorous
efficient	influencing	progressive	visionary
energetic	influential	promoting	well-intentioned
enlightened	ingenious		

UNDERBALANCED ENERGY

aimless	impractical	obtuse	unenthusiastic
aloof	inactive	slow	unfocused
amateurish	indifferent	spiritless	unimaginative
apathetic	inexperienced	submissive	uninformed
biased	lethargic	torpid	
bumbling	lifeless	unaffected	(The underbalance of
detached	lukewarm	uncertain	both master numbers
dull	negligent	undirected	are similar.)
feeble			

CHART **14** THE LIFE PATH PERIODS

GENERAL	The three Life Path Periods describe the probable general influences in the three phases of the life as aspects of the Life Path direction. See Chapter 28, page 485.
FIRST PERIOD	The Developmental Period of the Life Path spans youth and young adulthood. It often appears to display restrictive influences.
SECOND PERIOD	The Productive Period of the Life Path spans the important middle years, involving what is often the most productive period of the life. This period usually produces influences and opportunities for expansion.
THIRD PERIOD	The Integrative Period of the Life Path spans the later years of life. It sometimes describes influences supportive of reflection and retirement, sometimes influences supportive of bustling activity.
KARMIC PERIOD	If a Period is a 19/1, 13/4, 14/5, or 16/7 Period, the Period description will be modified by a strong negative impact.

TIME SPAN OF LIFE PATH PERIODS

Life Path	First Period	Second Period	Third Period
	Age	Age	Age
1	0–26	27–53	54 on
2 or 11/2	0–25	26–52	53 on
3	0–24	25–51	52 on
4 or 22/4	0–23	24–59	60 on
5	0–31	32–58	59 on
6	0–30	31–57	58 on
7	0–29	30–56	57 on
8	0–28	29–55	56 on
9	0–27	28–54	55 on

CHART **14**		**1**	INDIVIDUATION INDEPENDENCE ATTAINMENT
LIFE PATH PERIODS			

GENERAL   Influences emphasize:

> Being independent.
> Expressing one's individuality.
> Using your own original ideas.
> Leading and directing others.
> Achievement and recognition for achievement.

FIRST PERIOD

Although the subject, as a child and young adult, is likely to become aware of the power that comes with the development of the characteristics emphasized by the general influences, his environment makes it difficult for him to fully develop these traits. The environment may feel repressive, breed anxiety and intimidation, discourage originality or give little recognition for the individual's effort or achievement. Or, the environment may be free and open with so little direction that the subject may feel overwhelmed and frightened. The individual isn't likely to get much help from those close to him in achieving independence.

As the young adult moves into the world, he's likely to find himself in a more balanced environment, but with little background on which to build. He must teach himself how to be comfortable with being himself, being independent and having the courage to follow his own direction.

SECOND PERIOD

In this Productive Period, the subject is likely to be in an environment emphasizing his ability to make positive strides in the direction of the general influences. The environment is apt to encourage his forward-looking and original endeavors and reward his attainments with recognition and material gain.

THIRD PERIOD

In this Integrative Period, when there may be a desire for time for reflection, there's likely to be substantial movement instead. Attainments of this Period (and, sometimes, previous Periods) may receive recognition and lead to material gain.

19/1 KARMIC PERIOD

Problems relating to the following are likely to mar the Period unless the subject is willing to work to overcome the blockages:

Over-emphasis on self: egotism, stubbornness, dominance, aggression, selfishness.

Dependence: timidity, shyness, lack of confidence, insecurity.

CHART **14** LIFE PATH PERIODS	**2** RELATION COOPERATION

GENERAL	Influences emphasize:
	Being sensitive.
	Being tactful and cooperative.
	Promoting harmony.
	Working well with others rather than alone. Partnerships are likely to feel comfortable.
	Patience with details.
	Working with comparatively little recognition.
	Being friendly, affectionate.

FIRST PERIOD	Although the subject, as a child and young adult, is likely to become aware of the power that comes with the development of the characteristics emphasized by the general influences his environment probably makes it difficult for him to fully develop his sensitivity, in particular. He may find that his sensitivity is not only not nurtured, but that he must restrain his feelings or be berated for being too sensitive. He may become shy and uncertain for lack of any positive encouragement. He's likely to be more heavily influenced by his mother (or a surrogate mother) than by his father. The mother may be separated, divorced or widowed through a substantial part of the subject's childhood.
	As the young adult moves into the world, he's likely to find himself in a more balanced environment, but concern with his own needs may still not be encouraged. His sensitivity may begin to emerge, although probably painfully. He may find that he can mask his uncertainty by staying in the background. Insistence on his own needs and expression may cause problems which he feels ill-equipped to battle.

SECOND PERIOD	In this Productive Period, the subject is likely to be in an environment emphasizing his ability to make positive strides in the direction of the general influences. The environment is apt to encourage marriage and parenting. The subject may promote and maintain the harmony in many of his relations. He may often find himself in a background position, receiving little credit or recognition for his achievements.

THIRD PERIOD	In this Integrative Period, when there may be a desire for time for reflection, there is likely to be a supportive environment of warm close friends and family. There can be much satisfaction if there is not too much insistence on one's needs and tact used in dealing with others.

KARMIC PERIOD	Not applicable.

CHART **14** LIFE PATH PERIODS	**3** EXPRESSION JOY OF LIVING

GENERAL   Influences emphasize:

Light, enjoyable activities—travel, social activities, entertainment.
Being friendly, affectionate.
Developing personal expression, particularly verbal expression.
Opportunities to write, act or sing.
Developing artistic and creative abilities.

FIRST PERIOD

As a child and young adult, the subject is likely to become aware of the pleasures of friends and artistic pursuits. There's likely to be emphasis placed on creativity, possibly in such a way as to discourage the search for the deeper levels of originality, or with the application of pressure which may inhibit a shy or timid subject. There may be a tendency to waste the energies with subsequent frustration. Capricious or self-indulgent activity may, at times, overshadow healthier endeavors.

As the young adult moves into the world, he's likely to find himself in a more balanced environment. Artistic, verbal and social activities may be emphasized as avenues of expression leading to much pleasure.

SECOND PERIOD

In this Productive Period, the subject is likely to be in an environment emphasizing his ability to make positive strides in the direction of the general influences. The environment is apt to encourage the pleasures of life and the expression of the delight of living.

The tendency to waste energies in meaningless or frantic activities or to act capriciously or self-indulgently may be promoted by the permissive environment, with resultant frustration and loss of time and direction.

THIRD PERIOD

In this Integrative Period, when there may be a desire for time for reflection, there is likely to be a supportive environment of warm close friends and family. Emphasis is probably placed on enjoying life—little heed is likely to be given to status, power or recognition.

KARMIC PERIOD

Not applicable.

CHART **14** LIFE PATH PERIODS	**4**	LIMITATION ORDER SERVICE

GENERAL   Influences emphasize:

     Practical, realistic activities and solutions.
     Order, system, organization.
     Need for conscientious, dependable responses.
     Need for hard work, determined effort, constant application.
     Slowly developing opportunities and activities.

FIRST PERIOD

Although the subject, as a child and young adult, is likely to become aware of the power that comes with the development of the characteristics emphasized by the general influences, he is apt to be particularly aware of the limiting nature of the environment. He may see the environment as harsh and restrictive and there may be financial limitations which create or heighten the pressure. Little recognition is likely to be given to idealism, creativity or flights of fancy.

As the young adult moves into the world, he's likely to find himself in a more balanced environment, but still with emphasis on work, orderliness and practicality. The feeling of restriction is likely to persist.

SECOND PERIOD

In this Productive Period, the subject is likely to be in an environment emphasizing his ability to make positive strides in the direction of the general influences. The environment is apt to encourage hard, conscientious work. There may be financial limitations. It's important for the subject not to lose ambition, to move forward despite the seeming restrictions.

THIRD PERIOD

In this Integrative Period, when there may be a desire for time for reflection, there's likely to be emphasis on ongoing work and service. The feeling of limitation engendered by the restrictive nature of the work involved may cause aggravation and resentment. There may be financial limitations, too.

13/4 KARMIC PERIOD

Any tendency to be rigid, obstinate or dogmatic will increase the problems.

There's likely to be an excessively heavy work load or a restrictive type of work, either presenting substantial impediments so that the subject feels uncomfortably boxed in. Often, the nature of the work producing the obstruction can be changed if the subject is capable of analyzing the situation objectively.

| CHART **14**
LIFE PATH PERIODS | **5** CONSTRUCTIVE FREEDOM |

GENERAL Influences emphasize:
    Change—frequent, sudden, unexpected.
    Variety—new and different friends, work, interests.
      Many experiences, interesting adventures, travel.
    Freedom—little responsibility.
    Uncertain finances—likely to be plentiful some of the time, scarce at
      other times. May change with little warning.

FIRST PERIOD As a child and young adult, the subject is likely to become aware of the power and problems that come with freedom. Although the environment may well promote creative activity and allow a person to expand his talents, it also is apt to provide a continual feeling of restlessness. There's likely to be little responsibility to shoulder and little concern by others with teaching responsibility. There may be a fluctuating money supply which adds to the vagaries of the environment.

As the young adult moves into the world, he's likely to find himself in a more balanced environment, but with a continued emphasis on uncertainty and restlessness.

SECOND PERIOD In this Productive Period, the subject is likely to be in an environment emphasizing his ability to make positive strides in the direction of the general influences. If he can be comfortable with the many changes, he may feel free, released from the usual cares and responsibilities, revelling in the expansion of his horizons. Raising a family in an environment with this constant flux may present its own problems. His business life is likely to vary considerably from the norm.

THIRD PERIOD In this Integrative Period, when there may be a desire for time for reflection, there's likely to be substantial movement instead. It's not likely that there'll be much calm, but there may be satisfaction in the changing horizons. Fluctuations in the money supply are apt to add to the restlessness of the environment.

14/5 KARMIC PERIOD There is likely to be difficulty in choosing among the many opportunities available. Frustration and less constructive development than desired may occur.

Failure to profit from experience instead of repeating mistakes may cause dissatisfaction and may block the easy-going pleasures of this period.

Excessive appetite for physical stimulation—food, sex, drink, drugs— may cause problems.

CHART **14** LIFE PATH PERIODS	**6** BALANCE RESPONSIBILITY LOVE

GENERAL	Influences emphasize: Responsibilities—may cause feeling of restriction. Home, family, children. Giving and receiving love. Opportunities to serve and help others: teaching, counseling, healing. Promoting harmony.
FIRST PERIOD	As a child and young adult, the subject is likely to become aware of the powers and problems that come with responsibility. He may find himself in a loving, caring family. The domestic chores and activities are likely to be a large part of the early years. He may feel restricted in being asked to sacrifice some of his own needs for the welfare of others. He's not likely to find much encouragement in expressing his own individuality. As the young adult moves into the world, he's likely to find himself in a more balanced environment, but still with emphasis on responsibility and obligation. Domestic matters related to the family in which he was brought up or the family which he starts are apt to loom large. He may marry early.
SECOND PERIOD	In this Productive Period, the subject is likely to be in an environment emphasizing his ability to make positive strides in the direction of the general influences. The environment is apt to stress the pleasures, love and caring of a happy home and family along with the responsibilities this entails. This can be a fine time for marriage or the continuation of a marriage started in the First Period.
THIRD PERIOD	In this Integrative Period, when there may be a desire for time for reflection, there is likely to be a supportive environment of warm close friends and family. There's likely to be responsibilities even within this loving space, but the willingness to accept responsibility and work toward harmony will probably provide rich rewards.
KARMIC PERIOD	Not applicable.

CHART 14 LIFE PATH PERIODS	7 ANALYSIS UNDERSTANDING

GENERAL Influences emphasize:

Study: Learning, investigating, gaining skills, often in scientific, technical, religious or metaphysical fields.

Being alone: Usually more comfortable working alone. Marriage is likely to take much effort. May need the isolation to develop inner resources.

Little interest in material matters: There is likely to be little concern with practical affairs. There may be difficulties because of lack of money or material benefits.

FIRST PERIOD As a child and young adult, the subject may become aware of the powers that come with study and the development of the inner person, or, more likely the problems that come with not feeling close to anyone. He's apt to find himself in an environment where he has few friends, almost nobody who understands him, meeting with forces which tend to repress his real nature. He may withdraw, appear cool and detached. He may often feel that he has less opportunities than he would like and that his opportunities take too long to develop.

As the young adult moves into the world, he's likely to be alone, detached, concerned with developing inner peace, deep in study. He should be aware that marriage or the closeness of any relation is apt to present difficulties.

SECOND PERIOD In this Productive Period, the subject is likely to be in an environment emphasizing his ability to make positive strides through study and inner growth. There may be recognition for his mental accomplishments, his unusual awareness, his analysis and research. He may teach some complex or difficult subject, or he may find satisfaction in writing about the fundamentals he studies. He's likely to have to wait with patience for his opportunities to develop.

THIRD PERIOD In this Introspective Period, when there may be a desire for time for reflection, there's likely to be a quiet environment with emphasis on study and development of the inner person. The subject may have to learn to be content with few close friends or companions. He may have to learn to achieve peace of mind in a relatively lonely environment.

16/7 KARMIC PERIOD The subject is likely to be perceived as "different", causing problems with communication or making others feel that he is difficult to approach. His tendency to introspection or self-centeredness may add to the problem.

Permanent relations—marriage, business partnerships—may be difficult to maintain.

CHART 14
LIFE PATH PERIODS

8 MATERIAL SATISFACTION

GENERAL   Influences emphasize:

Business and commercial activity.
Possibility of success, recognition, status.
Financial and material gain.
Pragmatic orientation. Emotional bias is not likely to be helpful.
Organizational and management abilities.

FIRST PERIOD   As a child and young adult, the subject is likely to become aware of the power and problems that come with money and materialistic interests. He may find himself in an atmosphere of status and power, and the material freedom may confuse his ability to deal with money later on. Or, he may find himself in an environment where there is strain after money and a lack of material satisfaction, again tending to confuse his abilities in this area.

As the young adult moves into the world, he's likely to find himself in a more balanced environment, but still with a strong emphasis on money and materialistic interests. He may now begin to develop a better perspective on these matters.

SECOND PERIOD   In this Productive Period, the subject is likely to be in an environment emphasizing his ability to make positive strides in the direction of the general influences. There's probably a good deal of work to be accomplished, little time for play or concerns which stray from a realistic perspective.

THIRD PERIOD   In this Integrative Period, when there may be a desire for time for reflection, there's likely to be substantial movement instead. Retirement or a reduced work load may be possible, but there are likely to be continued business concerns or, at the least, concerns of a practical nature requiring work and attention.

KARMIC PERIOD   Not applicable.

| CHART **14**
LIFE PATH PERIODS | **9** SELFLESSNESS
HUMANITARIANISM |

GENERAL   Influences emphasize:

Drama and emotions.

Need for tolerance and compassion.

Need for an approach with little concern for personal interests.

Need for giving love without expecting it to be returned.

Humanistic, philanthropic or artistic endeavors.

Completion of major endeavors which provide the freedom to move forward. The completion is likely to be highly charged with emotion. The completion may not be desired by the subject, even though its ultimate ends will probably prove beneficial.

FIRST PERIOD   As a child and young adult, the subject is likely to become aware of the problems with selflessness and deep feelings. He's apt to find himself in an environment where selflessness is held up as an ideal, but he probably receives little input on what to do with his own personal needs. The environment is likely to be highly charged with emotion, although the emotions may not be expressed clearly. With this as background, the subject probably has difficulty with his own feelings. He's likely to feel most unsatisfied.

As the young adult moves into the world, he's likely to find himself in a more balanced environment, but with little background on which to build. He must learn to deal with the drama and emotion he's likely to find at this time.

SECOND PERIOD   In this Productive Period, the subject is likely to be in an environment emphasizing his ability to make positive strides in the direction of the general influences. He may be aware of a lack of personal satisfaction. Marriage is likely to require much effort as well as the foregoing of many personal needs.

THIRD PERIOD   In this Integrative Period, when there may be a desire for time for reflection, there's likely to be some quiet time for this, although there's probably a need to spend time helping others. Some of the personal needs probably aren't fulfilled.

KARMIC PERIOD   Not applicable.

CHART **14** LIFE PATH PERIODS	**11** ILLUMINATION

GENERAL	Influences emphasize: Philosophic, religious or metaphysical studies. Possibility of inspiration and illumination. Lack of concern with practical and material matters. Problems with associates, particularly business partners or spouse. Nervous tension. See the 2 influences also.
FIRST PERIOD	Always reduces to a 2 Period.
SECOND PERIOD	In this Productive Period, the subject is likely to be in an environment emphasizing his ability to make positive strides in the direction of the general influences. There's probably time for dreaming and for attempting to act on the dream. Don't expect much in the way of opportunity in the business world.
THIRD PERIOD	In this Integrative Period, when there may be a desire for time for reflection, there's likely to be some quiet time for this activity. There's probably time for dreaming and for attempting to act on the dream. The subject may advise others with more opportunity or potential to produce results.
KARMIC PERIOD	Not applicable.

CHART **14** **LIFE PATH PERIODS**	**22** MASTER BUILDER

GENERAL   Influences emphasize:

> Large scale business endeavors or endeavors with the potential for large scale influence.
> Idealistic approach to secure practical ends.
> Nervous tension.

> See the 4 influences also.

FIRST PERIOD   Not applicable. There are no 22 First Periods.

SECOND PERIOD   In this Productive Period, the subject is likely to be in an environment emphasizing his ability to make positive strides in the direction of the general influences. Leadership opportunities may allow a realization of deeply-held beliefs, but much continuous effort would be necessary to develop the ultimate potential.

THIRD PERIOD   In this Integrative Period, when there may be a desire for time for reflection, there's likely to be, instead, endeavors requiring continuous effort to develop ultimate potential. Retirement or even partial retirement isn't likely.

KARMIC PERIOD   Not applicable.

CHART **15** THE PINNACLES

GENERAL   The four Pinnacles describe the general influences during each of the four Pinnacle phases of the Life. See Chapter 29, page 499.

FIRST PINNACLE   The Developmental Pinnacle spans youth and young adulthood. It usually displays limiting influences.

SECOND PINNACLE

THIRD PINNACLE   The Second Pinnacle, or Productive Pinnacle A, and the Third Pinnacle, or Productive Pinnacle B, span the important middle years, involving what is often the most productive period of the life. These Pinnacles usually produce influences and opportunities for expansion.

FOURTH PINNACLE   The Integrative Pinnacle spans the later years of life. It sometimes describes influences supportive of reflection and retirement, sometimes influences supportive of bustling activity.

KARMIC PINNACLE   If a Pinnacle is a 19/1, 13/4, 14/5, or 16/7 Pinnacle, the Pinnacle description will be modified by a strong negative impact.

TIME SPAN OF PINNACLES

Life Path	First Pinnacle	Second Pinnacle	Third Pinnacle	Fourth Pinnacle
	age:	age:	age:	age:
1	0-35	36-44	45-53	54 on
2 or 11/2	0-34	35-43	44-52	53 on
3	0-33	34-42	43-51	52 on
4 or 22/4	0-32	33-41	42-50	51 on
5	0-31	32-40	41-49	50 on
6	0-30	31-39	40-48	49 on
7	0-29	30-38	39-47	48 on
8	0-28	29-37	38-46	47 on
9	0-27	28-36	37-45	46 on

CHART **15** THE PINNACLES	**1** INDIVIDUATION INDEPENDENCE ATTAINMENT

GENERAL Influences emphasize:

  Being independent.
  Expressing one's individuality.
  Using own original ideas.
  Leading and directing others.
  Achievement and recognition for achievement.

FIRST PINNACLE

Most of this period is probably spent learning how to use original ideas, how to lead, how to rely on oneself without being egotistical, stubborn, self-centered or dominating.

This is a good period for beginnings, but the potential is likely to be limited in this learning period.

SECOND PINNACLE

THIRD PINNACLE

Responsibilities and accomplishments will be based on the ability to develop the talents required by the general influences.

FOURTH PINNACLE

Any desire to retire or slow down is not likely to be fulfilled. Challenges, changes and activities are likely to continue.

Responsibilities and accomplishments will be based on the ability to develop the talents required by the general influences.

19/1 KARMIC PINNACLE

Problems relating to the following are likely to mar the Pinnacle unless the subject is willing to work to overcome the blockages:

Over-emphasis on self: egotism, stubbornness, dominance, aggression, selfishness.

Dependence: Timidity, shyness, lack of confidence, insecurity.

CHART **15** THE PINNACLES	**2** RELATION COOPERATION

GENERAL	Influences emphasize: Being sensitive. Being tactful and cooperative. Promoting harmony. Working with others rather than alone. Partnerships are likely to feel comfortable. Patience with details. Working with comparatively little recognition. Being friendly, affectionate.
FIRST PINNACLE	Most of this period is probably spent feeling oversensitive—being very aware and easily hurt or frightened. There may also be difficulties with expression. Efforts must be made to develop a comfortable expression of a better balanced sensitivity. Mother (or surrogate mother) is likely to be a strong influence. Father may be separated, divorced or dead.
SECOND PINNACLE **THIRD PINNACLE**	Responsibilities and accomplishments will be based on the ability to develop the talents required by the general influences.
FOURTH PINNACLE	A harmonious working environment or retirement is possible. Sensitivity and receptivity are likely to be of special importance.
KARMIC PINNACLE	Not applicable.

CHART **15** THE PINNACLES	**3** EXPRESSION JOY OF LIVING

GENERAL   Influences emphasize:

Light, enjoyable activities—travel, social activities, entertainment.
Being friendly, affectionate.
Developing personal expression, particularly verbal expression.
Opportunities to write, act or sing.
Developing artistic and creative abilities.

FIRST PINNACLE   There may be substantial opportunities to develop artistic or creative potential, but the subject may not recognize them or be willing to work as hard as may be required for the development of the opportunities. He may scatter energies by working on opportunities with little potential.

SECOND PINNACLE   Responsibilities and accomplishments will be based on the ability to develop the talents required by the general influences.

THIRD PINNACLE

FOURTH PINNACLE   A harmonious working environment or retirement is possible.
There's the possibility of travel, friends and much delight.

KARMIC PINNACLE   Not applicable.

CHART **15** THE PINNACLES	**4** LIMITATION ORDER SERVICE

GENERAL — Influences emphasize:

Practical, realistic activities and solutions.

Order, system, organization.

Need for conscientious, dependable responses.

Need for hard work, determined effort, constant application.

Slowly developing opportunities and activities.

FIRST PINNACLE — This may be a demanding period with the need to work hard at a young age.

There may be economic limitations and little time for youthful activities.

SECOND PINNACLE — Responsibilities and accomplishments will be based on the ability to develop the talents required by the general influences. There may be feelings of economic limitation.

THIRD PINNACLE

FOURTH PINNACLE — Any desire to retire or slow down is not likely to be fulfilled. There's likely to be little leisure and feelings of economic limitation.

Responsibilities and accomplishments will be based on the ability to develop the talents required by the general influences.

13/4 KARMIC PINNACLE — Any tendency to be rigid, obstinate or dogmatic will increase the problems.

There's likely to be either an excessively heavy work load or a restrictive type of work, either presenting substantial impediments so that the subject feels uncomfortably boxed in. Often, the nature of the work producing the obstruction can be changed if the subject is capable of analyzing the situation objectively.

CHART **15** THE PINNACLES	**5** CONSTRUCTIVE FREEDOM
GENERAL	Influences emphasize: Change—frequent, sudden, unexpected. Variety—new and different friends, work, interests. Many experiences, interesting adventures, travel. Freedom—little responsibility. Uncertain finances—likely to be plentiful some of the time, scarce at other times. May change with little warning.
FIRST PINNACLE	Variety and change produce exciting period, make it difficult to feel sense of completion. Dissatisfaction in attempts at building a foundation.
SECOND PINNACLE **THIRD PINNACLE**	Accomplishments and contentment will be based on the ability to be comfortable with the fluctuating environment.
FOURTH PINNACLE	Any desire to retire or slow down is not likely to be fulfilled. Change and variety are likely to continue. Accomplishments and contentment will be based on the ability to be comfortable with the fluctuating environment.
14/5 KARMIC PINNACLE	There is likely to be difficulty in choosing among the many opportunities available. Frustration and less constructive development than desired may occur. Failure to profit from experience instead of repeating mistakes may cause dissatisfaction and may block the easy-going pleasures of this period. Excessive appetite for physical stimulation—food, sex, drink, drugs—may cause problems.

CHART **15** THE PINNACLES	**6**	BALANCE RESPONSIBILITY LOVE

GENERAL   Influences emphasize:

Responsibilities—may cause feeling of restriction.
Home, family, children.
Giving and receiving love.
Opportunities to serve and help others: teaching, counseling, healing.
Promoting harmony.

FIRST PINNACLE   There is likely to be much duty and responsibility related to home and family. There may be strong feelings of limitation because of these pressures at a young age.

The opportunity for an early marriage is possible. This is not necessarily the most desirable course of action.

SECOND PINNACLE

THIRD PINNACLE   Responsibilities and accomplishments will be based on the ability to develop the talents required by the general influences. Home and family may take precedence over business matters.

FOURTH PINNACLE   A harmonious working environment or satisfying retirement is possible. The opportunity for the pleasures of home, marriage, love are likely to be present.

KARMIC PINNACLE   Not applicable.

| CHART **15** THE PINNACLES | **7** ANALYSIS UNDERSTANDING |

GENERAL   Influences emphasize:

Study: learning, investigating, gaining skills, often in scientific, technical, religious or metaphysical fields.

Being alone: usually more comfortable working alone. Marriage is likely to take much effort. May need the isolation to develop inner resources.

Little interest in material matters: there is likely to be little concern with practical affairs. There may be difficulties because of lack of money or material benefits.

FIRST PINNACLE   The subject may encounter difficulties because of a lack of friends. He may have difficulty getting the desired education because of parental pressures—or—he may be pressured into studies when he has little motivation because of his age.

SECOND PINNACLE

THIRD PINNACLE   Responsibilities and accomplishments will be based on the ability to develop the talents required by the general influences. Accomplishments may not produce financial benefits as desired or expected.

FOURTH PINNACLE   This may be a quiet, possibly lonely, time for the development of the inner person. It may be difficult to find comfortable companions.

16/7 KARMIC PINNACLE   The subject is likely to be perceived as "different", causing problems with communication or making others feel that he is difficult to approach. His tendency to introspection or self-centeredness may add to the problem.

Permanent relations—marriage, business partnerships—may be difficult to maintain.

CHART **15** THE PINNACLES	**8** MATERIAL SATISFACTION

GENERAL   Influences emphasize:

Business and commercial activity.
Possibility of success, recognition, status.
Financial and material gain.
Pragmatic orientation. Emotional bias is not likely to be helpful.
Organizational and management abilities.

FIRST PINNACLE   The subject may be involved in business or commercial activity at an early age. He may feel limited or restricted.

SECOND PINNACLE   Responsibilities and accomplishments will be based on the ability to develop the talents required by the general influences.

THIRD PINNACLE

FOURTH PINNACLE   Partial, if any, retirement is probably all that may be expected. There is likely to be a good deal of attention given to business or commercial endeavors.

KARMIC PINNACLE   Not applicable.

CHART **15** THE PINNACLES	**9** SELFLESSNESS HUMANITARIANISM

GENERAL — Influences emphasize:

Drama and emotions.

Need for tolerance and compassion.

Need for an approach with little concern for personal interests.

Need for giving love without expecting it to be returned.

Humanistic, philanthropic or artistic endeavors.

Completion of major endeavors which provide the freedom to move forward. The completion is likely to be highly charged with emotion. The completion may not be desired by the subject, even though its ultimate ends will probably prove beneficial.

FIRST PINNACLE — There may be a difficult completion of a situation involving work or love. Selflessness is often difficult for a young person, so this period is not likely to be easy.

SECOND PINNACLE

THIRD PINNACLE — Responsibilities and accomplishments will be based on the ability to develop the talents required by the general influences. There is likely to be much high drama and strong emotion.

FOURTH PINNACLE — There may be philanthropic or artistic endeavors allowing the subject to give much to the world. Retirement or partial retirement may be possible in conjunction with this work.

KARMIC PINNACLE — Not applicable.

CHART **15** **THE PINNACLES**	**11** ILLUMINATION

GENERAL   Influences emphasize:

> Philosophic, religious or metaphysical studies. Possibility of inspiration and illumination.
> Lack of concern with practical and material matters.
> Problems with associates, particularly business partners or spouse.
> Nervous tension.
>
> See the 2 influences also.

FIRST PINNACLE   It's probably difficult for the young person to use the general influences productively.

SECOND PINNACLE   Responsibilities and accomplishments will be based on the ability to develop the talents required by the general influences.

THIRD PINNACLE

FOURTH PINNACLE   Retirement or partial retirement is possible.

KARMIC PINNACLE   Not applicable.

CHART **15** **THE PINNACLES**	**22** MASTER BUILDER

GENERAL Influences emphasize:

> Large-scale business endeavors or endeavors with the potential for large-scale influence.
> Idealistic approach to secure practical ends.
> Nervous tension.
>
> See the 4 influences also.

FIRST PINNACLE It's probably difficult for the young person to use the general influences productively.

SECOND PINNACLE Responsibilities and accomplishments will be based on the ability to develop the talents required by the general influences.

THIRD PINNACLE

FOURTH PINNACLE Business endeavors with idealistic ends preclude retirement.

KARMIC PINNACLE Not applicable.

CHART **16** PERSONAL YEAR/UNIVERSAL YEAR

PERSONAL YEAR   A medium term cycle describing the yearly approach to events likely to produce growth and development. See Chapter 31, page 521. The Personal Year also describes the individual's position in the 9 Year Epicycle.

UNIVERSAL YEAR   A medium term cycle describing the general yearly trend of the world influences. See Chapter 31, page 519.

CHART **16**	**1**	INDIVIDUATION INDEPENDENCE ATTAINMENT
PERSONAL YEAR/UNIVERSAL YEAR		

PERSONAL YEAR

Start of a 9 Year Epicycle—a time of change, progress, new BEGIN-NINGS. The subject's actions this year will have a significant effect on the course of the next nine years. Inability to begin a venture now may delay prospects until the following Epicycle.

The subject should clarify his goals and start working toward their achievement. He should seek out the opportunities and take advantage of them without hesitation. If the odds are encouraging, chances should be taken. (The opportunities should be studied carefully, though, because impulsiveness isn't likely to be helpful.) The individual can plan and begin a new venture—or make changes or expand an existing venture—or, at least, broaden his interests and activities. Power is high this year—it's a time to ACT. Hard work may be necessary to get a venture moving.

Independence should be emphasized. If there are areas of dependency, this is a fine time to work on them. If existing conditions have been bothering the subject for some time, this is the time to start to break free. This is a time also, to express courage and assertiveness, to act confidently and self-reliantly. Individuality should also be stressed.

This is one of the years of the Epicycle in which an important change is likely. The change is probably due to the individual's own efforts.

UNIVERSAL YEAR

New endeavors and the expansion of existing endeavors. Planning for the future.

A sense of beginning.

CHART **16**	**2** RELATION COOPERATION
PERSONAL YEAR/UNIVERSAL YEAR	

PERSONAL YEAR

A year to wait while ventures begun last year develop slowly. Time is vital for plans to fully mature.

The subject should stay in the background and WAIT for developments. He shouldn't make much effort to move endeavors ahead. Action usually isn't necessary at this time and is likely to force conditions into less constructive channels. Aggressiveness is often followed by problems. The subject must be prepared for delays, detours, stoppages and must be patient.

He should concentrate on working with others in a spirit of COOPERATION, relating to others tactfully and with consideration. Harmony should be emphasized. The details must be taken care of when necessary. The subject may give time and effort to further another's work.

Emotions and sensitivity need to be kept in balance. Difficulty with self-control is likely to heighten the nervous tension and provoke disharmony.

UNIVERSAL YEAR

Emphasis on development of balance, peace and harmony.
Diplomatic missions.
Reconciliations.

A sense of cooperation.

CHART 16
PERSONAL YEAR/UNIVERSAL YEAR

3 EXPRESSION
JOY OF LIVING

PERSONAL YEAR

A special lighter year! Though there are opportunities to expand and develop, the keynote of this year is the experiencing of pleasure and happiness and the expressing of the JOY OF LIVING. (If the Essence or the Transits have a substantially darker tone, the pleasure and happiness are likely to be considerably muffled or completely submerged.)

The subject should approach experiences, if possible, with joy, cheer and enthusiasm. He should enjoy friends, lead an active social life, delight in enjoying himself with a minimum of the cares of responsibility. He shouldn't, though, indulge only in superficial or capricious activities. He should try to be there for others with vibrance and vitality. He may enjoy the deep delights of love and romance.

The subject should concentrate on opportunities for self-improvement, particularly along the lines of his CREATIVE TALENTS. He should use intuition, imagination and inspiration. Advancement or recognition is possible. He may want to particularly emphasize endeavors involving words such as acting, singing or writing.

It's important to handle emotions constructively. The individual should try not to waste energies. He may enjoy the satisfaction and accomplishment of bringing projects to a satisfactory conclusion. Self-indulgence or extravagance are likely to impede progress and downgrade the chance of experiencing pleasures.

UNIVERSAL YEAR

Delight in pleasure.
Emphasis on social life, entertainment.
A sense of the joy of living.

CHART **16**	**4** LIMITATION ORDER SERVICE

ERSONAL YEAR/UNIVERSAL YEAR

PERSONAL YEAR

A year to stabilize ventures, to establish a secure base for future development.

The subject must concentrate on hard work, mental and/or physical, WORK to put a solid base under his endeavors. He will have to search out and strengthen the weak areas, take care of all the details, put everything in order, ready for potential growth. He should proceed in a practical and rational manner, making the most of his ability to organize and manage.

The subject should be sure to meet his obligations. If work is shirked, the resulting leisure isn't likely to be enjoyable. The work may be long and unremitting, but there's much satisfaction to be obtained from its completion. Progress is apt to be slower than expected. The subject shouldn't depend on luck or dreams—they're not much help at this time.

He should be efficient, economical and rational with financial matters and establish a solid foundation here, too, for the future.

The subject can counteract any feelings of limitation or restriction by periodically interspersing some play to relieve the pressure of the work load. He should check on health matters when necessary.

UNIVERSAL YEAR

Economic problems.
Scarcity of jobs.
Financial difficulties.

A sense of work to be accomplished to alleviate problems.

CHART **16**	**5** CONSTRUCTIVE FREEDOM
PERSONAL YEAR/UNIVERSAL YEAR	

PERSONAL YEAR

A year to expand horizons, to grow and change, to delight in the variety of experience. This is a time to enjoy new friends, new opportunities, adventure, excitement, social activities, to revel in FREEDOM.

The subject should concentrate on feeling loose and free. He should move away from old routines, but do it constructively. If he's bogged down, this is a good time to seek out new directions. The opportunities now lie with the new and progressive. Involvement with detail work is likely to feel confining.

The subject must be careful not to scatter his energy in all directions. If there's restlessness or impulsiveness, there's likely to be interferences which cut down the potential of the free-wheeling opportunities.

This is one of the years of the Epicycle in which an important change is likely—probably a change of residence, work or family situation. The change may not be due to the subject's initiative, but the ultimate effect is dependent on his ability to take advantage of the change and use it to help in his forward movement.

UNIVERSAL YEAR

International activities.
New and unusual ventures.
Dynamic progress.

A sense of excitement and adventure.

| CHART **16**
PERSONAL YEAR/UNIVERSAL YEAR | **6** BALANCE
RESPONSIBILITY
LOVE |

PERSONAL YEAR

A year to concentrate on home life, the duties and RESPONSIBIL-ITIES of the FAMILY and close community. The individual should guard against being a doormat or a martyr but must understand the occasional need for sacrifice.

This is a time to help serve the spouse, children, parents and close friends. When necessary, the subject may have to take care of the infirm or elderly. He must make adjustments and work for harmony and balance—this is a good time to resolve tensions. The individual should talk matters over with family and friends, understand and consider everyone's needs, try to be as unselfish and giving as possible.

The subject may enjoy the deep quiet pleasures of romance, love and/or marriage. The more love and affection given, the more returned. This is a good year to get married or to continue in marriage—as long as emotions are balanced and clearly, openly expressed. There's likely to be a good deal of feeling—any attempts to hide or disguise feelings are apt to backfire.

Endeavors outside the home are probably moving slowly. He should give them the attention they need without neglecting domestic responsibilities. The individual must learn to accept the slow pace as well as the many demands on his time (and, often, money). He must have faith that movement is occurring even though it may not be visible to him.

UNIVERSAL YEAR

Interest in welfare, education.
Emphasis on family life.
A sense of close belonging.

CHART **16**	**7** ANALYSIS
PERSONAL YEAR/UNIVERSAL YEAR	UNDERSTANDING

PERSONAL YEAR

A special INTROSPECTIVE year! A vital pause between the intense activities of the 4,5 and 6 Personal Years and the powerful 8 Personal Year. A time to gain an understanding of the self by spending much time in contemplation.

The subject should concentrate on spending time alone or in quiet activities, as free from outside responsibilities as possible. He should try to get away from business pressures. This is a good time to meditate, examine inner depths, rely on the intuition. It's a year to study the past and present—plan for the future. The subject should take little action but rather wait for developments. Associations and experiences may be completed and he may experience some loneliness at times.

The individual should work to develop inner power and spiritual awarenesses. He may develop a broader faith. He may find that new interests are awakened along with new understandings. There may be a desire to study, research, teach or write about technical, scientific, religious or occult subjects, to delve into the fundamentals. This may be the time to lay the theoretical groundwork for later expansion into the business world.

Appearances of coolness or detachment may irritate or alienate others who don't understand the subject's current interests or activities. He shouldn't fight and shouldn't force issues but, instead, use a minimum of quiet explanation. If there are feelings of limitation or confusion, he must wait patiently for the development of more clarity. He should check on health matters when necessary.

UNIVERSAL YEAR

Spiritual, religious or occult expansion.
Inward searchings and studies.

A sense of inner development.

| CHART **16**
PERSONAL YEAR/UNIVERSAL YEAR | **8** MATERIAL SATISFACTION |

PERSONAL YEAR

The ultimate year of ACTION in the Epicycle. The subject's abilities are likely to be operating more effectively now than at any other time in the nine years—if there's a time for ACCOMPLISHMENT, *this is it!* He should take advantage of the situation.

Ventures begun in the 1 Personal Year, then expanded, revised, analyzed in the intervening years, may well come to fruition *now*. The subject should use all available energy and take action at this time for maximum impact. Much of the benefit is likely to accrue in the business world, but all areas of the life are susceptible to the effects of the current dynamic energy. This doesn't mean the individual can do anything, but he can probably do more than at any time in the past seven years.

There are apt to be many opportunities as well as advancement, achievement, recognition and improvement in the financial status. This year can be the fitting culmination of the work that has gone before. (If little work and effort have preceded this year, there may still be benefits, but of a considerably smaller magnitude.)

The subject should approach opportunities in a businesslike manner displaying efficiency, practicality, executive ability and good judgment. He should impress others with his resourcefulness and sustained effort. If possible, he should exude authority and self-confidence while avoiding an emotional and sensitivity imbalance. He must be realistic—he can't act on impractical dreams or visions. He has to keep a sense of perspective at all times.

The work load may deplete the energy. If a strain is present, the level of activity should be lowered. The subject should check on health matters when necessary.

UNIVERSAL YEAR

Plentiful jobs and money.
Progress in material matters—new products, increased productivity.
A sense of material well-being.

CHART **16**	**9** SELFLESSNESS HUMANITARIANISM

PERSONAL YEAR

The end of the Epicycle, the closing of one phase of experience. COMPLETION is the watchword.

The subject should finish and leave behind as many as possible of the areas that have acted as obstacles. He should let go of these negatives—it's easier now than at any other time in the Epicycle. Now is the time to give up relationships that no longer have meaning. Some experiences or people may go out of the life and leave a deep feeling of loss. If experiences or relations show signs of ending, the subject shouldn't fight the ending—rather, he should work to reach a constructive conclusion.

This is the time to complete the good and meaningful experiences which seem to be ready to give way to the new. The subject should carry forward only those experiences and relations with promise for positive development in the approaching Epicycle.

He should give some thought to areas to develop when the 1 Personal Year commences. He shouldn't start anything new at this time, if possible, especially something major like marriage or a new business, although beginnings can be made during the closing months of this year when the vibrations of the coming year can be felt. Activities started in a 9 Personal Year often end prematurely.

The individual must be prepared to experience much drama and emotion. He should express love and compassion, although little may be returned. There may be artistic or creative endeavors.

The subject should check on health matters when necessary.

This is one of the years of the Epicycle in which an important change is likely. The change may be initiated by the individual's efforts or by others' efforts.

UNIVERSAL YEAR

The old tends to fade away.

Religious or spiritual movements emphasizing love and understanding.

A sense of completion.

| CHART **16** | **11** ILLUMINATION |
| PERSONAL YEAR/UNIVERSAL YEAR | |

PERSONAL YEAR

A year in which heightened sensitivity is emphasized. By tuning in to experiences in a special way, expanded awarenesses may be received.

The subject may want to concentrate on experiences involving spiritual or occult matters. Understanding of these experiences may contribute to **INNER DEVELOPMENT** and a deeper use of the intuition.

The individual should prepare for considerable nervous tension, although, even with preparation, there are apt to be difficulties which may detract from the ability to absorb the new awarenesses.

The emphases stressed by the 2 Personal Year are also in effect.

UNIVERSAL YEAR

Metaphysical or religious experiences.
Idealistic developments.

A sense of illumination.

CHART **16**	**22** MASTER BUILDER
PERSONAL YEAR/UNIVERSAL YEAR	

PERSONAL YEAR

A year with possibilities for progress on significant projects or progress on ventures with significant influence. The subject should approach these endeavors only if he is feeling idealistic and extremely capable. Status, recognition and financial gain may result if there are pure humanitarian motives with little concern for personal gain.

Heightened nervous tension usually accompanies the SIGNIFICANT OPPORTUNITIES. The tension is likely to complicate the relation with others and impede progress.

Maturity and high-level power are necessary for advancement. If there are any doubts, revert to the emphases stressed by the 4 Personal Year. Even when the opportunities of the 22 Personal Year are experienced, the emphases of the 4 Personal Year remain in effect.

UNIVERSAL YEAR

Large scale ventures to benefit mankind.
Idealistic endeavors.

A sense of prodigious opportunities.

CHART 17 THE ESSENCE

ESSENCE	A medium term cycle describing probable events or the probable trend of events. See Chapter 32, page 537. Sometimes, desirable means of dealing with the events are also described. These are *not* integral to the Essence itself.
ADDITIONAL EMPHASIS	The number behind the Essence, if there is one, describes an additional emphasis. The karmic Essences—19/1, 13/4, 14/5, 16/7—describe especially significant emphases.
LONG PERIOD OF AN ESSENCE	A long period, five or more years of an Essence, describes a significant emphasis.
ESSENCE AND PERSONAL YEAR WITH SAME NUMBER	Description of the strong negative potential with repeated numbers and some approaches to alleviate the difficulties.

| CHART **17** | **1** | INDIVIDUATION INDEPENDENCE ATTAINMENT |
| THE ESSENCE | | |

1 ESSENCE

Events and opportunities emphasize BEGINNINGS, CHANGE and PROGRESS, such as:

Development of new ideas.
Expanding existing interests.
Increasing status and/or recognition.
Meeting new friends or business associates.
Turning avocation into vocation.

Sometimes, one strong change triggers a sequence of events which forces substantial alterations in almost every facet of the life.

ADDITIONAL EMPHASES

10/1 Similar to the 1 Essence but with a bit more intensity.

19/1 Usually a strong impact on the life.

Opportunities to achieve independence by changing existing limiting situations. The achievement of independence takes much effort, because the subject is likely to feel beset with obstacles and problems. The overcoming of the difficulties is likely to involve important lessons leading to development and growth.

28/1 Opportunities for progress are likely to stress business ventures which emphasize cooperation with others. Too much emphasis on money, status or power is apt to limit advancement.

LONG PERIOD OF 1 ESSENCE

This long period may bring a series of dramatic ongoing changes in the life, or one substantial change with many years between the onset and the conclusion of the direct effects.

1 ESSENCE WITH 1 PERSONAL YEAR

A great deal of stimulation and ample opportunities may make it difficult to clearly perceive the best direction. There may be false starts and dead ends with resultant frustration. The subject should realize that he can't take advantage of all the opportunities. He must pick and choose carefully, always with an eye on the future benefits rather than the current utility.

CHART **17** THE ESSENCE	**2** RELATION COOPERATION

2 ESSENCE

Events and opportunities emphasize COOPERATION and PA-TIENCE, such as:

  Developing relations and associations.
  Working as part of a group to satisfy mutual needs.
  Helping others with their needs.
  Carefully completing details.

Developments are likely to take longer than first expected but us-ing additional effort isn't apt to help. It may even be detrimental or cause potential opportunities to disappear. Delays and tem-porary stoppages may often be frustrating, but they may actually improve the ultimate timing needed for reaching goals.

High emotions and high sensitivity are likely. When faced with an emotional situation, the subject should deal with it directly rather than side-stepping it.

Lowered energy and vitality may be experienced.

ADDITIONAL EMPHASES

  11/2   See the 11 page.

  20/2   Similar to the 2 Essence but with a bit more intensity.

  29/2   See the 11 page.

LONG PERIOD OF 2 ESSENCE

This long period may produce nervous tension due to prolonged high emotions and/or deep frustration due to delays.

2 ESSENCE WITH 2 PERSONAL YEAR

Emotional conflicts may heighten the tension, upset the sensitiv-ity, affect the health. Self-control and a disciplined approach can help maintain a harmonious balance.

A sense of perspective in relation to the delays and difficulties will help relieve frustration. The subject must learn that plans move forward despite the occasional detours.

CHART **17** THE ESSENCE	**3** EXPRESSION JOY OF LIVING

3 ESSENCE

Some events and opportunities emphasize the JOY OF LIVING, such as:

> Meeting new friends, renewing old friendships.
> Engaging in love affairs.
> Receiving pleasure through children.
> Expanding social activities.
> Traveling.

Some events and opportunities emphasize EXPRESSION, such as:

> Producing creative work, particularly with words—singing, acting, writing.
> Advancing talents with classes or study.
> Starting or expanding business interest involving creative endeavors.
> Turning creative avocation into vocation.

Honestly expressed emotions can aid developments, while disguised or repressed feelings are likely to interfere with growth.

Optimism and enthusiasm are apt to open doors, while pessimism and a critical attitude may interfere with opportunities.

The subject should maintain self-discipline to avoid wasting energies or acting capriciously or self-indulgently.

ADDITIONAL EMPHASES

12/3 Advancement of creative abilities may be related to opportunities provided by new or old friends.

21/3 Heightened emotions and sensitivity may cause problems and interfere with opportunities.

30/3 Similar to the 3 Essence but with a bit more intensity.

LONG PERIOD OF 3 ESSENCE

This long period may allow broad creative development in a beautiful and happy time. (When the Transits have a substantially darker tone, the beauty and happiness is likely to be considerably muffled or completely submerged.)

3 ESSENCE WITH 3 PERSONAL YEAR

Unless the subject can maintain strong self-discipline, there's likely to be a considerable waste of energy, a restlessness leading to frivolous and superficial activity, a resultant feeling of lack of pleasure or accomplishment and accompanying frustration.

CHART **17** THE ESSENCE	**4** LIMITATION ORDER SERVICE

4 ESSENCE   Events and opportunities emphasize WORK, such as:

Putting a solid base under a business venture.
Expanding a business.
Ordering or managing affairs.
Dealing with financial matters with a sense of economy.

Development of opportunities requires a practical and realistic view along with hard work, effort, discipline and determination.

Opportunities are likely to feel limiting or restrictive. Progress is usually much slower than expected. The subject should cultivate an awareness of forward movement rather than restriction.

The subject should check on health matters when necessary.

ADDITIONAL EMPHASES

13/4 Usually a strong impact on the life.

Much continual hard work is likely to feel severely restrictive. The subject must accept the responsibility for the work and accomplish it or the restrictive feelings become more intense. Feelings of limitation often grow from the subject's point of view rather than from the work itself.

22/4 See 22 page.

31/4 Much hard work using creative talents can lead to achievement and advancement in business ventures.

LONG PERIOD OF 4 ESSENCE

This long period may bring unremitting hard work with resultant feelings of limitation.

4 ESSENCE WITH 4 PERSONAL YEAR

Feelings of limitation or restriction are likely to be strong. Often, the feelings are related to the subject's point of view as much as or more than to the actual work in hand. The subject should reevaluate his position if there are feelings of being in a rut or plodding along blindly. He should clarify the obstacles and take steps to remove them.

CHART **17** THE ESSENCE	**5** CONSTRUCTIVE FREEDOM

5 ESSENCE

Events and opportunities emphasize FREEDOM, such as:

Experiencing the sudden, unexpected, unusual.
Dealing with constant change and activity.
Engaging in ventures stressing progress.
Enjoying new ideas and experiences.
Meeting new friends.
Traveling.

The subject shouldn't waste energy and go off in every direction. There's likely to be far more opportunity than he can possibly use. He must pick and choose for maximum positive impact on his development.

ADDITIONAL EMPHASES

14/5   Usually a strong impact on the life.

Significant breakthroughs involving freedom are possible.

Many opportunities make choices difficult. The subject should not work only on his own needs or he is likely to alienate others who can help with forward progress. He must focus his energy for maximum benefit.

23/5   Opportunities are likely to derive from use of the creative talents and sensitivity to others.

32/5   Opportunities are likely to derive from use of the creative talents and sensitivity to others.

LONG PERIOD OF 5 ESSENCE

A free-wheeling period. Unless some self-discipline is exercised, most of the energy is likely to be scattered with little accomplishment. Ultimately, there may be feelings of deep frustration.

5 ESSENCE WITH 5 PERSONAL YEAR

Freedom may be misused—by mistaking constant change for forward movement; by getting lost in physical pleasures—food, drink, sex, drugs; by emphasizing self-centered interests with little concern for others. Unless the subject can develop a balanced approach, the opportunities for freedom and change as well as the possibilities for fun and constructive development are likely to prove elusive.

CHART **17** THE ESSENCE	**6** BALANCE RESPONSIBILITY LOVE

6 ESSENCE
Events and opportunities emphasize RESPONSIBILITY and DOMESTIC AFFAIRS, such as:

Handling responsibility involved with home and family.
Experiencing love; getting married or continuing marriage.
This is the best Essence for marriage. A new or continuing marriage may be beautiful if both partners are unselfish. Problems in love and marriage are likey if dominance or self-centeredness is present.
Relating to children.
Serving close community.

ADDITIONAL EMPHASES

15/6 If single, the subject is likely to experience enjoyable social time with a tendency to bypass some responsibilities.
If married, there are likely to be some unsettled areas, occasionally significant problems, if care is not exercised in using freedom.

24/6 Responsibilities related to family, children or parents may feel limiting or restrictive.

33/6 Social activities, trips, creative endeavors center around the home and family.

LONG PERIOD OF 6 ESSENCE
This long period may bring ongoing domestic responsibilities. Lack of acceptance of these responsibilities is likely to bring feelings of restriction. Acceptance of these obligations is apt to bring much love in return.

6 ESSENCE WITH 6 PERSONAL YEAR
Feelings of restriction are likely to be due to heavy family responsibilities, or, at the least, the subject's view of those responsibilities. Much emotion is likely to be in the air. Clear expression and a willingness to share feelings may lead to a better balance. Failure to communicate the feelings may lead to confusion and difficulties.

| CHART **17** THE ESSENCE | **7** ANALYSIS UNDERSTANDING |

7 ESSENCE

Events and opportunities emphasize STUDY and INTROSPEC-TION, such as:

> Writing about scientific, religious or metaphysical subjects.
> Involvement in research or educational pursuits.
> Looking for an understanding of fundamentals.
> Pursuing new interests, often in a field completely different than any in which there's been previous experience.
> Withdrawing for reflection and meditation.
> Searching for inner peace and faith.
> Learning to be comfortable with quiet and repose.

ADDITIONAL EMPHASES

16/7 Usually a strong impact on the life.

A difficult transition period with substantial changes possible in the life pattern. At the end of the period, the subject is often in a better position than at the beginning, but the period provides little in the way of signposts. It is difficult or impossible to clearly comprehend the direction to take. The apparent direction must often be accepted on instinct. Confusion, negativity and frustration may be felt until a final understanding is reached. The turmoil of the period often negates any attempts at study, reflection, or meditation. Much of the energy at this time is devoted to clarifying and searching for the different stages leading to a final breakthrough. With its significant difficulties, this Essence is a fine time to learn the meaning of faith.

25/7 Research or study may be conducted as a member of a group. Sensitivity may be high. Ultimately, a sense of freedom or release may be experienced.

34/7 Use of the creative talents will help in research or study. A good deal of ongoing work is involved here, often leading to feelings of limitation.

LONG PERIOD OF 7 ESSENCE

This long period may point to an extended study time or spiritual retreat. The introspective nature of the work may mean a withdrawal from family and social activities as well as many everyday pursuits.

7 ESSENCE WITH 7 PERSONAL YEAR

Withdrawal, accompanied by moodiness, depression, strong feelings of limitation and emotional discomfort. The subject probably needs more relation to others, more feeling that others care. He should seek help rather than waiting for it to come.

CHART **17** THE ESSENCE	**8** MATERIAL SATISFACTION

8 ESSENCE

Events and opportunities emphasize BUSINESS, such as:

Advancing in the business world and community.

Improving professional standing and reputation.

Receiving financial gain.

Building or expanding current venture, often with dynamic possibilities.

Traveling, possibly on business matters.

Organizational, managerial and executive skills will allow maximum development of opportunities. Practical and rational judgments can win others' confidence and open doors.

Continuous effort and hard work will probably be required to develop the possibilities.

ADDITIONAL EMPHASES

17/8 Unique or unusual ideas are likely to lead to advancement, financial gain and a more independent position.

26/8 Heavy responsibilities must be handled with sensitivity. Too much emotion or poorly expressed emotion is likely to prove detrimental.

35/8 Free-wheeling use of creative talents is likely to lead to advancement, financial gain. The subject should temper the expansive ideas with a sense of practicality for best results.

LONG PERIOD OF 8 ESSENCE

This long period may bring a major business development likely to require a sustained effort. There may be significant rewards for the future. A one-track approach for any extended period is usually disappointing in its ultimate unfolding. The subject should be sure there are some varied interests in his life or run the risk of later regrets and resentment.

8 ESSENCE WITH 8 PERSONAL YEAR

There may be a tendency to strain after money, power or status. The opportunities are there, but undue strain or little concern with others' needs may alienate associates and hurt the potential. Too much strain or too much feeling left unexpressed can affect the health and business prospects.

| CHART **17** THE ESSENCE | **9** SELFLESSNESS HUMANITARIANISM |

9 ESSENCE

Events and opportunities emphasizing DRAMA, EMOTIONS and/or COMPLETION, such as:

Experiencing events of significance filled with much feeling.
Tolerance, compassion and sensitivity can be of great help.

The ending (usually unexpected) of a meaningful experience or close personal relation.
There may be much emotional confusion relating to the ending. (Endings usually indicate a change of interests or the subject moving apart from a close relation—only occasionally is death involved.) The ending usually allows the subject more freedom, but this probably isn't apparent at the time it happens.

Involvement with romance and love affairs.
There may be high emotions and confusion. The lesson may have to be learned that ultimate love doesn't restrict, but rather supports freedom. This lesson may be a difficult one.

Involvement with ventures related to humanitarian, philanthropic or creative endeavors.

ADDITIONAL EMPHASES

18/9 Business opportunities leading to more independence may relate to humanitarian, philanthropic or creative endeavors.

27/9 Unusual viewpoint often expressing extreme sensitivities may aid development of humanitarian, philanthropic or creative endeavors.

36/9 Much responsibility is likely to be involved in humanitarian, philanthropic or creative endeavors.

LONG PERIOD OF 9 ESSENCE

This long period may bring protracted emotional strain or protracted endings.

9 ESSENCE WITH 9 PERSONAL YEAR

Completions are likely to be difficult. High emotions may cause strain. Clear thought and action are probably impeded.

CHART **17** THE ESSENCE	**11** ILLUMINATION

11 ESSENCE	Often, a strong impact on the life.
	Events and opportunities emphasize SPIRITUAL MATTERS and ILLUMINATION.
	There may be some new awareness of great importance which supports the development of faith and inner peace. Sometimes, the new understandings have a profound effect on the entire life, although it's likely to take time for the changes to develop. Looking back, it may be possible to pinpoint an 11 Essence as a time of a major shift in the life.
	Heightened sensitivity may cause problems and misunderstandings. It may also attract new friends who appreciate the sensitivity.
	Nervous tension may alienate some, make difficulties with others. Nervousness may affect the subject's ability to express feelings with clarity.
	See the 2 Essence also.

ADDITIONAL EMPHASES	
29/11	Extreme sensitivity and nervous tension produce problems with relations.

LONG PERIOD OF 11 ESSENCE	This long period may allow time for study and development of new awareness for maximum impact.
	Heightened sensitivity and nervous tension for a prolonged period are likely to place a substantial strain on close relationships.

11 ESSENCE WITH 11 PERSONAL YEAR	Extreme nervous tension and extreme heightened sensitivity makes for problems with relationships. New and unusual awarenesses may cause inner conflict. Communication of these awarenesses is likely to present its own difficulties.

CHART **17** THE ESSENCE	**22** MATERIAL MASTER

22 ESSENCE	Often, a strong impact on the life.
	Events and opportunities emphasize SIGNIFICANT VEN-TURES.
	Opportunities for significant projects or ventures with the potential for significant influence are likely to come to the subject's attention. Unless the subject possesses a significant power potential, he may be accepting a difficult burden.
	Opportunities are likely to emphasize idealistic ends. Unless the subject is extremely altruistic, he may be taking on more than he can handle. There may be benefits here, including recognition, status and financial gain, but these benefits can only be achieved by operating with pure humanistic or philanthropic motives.
	Considerable nervous tension is likely.
	It is usually easier to revert to the 4 Essence. Although the potential for accomplishment is considerably less with the 4, the tension and pressure are significantly reduced.
ADDITIONAL EMPHASES	Not applicable.
LONG PERIOD OF 22 ESSENCE	This long period may bring the possibility of prodigious achievement. Enormous pressure and high nervous tension may be constantly present.
22 ESSENCE WITH 22 PERSONAL YEAR	Extreme nervous tension is likely to affect the possibility of progress. Large-scale business problems and problems with family and business associates probably make life complex and uncomfortable. It is usually more productive to revert to 4·4 energy rather than struggle with the 22·22.

CHART **18** THE TRANSITS

TRANSITS   Medium term cycles describing probable events or the probable trend of events. See Chapter 32, page 537.

| CHART **18**
THE TRANSITS | **1** | INDIVIDUATION
INDEPENDENCE
ATTAINMENT |

A = 1

Important change.
> Often, change of residence.
> Sometimes, change of work situation.

Important decision.
> Significant implications for the future.

Much activity, possibly travel.

New people.
> Business or personal relations.

New opportunities.

A·A
A·J
A·S
J·S

Difficult to choose right opportunities because of excessive activity.
Frustration may result from inability to focus energies for positive results.

J = 10/1

Important change.
> Often, change of residence.
> Sometimes, change of work situation.

Shift in business responsibilities.
> Potential for increased status and responsibility.
> Financial gain.

New people.
> > Business or personal relations.

J·J

Difficult to focus required energy for business affairs because of excessive activity.
The development of the available business opportunities, therefore, may fall short
of the potential.

S = 19/1

Sudden or unexpected change.
> In family, personal relations or work situations.
> May trigger additional changes.
> Implications for the future.
> Adjustments due to change may need time well beyond this year.

Strong emotions.

Unexpected or unusual love affairs.

Creative urges or unusual ideas.

S·S

Emotional upset may be brought on by change.

CHART **18** THE TRANSITS	**2** RELATION COOPERATION

B = 2

Opportunities develop through cooperative efforts.
    Partnerships or group activities.
    Problems likely if there's lack of cooperation.
Beautiful love affairs.
Possibility of marriage.
Emotions may run high and sensitivities may be disturbed.
    Tension may be reduced by patience and joint efforts.
Lowered vitality. Attend to matters of health.

B·B
B·K
B·T
K·T

Tense, nervous period. Possibility of emotional upsets.

K = 11/2

See 11 page.

T = 20/2

Change.
    Often change of residence.
Opportunities develop through cooperative efforts.
    Partnerships or group activities.
    Complications in partnerships or group activities may cause problems.
Love affairs.
    May lead to marriage or affect existing marriage.
Emotions may run high and sensitivities may be disturbed.
    Delays, detours may result.
    Maintain strong self-discipline.
    Reduce stress by spending some time alone.
Lowered vitality and high tension. Attend to matters of health.

T·T

Tense, nervous period. Possibility of substantial emotional upsets.

CHART **18**	**3** EXPRESSION
THE TRANSITS	JOY OF LIVING

C = 3

Friends.
    Meeting new friends, renewing old friendships.
    Enjoyable social activities.
Creative enterprise.
    Advancement by developing talents.
Expansive potential.
    In business or in living conditions.
    May lead to problems with spouse, sometimes aggravated by love affairs.
Extravagant or self-indulgent actions.
    Create difficulties and interfere with opportunities.

C·C
C·L
C·U
L·U

Tendency to scatter energies is likely to cause frustration, interfere with advancement possibilities.

L = 12/3

Friends.
    Meeting new friends, renewing old friendships.
    Enjoyable social activities.
    Love and romance.
Creative enterprise.
    Advancement by developing talents.
Home, marriage, children.
    Pleasure and happiness.
    Added understandings come with honestly expressed feelings.
Travel.
Extravagant or self-indulgent actions.
    Create difficulties and interfere with opportunities.

L·L

Tendency to indolence or selfishness is likely to interfere with advancement possibilities.

U = 21/3

Creative enterprise.
    Advancement by developing talents.
    Lack of confidence may interfere with opportunities.
Unusual love affairs.
    Emotional confusion.
    May interfere with opportunities.
Heightened emotions and sensitivity.
    Poorly expressed or repressed emotions create difficulties.
    Problems with spouse and children.
    Delay major decisions, especially financial decisions, until clear thinking is possible.

U·U

Heightened emotional confusion. Work to understand and express deep feelings clearly and honestly to alleviate difficulties.

| CHART **18** THE TRANSITS | **4** LIMITATION ORDER SERVICE |

D = 4

Much work.
　　Lack of application brings problems.
Practical time, particularly in business matters.
　　Responsibilities.
　　Need for organization.
Build stable base.
　　In business and personal life.
Travel.
Lowered energy. Attend to matters of health.

D·D
D·M
D·V
M·V

Feelings of limitation and restriction, usually due to the unremitting nature of the work.

M = 13/4

Much work.
　　Lack of application brings problems.
Practical time, particularly in business matters.
　　Responsibilities.
　　Need for organization.
　　Opposition possible from business associate.
Finances.
　　Financial advancement possible with careful approach.
Feelings of limitation and restriction.
　　Usually due to unremitting nature of the work.
Love affairs or marriage.
Travel.
Lowered energy. Attend to matters of health.

M·M

Pressure of unremitting work may affect health.

V = 22/4

See 22 page.

CHART **18** THE TRANSITS	**5** CONSTRUCTIVE FREEDOM

E = 5

Sudden, unexpected, unusual and/or exciting events.
Constant change and activity.
Change possible.
   In residence.
   In work situation.
New friends.
   Desire for freedom may bring separation from old friends.
Love affairs.
   May be exciting but often short-lived.
Sudden marriage or separation.
   Restlessness or impulsiveness may motivate actions.
Fluctuating finances.
Travel.

E·E
E·N
E·W
N·W

Haste, impulsiveness, scattering of energy may impede potential benefits.

N = 14/5

Sudden, unexpected, unusual and/or exciting events.
Constant change and activity.
   Possible change in work situation.
New friends.
   Desire for freedom may bring separation from old friends.
Love affairs.
   Sudden, unusual, often short-lived.
Marriage.
   Close if unsettled areas have been previously resolved.
   Lack of balanced emotions cause problems.
Fluctuating finances.
Travel.

N·N

Haste, impulsiveness, scattering of energy may impede potential benefits.

W = 23/5

Sudden, unexpected, unusual and/or exciting events.
   Sudden happenings may be emphasized.
   Little feeling of stability.
Constant change and activity.
Love affairs.
   Sudden, exciting, often short-lived.
Marriage.
   Restlessness emphasizes instability.
   Lack of balanced emotions cause problems.
Travel.
Attend to health matters.

W·W

Haste, impulsiveness, scattering of energy may impede potential benefits.

CHART **18** THE TRANSITS	**6** BALANCE RESPONSIBILITY LOVE

F = 6

Home and family.
    Children bring pleasures and problems.
    Responsibilities.
        Domestic responsibilities may feel restrictive.
        Accept only duties which feel comfortable.
        If feelings of being a doormat exist, lighten the load or the resentment will increase the difficulties.
    Love and romance.
        High level; good period to marry or continue marriage.
        Selfishness brings problems.

F·F
F·O
F·X
O·X

Responsibilities feel uncomfortable and difficult to remove or reduce. Feelings of restriction, resentment and frustration.

O = 15/6

Home and family.
    May be very strong interest.
    Much caring and affection.
    Children bring pleasures and problems.
    Responsibilities.
        Domestic responsibilities may be substantial but satisfying.
        Accept only level of responsibility that is comfortable or expect problems.
    Love and romance.
        High level if can give of self freely.
        Good period to marry or continue marriage.
        Protecting self by withholding feelings likely to cause problems.
    Travel.

O·O

Responsibilities feel extremely restrictive. Subject sometimes feels trapped and resentful.

X = 24/6

Home and family.
    Responsibilities.
        Primarily domestic responsibilities.
        Sacrifices may be necessary.
    Love and romance.
        High level; good period to marry or continue marriage.
        Express feelings openly and clearly to avoid difficulties.
    Strong emotions.
        Differences between parents and children may cause strain.
    Travel.

X·X

Likely to be emotional confusion relating to differences between parents and children. A great deal of this stress and strain is apt to make the home life difficult and significantly affect other areas of the life.

CHART **18** THE TRANSITS	**7** ANALYSIS UNDERSTANDING

G = 7

Study, research, furthering the education.
Expansion in business world.
   Advancement in position.
   Financial gain.
Unusual friends or lovers.
   May cause emotional difficulties.
Tendency to secrecy, introspection.
   May be moody, critical.
Attend to matters of health.

G·G
G·P
G·Y
P·Y

Withdrawal or emotional confusion are likely to block possibilities for progress.

P = 16/7

Study, research, furthering the education.
   May investigate new interests requiring courage of the convictions.
Advancement in business world.
   Slower than expected; may require much patience.
   Advancement likely to be related to previous study, research or education.
Problems with partners or spouse.
   Love affairs may cause emotional difficulties.
   Lack of clear communication brings confusion.
Tendency to secrecy, introspection.
   May be moody, critical, occasionally depressed.
Attend to matters of health.

P·P

Withdrawal or emotional confusion are likely to block possibilities for progress.

Y = 25/7

Study, research, meditation, furthering the education.
New interests.
   May be based on insights gained from meditation.
   Old interests may be abandoned to pursue new.
Increase in spiritual awareness.
   Concern with fundamentals and deep understandings.
   Possible psychic experiences.
Problems with partners, spouse.
   Precipitated by new interests, desire to be alone.
   Lack of clear communication brings confusion.
Tendency to secrecy, introspection.
   May withdraw.
   May be difficult for others to understand.
   May be shy, not want to reveal new thoughts.
Attend to matters of health.

Y·Y

Withdrawal, emotional confusion, misunderstanding or loneliness are likely to block possibilities for progress.

| CHART **18** THE TRANSITS | **8** MATERIAL SATISFACTION |

H = 8

Advancement in business.
  Significant change in authority possible.
  Practical, efficient approach likely to be rewarded.
  A time to build a solid base for future expansion.
Possible financial gain.
  Strain after money blocks possibilities.
  Selfishness interferes with opportunities.
Business affairs may add strain to personal life.
  Repressed feelings in business dealings may obstruct personal affairs.
Travel, possibly on business matters.

H·H
H·Q
H·Z
Q·Z

Possibility of overwork and strain after money. Personal affairs may be neglected in favor of business concerns, bringing problems.

Q = 17/8

Advancement in business.
  Significant change in authority possible.
  Unique or unusual approach may expand or redirect business venture. Care should be taken that "different" approach doesn't alienate potential backers.
Possible financial gain.
  Strain after money blocks possibilities.
  Selfishness interferes with opportunities.
Emotional difficulties.
  Temperamental displays or unclear or repressed feelings may cause personal or business conflicts.
Unusual friends.
  May be helpful in business ventures.

Q·Q

Unusual approach or emotional confusion is likely to interfere strongly with business ventures. Good judgment and a balanced temperament may take substantial effort.

Z = 26/8

Advancement in business.
  Significant change in authority possible.
  Increased reputation and prestige possible.
Possible financial gain.
  Needs good judgment and responsible effort.
Love affairs.
Marriage.
  Possible unusual marriage or unusual spouse.
  Problems unless emotional discipline maintained.
Sensitivity and high emotions.
  Particularly with spouse, close friend or associate.

Z·Z

Over-sensitivity or poorly expressed or repressed emotions may cause difficulties with spouse, close friend or associate.

CHART **18** THE TRANSITS	**9** SELFLESSNESS HUMANITARIANISM

I = 9

Events of significance.
> Often a dramatic time of the life.
> A tolerant and sensitive attitude will be helpful.

Possibility of delays.

Strong emotions likely.
> Deep feelings, high sensitivity, loving and giving will help in ventures. Emotional confusion, repressed feelings, oversensitivity are likely to impede development.
>> A fine balance is necessary but takes effort to maintain.
> Nervous tension, worry or moodiness may be difficult to avoid.

Business opportunities.
> Often related to humanitarian or philanthropic endeavors.

Attend to matters of health, possibly related to emotional upsets.

I·I
I·R

Conflicts and problems stemming from strong emotions and high sensitivity. Considerable delays and uncomfortable endings.

R = 18/9

Events of significance.
> Often a dramatic time of the life.
> A tolerant and sensitive attitude will be helpful.

Possibility of delays.

Strong emotions likely.
> Opportunity to use self-discipline so emotions can be expressed for positive results.

Love and marriage.
> High level possible if emotions are balanced.

Business opportunities.
> Often related to humanitarian or philanthropic endeavors.
> Understanding of others' needs opens doors.

R·R

Considerable delays and uncomfortable endings.

CHART 18
THE TRANSITS

11 ILLUMINATION

K = 11/2   Important spiritual awareness or psychic experience possible.
Opportunities develop through cooperative efforts.
    Partnerships or group activities.
    Problems likely if there's lack of cooperation.
Unusual experiences.
    Unique friends.
    Unusual love affairs.
Emotions may run high and sensitivities may be disturbed.
    Interruptions, misunderstandings.
    Nervous tension is likely to affect relationships.
Attend to matters of health.

K·K   Tense, nervous period. Possibility of substantial emotional upsets.
K·B
K·T

CHART **18**
THE TRANSITS

22 MASTER BUILDER

V = 22/4   Significant projects or ventures with the potential for significant influence.
Practical point of view and idealistic approach needed.
Imagination and intuition required.
Ventures may relate to long-standing dreams.
Much work.
Lack of application brings problems.
Travel.
Nervous tension.
Extravagance is likely to defeat objectives.

V·V   Heightened nervous tension likely to interfere with activities, particularly with relationships. May require scaling down activities to more manageable, less pressure-filled levels.

V·D
V·M   Feelings of limitation and restriction, usually due to the unremitting nature of the work.

CHART 19 PERSONAL MONTH/PERSONAL DAY

PERSONAL MONTH   A short term cycle describing the approach to events for a given month likely to produce growth and development. See Chapter 34, page 581.

PERSONAL DAY   A short term cycle describing the approach to events for a given day likely to produce growth and development. See Chapter 35, page 595.

CONTRIBUTING AND IMPEDING TRAITS   Character traits likely to produce positive results and other character traits likely to contribute to a disappointing time.

CHART **19**	**1**	INDIVIDUATION INDEPENDENCE ATTAINMENT

PERSONAL MONTH/PERSONAL DAY

PERSONAL MONTH

The subject should take the steps he's been contemplating.
  Now is the time to act.
  He shouldn't be afraid to take a chance if the odds are encouraging.

A time of change.
  The subject should make the change or move closer to making the change in the future.
  He should break up old conditions he doesn't like or attack a weak point.

A time to begin something new.
  The subject should begin a new activity, friendship, relation, vocation.
  At the least, a different phase of an existing experience should be begun.

The subject should be himself.
  He should emphasize his individuality and uniqueness.
  He should express his originality and creativity.
  He shouldn't overdo it and irritate or alienate others.

19/1 PERSONAL MONTH

Obstacles to taking advantage of opportunities may result from:
  Egotism, self-centeredness, domination, over-aggressiveness,
                                or
  Laziness, fear, timidity, inability to act decisively.

PERSONAL DAY

The start of the daily Epicycle. Potentially, one of the more dynamic days of the month.

A day to make a beginning or a change, to put a new plan into action. The activities on a 1 Personal Day seem to receive an extra impetus, but the activities must reflect a sense of commitment, a desire to make things happen and a capability of getting the job under way. Without these attributes, the activities will tend to fizzle and produce minimum impact.

19/1 PERSONAL DAY

Self-centeredness, over-aggression, fear or indecisiveness are likely to impede progress on a 19/1 Personal Day. If any of these characteristics are present, use the day to try to change or overcome these tendencies. *Don't* use the day for significant beginnings—you're liable to get off on the wrong foot.

CONTRIBUTING AND IMPEDING TRAITS

A 1 Personal Month or 1 Personal Day is likely to produce positive results when the subject is:
  Assertive, ambitious, authoritative, vigorous, progressive.

A 1 Personal Month or 1 Personal Day is likely to be disappointing when the subject is:
  Overly aggressive, egotistic, impatient, selfish, fearful, submissive or stubborn.

CHART **19**	**2** RELATION COOPERATION
PERSONAL MONTH/PERSONAL DAY	

PERSONAL MONTH

A time to be quiet, understanding.
    The subject should be sensitive to the subtleties.
    He should keep his emotions in balance.
    He should be considerate.

A time to wait for developments.
    The subject should exercise patience.
    He shouldn't make much effort to push endeavors ahead.

A time to cooperate with others on own projects or others' ventures.
    The subject should work quietly for harmony.
    He should take care of the details.

PERSONAL DAY

A day with little direct feeling of power, although developments may progress of their own accord. The subject should try to be aware of the subtle nuances—he may learn something of significance for the future. This could be a pleasant, but probably quiet, social time. It's a good day to cooperate with others in their work or to enjoy one's own routine. The subject should help the routine move forward smoothly, without changing or even attempting to change direction.

CONTRIBUTING AND IMPEDING TRAITS

A 2 Personal Month or 2 Personal Day is likely to produce positive results when the subject is:
    Relaxed, responsive, tactful, gentle, supportive.

A 2 Personal Month or 2 Personal Day is likely to be disappointing when the subject is:
    Meddling, oversensitive, scheming, apathetic, tactless or inconsiderate.

| CHART **19**
PERSONAL MONTH/PERSONAL DAY | **3** EXPRESSION
JOY OF LIVING |

PERSONAL MONTH

A time to enjoy oneself.
  The subject should move responsibilities past this month if possible.
  He should express his happiness and delight so it's contagious.
A good time to vacation and travel.

A time to express oneself.
  Artistic creation—art, music, writing, etc.
  A time to use imagination, intuition, inspiration.

A time to spend with friends.
  The subject should enjoy a lively social life.
  He should entertain or be entertained.

PERSONAL DAY

A day, simply, to have a good time, usually with others. The subject should schedule visits with friends, social affairs or entertainment of all sorts. He should make his delight contagious if possible—express his pleasure in the day with all the cheer and enthusiasm he feels, express the beauty in the world with his creative talents. This is a good day to practice a musical instrument, to paint a landscape, to write a poem. In many ways, the simplest of the days in the daily Epicycle—in another sense, one of the most profound.

CONTRIBUTING AND IMPEDING TRAITS

A 3 Personal Month or 3 Personal Day is likely to produce positive results when the subject is:
  Enthusiastic, friendly, imaginative, optimistic, joyful.

A 3 Personal Month or 3 Personal Day is likely to be disappointing when the subject is:
  Superficial, extravagant, ostentatious, critical, inhospitable or worrying.

CHART **19**	**4**	LIMITATION ORDER SERVICE
PERSONAL MONTH/PERSONAL DAY		

PERSONAL MONTH

A time to work hard.
> The subject should build a solid foundation.
> He should strengthen weak areas.
> He should take care of the details.

A time to put everything in order for possibility of future expansion.
> The subject should proceed practically, rationally.
> He should organize, systematize.

A time to try to clarify and understand the feelings of limitation.
> The subject should clarify the limitations of his own making and plan to eliminate them.
> He should clarify the limitations due to his point of view and work on shifting that point of view.
> He should clarify the limitations which are comparatively unchangeable and study how to deal with them in a more satisfactory manner.

A time to take care of the health.

13/4 PERSONAL MONTH

Feelings of limitation or restriction are likely to be strongly emphasized by:
> Rigidity, obstinacy, dogmatism,
> or
> Laziness, inability to apply self to the work at hand, tendency to disorganization.

PERSONAL DAY

A day to complete routine tasks, to keep the nose to the grindstone. This is a good time to put a sustained effort forward, particularly when there's involvement with a not so agreeable chore. The subject should make sure to stay in line, not look for anything new. If he finds a new opportunity, it may be more difficult to deal with than on some more propitious days. The subject isn't likely to look forward to a 4 Personal Day, but he'll find it's vital to make the rest of the daily Epicycle go. He may even end up with the satisfaction of getting those jobs out of the way that have been around too long.

13/4 PERSONAL DAY

Feelings of limitation or restriction, resistance, laziness or disorganization are likely to impede progress on a 13/4 Personal Day. If any of these characteristics are present, the day should be used to try to change or overcome these tendencies. The day shouldn't be used for anything but straightforward routine tasks—any other work is likely to present problems rather than opportunities.

CONTRIBUTING AND IMPEDING TRAITS

A 4 Personal Month or 4 Personal Day is likely to produce positive results when the subject is:
> Serious, constructive, methodical, practical, conscientious.

A 4 Personal Month or 4 Personal Day is likely to be disappointing when the subject is:
> Resistant, stubborn, contrary, unfocused, lazy or disorganized.

CHART **19**	
PERSONAL MONTH/PERSONAL DAY	**5** CONSTRUCTIVE FREEDOM

PERSONAL MONTH

A time to expand horizons.
  The subject should enjoy new people, places, opportunities, activities.
  He may enjoy adventure and excitement.
  He may enjoy social activities.

A time to exploit changes.
  The subject should initiate changes or, at the least, take advantage of them.
  He should drop the old, look for the new.
  He should take a chance if the odds are encouraging.

A time to feel loose and free.
  The subject should have fun, make a splash.
  He should enjoy the different, unusual, unexpected.
  He should take a vacation or travel.
  He should try to minimize responsibilities (but if there are responsibilities, they should be attended to.)

14/5 PERSONAL MONTH

Obstacles to taking advantage of opportunities may result from:
  Erratic nature.
  Repeating mistakes instead of profiting from experience.
  Fear of freedom. Fear of taking risks.
  Excessive appetite for physical stimulation—food, drink, drugs or sex.

PERSONAL DAY

Potentially, one of the more dynamic days of the month.

A day for the subject to try something new or to make an important change. He's likely to feel freer, more buoyant, willing to take a risk. And the vibrations are with him! If ever there's a day that will add positive energy to even the wildest of ideas, the 5 Personal Day is it! If there's something that the subject has been wanting to do, something that's a little risky or scary, he should save it for a 5 Personal Day and move forward on it then with all the enthusiasm he can muster.

The subject can have a good time, too. If he exploits the sense of adventure and excitement that's in the air, he can end up greatly exhilarated.

14/5 PERSONAL DAY

Restlessness, fear of taking risks, excessive appetite for physical stimulation—any or all are likely to impede progress on a 14/5 Personal Day. If any of these characteristics are present, the day should be used to try to change or overcome these tendencies. The subject shouldn't try something new unless it feels like the right thing to do. Otherwise, it's not likely to work out in his favor.

CONTRIBUTING AND IMPEDING TRAITS

A 5 Personal Month or 5 Personal Day is likely to produce positive results when the subject is:
  Adventurous, flexible, imaginative, resourceful.

A 5 Personal Month or 5 Personal Day is likely to be disappointing when the subject is:
  Thoughtless, irresponsible, nervous, fearful or uncertain.

CHART **19**	**6**	BALANCE RESPONSIBILITY LOVE
PERSONAL MONTH/PERSONAL DAY		

PERSONAL MONTH

A time to concentrate on the duties and responsibilities of domestic life.
   The subject should take care of needs of spouse, children, parents, possibly close friends.
   He should put other's needs before his own.
   He should help provide a harmonious, beautiful environment in the home.

A time to enjoy the pleasure of romance, love and/or marriage.
   The more affection and love given, the more returned.

A time to enjoy children and the pleasures of children's activities.

A time to express oneself.
   Artistic creation—art, music, writing, etc.
   A time to use imagination, intuition, inspiration.

PERSONAL DAY

A day to enjoy home and family. There may be work to accomplish around the house, there may be activities to attend with spouse and children, there may be simply the pleasures of domestic life. There may also be quarrels to be mediated, hurt feelings to be soothed, special service or assistance to be given.

The subject should give out much in the way of friendship, affection, love—as much or more will probably be returned.

CONTRIBUTING OR IMPEDING TRAITS

A 6 Personal Month or 6 Personal Day is likely to produce positive results when the subject is:
   Friendly, loving, giving, understanding, sympathetic.

A 6 Personal Month or 6 Personal Day is likely to be disappointing when the subject is:
   Interfering, over-emotional, unforgiving, worrying, intolerant, uninvolved or selfish.

CHART **19** PERSONAL MONTH/PERSONAL DAY	**7** ANALYSIS UNDERSTANDING

PERSONAL MONTH	The subject should spend time alone. He should meditate, reflect, analyze. He should review the past and present, plan for the future. He should learn to be content alone. He should try, as much as possible, to be relieved from business pressures or family responsibilities. A time to develop inner power, spiritual awareness. The subject may want to look into religious, metaphysical or occult ventures. A time to explore fundamentals. Studying, researching, writing or teaching. A time to take care of health.
16/7 PERSONAL MONTH	Others may be confused, disconcerted or alienated causing interference with quiet activities because of: Inflexibility, self-containment, "different" wavelength, or Timid, shy, retiring manner.
PERSONAL DAY	A day to spend at least some time alone getting in touch with deep inner feelings, inner power, special awarenesses possibly still in the process of formation. A good time to review the last few days or weeks and plan for the next few days or weeks. The subject should make time, if possible, for at least a little quiet meditation and observe how much this contributes to his life. He should leave beginnings and changes for another day. He shouldn't expect any dramatic developments on this day, either.
16/7 PERSONAL DAY	A "different" wavelength, self-centeredness, an argumentative attitude or a withdrawn manner are likely to make the subject difficult to approach. Others may be disconcerted or confused, causing possible problems in business or family matters. Explaining oneself clearly may alleviate difficulties but clear communication, unclouded by emotion, may be difficult at this time.
CONTRIBUTING OR IMPEDING TRAITS	A 7 Personal Month or 7 Personal Day is likely to produce positive results when the subject is: Contemplative, peaceful, poised. A 7 Personal Month or 7 Personal Day is likely to be disappointing when the subject is: Critical, inflexible, withdrawn, over-analytical.

CHART 19

8 MATERIAL SATISFACTION

PERSONAL MONTH	A time to act dynamically.

A time to act dynamically.
> The subject is likely to have more ability to make things happen, particularly in regard to business or material matters, than in any other Personal Month.
> He should act decisively for maximum impact.

A time to take advantage of opportunities.
> Possibility of advancement, recognition.
> Possibility of financial improvement.
> Possibility of business expansion.

The subject should approach matters in a businesslike manner.
> He should act practically and realistically.
> He should express himself with authority and self-confidence.

PERSONAL DAY

A day when the subject possesses a great deal of ability to make things happen—potentially, one of the more dynamic days of the month. A decisive use of power today is likely to register a maximum impact, particularly in business or financial matters. This is a good time to make things happen the way the subject wants—an especially fine time to discuss or sign a contract or agreement. An action now may prove significant in regard to accomplishment, advancement and/or financial improvement. The subject should explore ventures with an understanding of others' needs and desires.

CONTRIBUTING AND IMPEDING TRAITS

An 8 Personal Month or 8 Personal Day is likely to produce positive results when the subject is:
> Confident, dynamic, organized, realistic, discriminating.

An 8 Personal Month or 8 Personal Day is likely to be disappointing when the subject is:
> Bullying, impatient, over-ambitious, unreasonable, careless, impractical or lacking in confidence.

CHART **19**	**9** SELFLESSNESS
PERSONAL MONTH/PERSONAL DAY	HUMANITARIANISM

PERSONAL MONTH

A time to complete experiences, activities, relationships.
    The subject should end ventures as constructively as possible.
    He should expect drama and strong emotions.

The subject should be prepared to help others.
    He should work at philanthropic or humanistic endeavors.
    He should give of himself with little thought of reward.
    He should be generous, kind, compassionate.

A time to express oneself.
    Artistic creation—art, music, writing, etc.
    A time to use imagination, intuition, inspiration.

PERSONAL DAY

The end of the daily Epicycle.

A day for completions. It's usually easier to complete a matter on a 9 Personal Day than on any other day. Some ventures are never particularly easy to end, but even these are probably more satisfactorily finished on a 9 Personal Day. Endings, of course, tend to be connected to much drama and emotion. Today, with or without the endings, there's likely to be heightened feelings displayed. The subject should try to be sensitive to everyone, to be compassionate and understanding no matter what the situation. He shouldn't continue an experience which he wants ended just because the emotions are higher than expected; he should act with an awareness of others' needs and desires.

CONTRIBUTING OR IMPEDING TRAITS

A 9 Personal Month or 9 Personal Day is likely to produce positive results when the subject is:
    Charitable, broadminded, compassionate, forgiving, sensitive, tolerant.

A 9 Personal Month or 9 Personal Day is likely to be disappointing when the subject is:
    Intolerant, over-emotional, self-centered, insensitive, unfeeling or inflexible.

| CHART **19**
PERSONAL MONTH/PERSONAL DAY | **11** ILLUMINATION |

PERSONAL MONTH

A time for inner growth and heightened sensitivity.

Psychic or spiritual experiences are possible.
New awarenesses.
Inspiration.
Illumination.

Nervous tension is likely.

See 2 Personal Month also.

PERSONAL DAY

A day to heed inner voices and to grow in understanding and sensitivity. Unless there's an 11 core element, there's usually little awareness of the possibilities and the 11 Personal Day is generally reduced to a 2 Personal Day. Even with an 11 core element, advantage can only occasionally be taken of these particular energies.

Nervous tension is likely.

See 2 Personal Day also.

CONTRIBUTING AND IMPEDING TRAITS

An 11 Personal Month or 11 Personal Day is likely to produce positive results when the subject is:
Idealistic, intuitive, sensitive.

An 11 Personal Month or 11 Personal Day is likely to be disappointing when the subject is:
Fanatical, unfocused, apathetic.

CHART **19**	**22** MASTER BUILDER
PERSONAL MONTH/PERSONAL DAY	

PERSONAL MONTH

A time to start or advance on significant projects or ventures with significant influence.

Recognition and financial gain are possible if the subject has pure humanitarian motives and little concern with personal gain.

Nervous tension is likely.

See 4 Personal Month also.

PERSONAL DAY

A day with vast power potential. Unless there's a 22 core element, there's usually little awareness of the possibilities and the 22 Personal Day is generally reduced to a 4 Personal Day. Even with a 22 core element, advantage can only occasionally be taken of this particular energy.

Nervous tension is likely.

See 4 Personal Day also.

CONTRIBUTING AND IMPEDING TRAITS

A 22 Personal Month or 22 Personal Day is likely to produce positive results when the subject is:
  Dynamic, humanitarian, idealistic, inspirational, visionary.

A 22 Personal Month or 22 Personal Day is likely to be disappointing when the subject is:
  Lacking in confidence, concerned with personal gain, indecisive.

CHART 20 THE EPICYCLE

NINE YEAR EPICYCLE, MONTH BY MONTH

This chart describes the complete nine year Epicycle, month by month. See Chapter 31, page 524, and Chapter 34, page 584.

In the first two months of each year, the waning effect of the preceding Personal Year is noted. In the last three months of each year, the developing effect of the approaching Personal Year is noted.

CHART **20** THE EPICYCLE	**1**	INDIVIDUATION INDEPENDENCE ATTAINMENT

1
PERSONAL
YEAR

A time to plan and begin.
A time to make changes, expand.
    The subject should take action.
He should be prepared for an important change.

	SEPTEMBER 1 PERSONAL MONTH New plans or activities may be placed on course or expanded dramatically. Advantage may be taken of progressive opportunities.

JANUARY 2 PERSONAL MONTH
A time to wait for developments on plans made at end of last year.
End of 9 Personal Year: Time should be allowed for satisfactory endings without forcing situations.

OCTOBER 2 PERSONAL MONTH
Quietly work toward harmony after three month forward surge.
Start of 2 Personal Year: Developments should be watched with great patience while waiting.

FEBRUARY 3 PERSONAL MONTH
Creative and verbal talents may be used to initiate changes. Friends may open doors.
End of 9 Personal Year: An imaginative approach may be used to end an activity ready for completion.

NOVEMBER 3 PERSONAL MONTH
Inspiration, enthusiasm and joie de vivre may be used to involve others in new ventures.
Start of 2 Personal Year: Friends and social life may be enjoyed, but emotions must be kept in balance.

MARCH 4 PERSONAL MONTH
Changes may be initiated with hard work. Organization and detail work may be necessary to get new ventures under way.

DECEMBER 4 PERSONAL MONTH
Foundation for future developments may begin. Hard work now will pay off later.
Start of 2 Personal Year: Things should be allowed to fall into place without force or persuasion.

APRIL 5 PERSONAL MONTH
Exciting opportunities may be exploited for beginnings, progress and expansion. Travel may present unusual or unexpected possibilities.

MAY 6 PERSONAL MONTH
Changes may be instituted related to home, family or lovers. Serving others may open new avenues. Emotional balance is important.

JUNE 7 PERSONAL MONTH
Goals, progress should be clarified. Change and forward development may be planned. Time may be spent in quiet contemplation of the unfolding Epicycle.

JULY 8 PERSONAL MONTH
Decisive move forward, particularly in relation to material or financial matters possible. Business ventures may be started or expanded.

AUGUST 9 PERSONAL MONTH
Plans may be completed for forward movement in this Epicycle. Roadblocks to progress, independence may be eliminated.

CHART **20** **THE EPICYCLE**	**2** RELATION ASSOCIATION

2
PERSONAL
YEAR

A time to wait, cooperate.
A time to stay in the background.
  The subject should be receptive.

  (Receptive 11 Personal Year is sometimes substituted for the 2 Personal Year.)

	AUGUST 1 PERSONAL MONTH Areas requiring tact and diplomacy advanced quietly. Ventures progress with little direct effort; sensitivity and emotional balance may assist.
	SEPTEMBER 11/2 PERSONAL MONTH *2 Personal Month:* Progress may be behind-the-scenes. Issues should not be forced. *11 Personal Month:* New awarenesses may increase sensitivity. Nervous tension may interfere with opportunities.
JANUARY 3 PERSONAL MONTH Friends and social life may be enjoyed while awaiting developments. Artistic talent may be used for avocation. *End of 1 Personal Year:* Friends may advance opportunities if not pressured.	**OCTOBER** 3 PERSONAL MONTH Creative talents and heightened sensitivity may be used to expand quietly and cautiously. *Start of 3 Personal Year:* Verbal ability and imagination may be of considerable significance.
FEBRUARY 4 PERSONAL MONTH Others may be helped with their work in a sensitive manner. *End of 1 Personal Year:* Hard work progresses but in an unobtrusive way, on ventures started last year.	**NOVEMBER** 13/4 PERSONAL MONTH Feeling of limitation is likely to be strong. Work takes much time but results may be less than desired. *Start of 3 Personal Year:* Feelings may be lightened by spending time socializing and entertaining.
MARCH 5 PERSONAL MONTH New people, travel and unusual may be enjoyed. Opportunities should be accepted to advance as long as they flow readily and without pressure. Long-shot possibilities should be ignored.	**DECEMBER** 5 PERSONAL MONTH Expansive opportunities may be exploited with a bit more vigor than in previous months though still not aggressively. *Start of 3 Personal Year:* Fun and adventure can be enjoyed—activity likely to point to next year.
APRIL 6 PERSONAL MONTH Devotion to home and family—the pleasures of friendship, love and affection may be enjoyed. Family members may be helped in their work with sensitivity.	
MAY 7 PERSONAL MONTH Development of ventures started last year may be examined; desirable path for remainder of this year may be clarified; commitment to patient waiting should be renewed.	
JUNE 8 PERSONAL MONTH Power may be used to help others with their projects with spirited cooperation. Aggressive forward moves shouldn't be encouraged.	
JULY 9 PERSONAL MONTH Completion of waiting period for some phase of experience expressing progress. Conclusion of a cooperative effort likely.	

| CHART **20** THE EPICYCLE | **3** EXPRESSION JOY OF LIVING |

3 PERSONAL YEAR

A time to express the joy of living.
A time to concentrate on self-improvement.
The subject should take action.

JULY 1 PERSONAL MONTH
Enthusiastic advance, exploiting creativity, imagination and verbal skills. Opportunities created by friends or social situations may be developed.

AUGUST 11/2 PERSONAL MONTH
2 Personal Month: Developments should be awaited on last month's actions. Friends' endeavors may be helped with subject's creative input.

11 Personal Month: Others may be inspired by transmitting feelings of joyous awareness. Progress can be blocked by over-sensitivity.

SEPTEMBER 3 PERSONAL MONTH
Expanding creative ability and artistic or verbal talents may be used to advance. Friends and social life, travel and entertainment may be enjoyed.

JANUARY 4 PERSONAL MONTH
Foundations may be firmed up with hard work, imagination and creative input.

End of 2 Personal Year: Friends should be approached diplomatically to help with the work.

OCTOBER 4 PERSONAL MONTH
A time to organize and take care of the details of opportunities advanced by creative impulses.

Start of 4 Personal Year: Excessive work likely to feel limiting.

FEBRUARY 5 PERSONAL MONTH
Friends, adventure and travel may provide opportunities for expansion. Freer feelings are possible than all of last year.

End of 2 Personal Year: Some caution should be exercised in moving forward.

NOVEMBER 14/5 PERSONAL MONTH
Opportunities for creative advancement may be impeded by restlessness or impulsiveness.

Start of 4 Personal Year: Work to be accomplished now seems decidedly out of place.

MARCH 6 PERSONAL MONTH
The joy of living may be expressed with family and close friends. Creativity and inspiration may be used to ensure harmony in the domestic life.

DECEMBER 6 PERSONAL MONTH
Merriment, enthusiasm and joy center around home, family. Creative endeavors may help to serve others.

Start of 4 Personal Year: Domestic duties may feel restrictive at the end of this expansive year.

APRIL 7 PERSONAL MONTH
Creative talents may be developed by spending time working alone, exploring possibilities of artistic and verbal skills. Use of talents during rest of the year should be contemplated.

MAY 8 PERSONAL MONTH
Forward dynamic movement using creative approach may be used, particularly to further business interests. Friends and social skills may unlock doors.

JUNE 9 PERSONAL MONTH
Creative preparation may be completed for new or expanded venture. If friendship is ending, tolerance and compassion should be expressed.

CHART **20** THE EPICYCLE

4 LIMITATION ORDER SERVICE

4 PERSONAL YEAR	A time to work hard, take care of the details. A time to put everything in order. The subject should take action only in order to consolidate. (Active 22 Personal Year is sometimes substituted for the 4 Personal Year.)

	JUNE 1 PERSONAL MONTH Much work may be required to take advantage of somewhat muted opportunities. Increased independence may depend on working hard to break up old conditions.
	JULY 11/2 PERSONAL MONTH *2 Personal Month:* Hard work in cooperation with others likely. Progress may be difficult to see. *11 Personal Month:* Inner growth may be related to thoughts about work and responsibility. Nervous tension may add to restrictive feelings.
	AUGUST 3 PERSONAL MONTH Break from work if possible—a time to socialize, play and travel. First pause in pressure since beginning of year—another difficult month to follow. Lots of work yet to come.
	SEPTEMBER 13/4 PERSONAL MONTH Harshly restrictive work load likely to bring feelings of limitation. Responsibilities should be handled with awareness of foundation being built for future growth.
JANUARY 5 PERSONAL MONTH Much activity and excitement. Opportunities may be misleading since much more work is required than is at first apparent. *End of 3 Personal Year:* Joy of living may be expressed but duties must not be neglected.	**OCTOBER 5 PERSONAL MONTH** New people, adventures and excitement may be enjoyed as foil for continuing organization and work. Work should not be neglected or there may be regrets later. *Start of 5 Personal Year:* Some feelings of expansion may provide relief in difficult year.
FEBRUARY 6 PERSONAL MONTH Much work and organization in family and home matters. Others' needs may take preference over needs of the subject. *End of 3 Personal Year:* Pleasures of spouse and children may be enjoyed.	**NOVEMBER 6 PERSONAL MONTH** Harmony at home may require special effort related to family duties and responsibilities. *Start of 5 Personal Year:* Domestic fun and excitement may be enjoyed as welcome respite from work.
MARCH 7 PERSONAL MONTH Time may be spent alone to analyze duties and responsibilities. Work should be planned to build desirable foundation.	**DECEMBER 7 PERSONAL MONTH** Progress since start of the Epicycle should be evaluated. Direction of future activity can be planned. *Start of 5 Personal Year:* Work and planning may feel restrictive with excitement of next year becoming apparent.
APRIL 8 PERSONAL MONTH Business or material interests may be advanced by working hard and organizing. Significant effort may be required, but likely to bring possibilities of advancement.	
MAY 9 PERSONAL MONTH Activity or relation with limiting tendencies may be completed. Working hard on humanistic or philanthropic ventures may be satisfying.	

CHART **20** THE EPICYCLE	**5** CONSTRUCTIVE FREEDOM

5 PERSONAL YEAR
A time to make changes, expand.
A time to seek new directions.
　　The subject should take action.
　　He should be prepared for an important change.

	MAY 1 PERSONAL MONTH Dynamic forward move with expansive, progressive opportunities possible. Unusual or unexpected support may be combined with own enthusiasm for advancement.
	JUNE 11/2 PERSONAL MONTH *2 Personal Month:* Expansive possibilities may develop by helping others with their ventures. *11 Personal Month:* Spiritual expansion leading to new directions is possible. Heightened sensitivity may increase awareness of opportunities.
	JULY 3 PERSONAL MONTH Time for pleasure with friends, travel and adventure. Joy of living may be expressed in unusual, unique or unexpected experience with related changes leading to expansion.
	AUGUST 13/4 PERSONAL MONTH Failure to accomplish work now may interfere with possibilities later this year. Even minor tasks may feel restrictive after several months of free-wheeling expansion.
	SEPTEMBER 14/5 PERSONAL MONTH Heightened excitement, activity and opportunities. Pleasure and expansion may be impeded by restless nature or excessive appetite for physical stimulation.
JANUARY 6 PERSONAL MONTH Changes and expansion in home and family may create new sense of excitement and adventure in domestic life. *End of 4 Personal Year:* Family duties requiring hard work should not be neglected.	**OCTOBER 6 PERSONAL MONTH** Excitement and activity in family activities or relating to friendship, affection or love. *Start of 6 Personal Year:* Domestic duties liable to be present. Should be started, at the very least.
FEBRUARY 7 PERSONAL MONTH A time alone for study or meditation may lead to changes and new directions. Restlessness and introspective needs may conflict. *End of 4 Personal Year:* A time to plan means of taking advantage of new awarenesses.	**NOVEMBER 16/7 PERSONAL MONTH** Self-centered or retiring manner and "different" wavelength hampering communication may interfere with opportunities for expansion. *Start of 6 Personal Year:* Reflection and domestic issues may block excitement and opportunities.
MARCH 8 PERSONAL MONTH Realistic, practical approach with combined dynamic awareness of new directions may begin, change or expand business ventures.	**DECEMBER 8 PERSONAL MONTH** New people and opportunities, particularly in the business world, may point dramatically in progressive directions. *Start of 6 Personal Year:* Business and domestic interests must be in harmony to allow expansion.
APRIL 9 PERSONAL MONTH An important relation or experience may founder or end, allowing pursuit of different, more progressive course. Deep feelings are likely to be involved.	

CHART 20 **THE EPICYCLE**	**6** BALANCE RESPONSIBILITY LOVE

6 PERSONAL YEAR

A time to take care of family responsibilities.
A time to work for harmony.
The subject should be receptive.

APRIL 1 PERSONAL MONTH
Breakdown of old conditions likely to be helpful with home and family. New start of activity or relation may add to balance in domestic life.

MAY 11/2 PERSONAL MONTH
2 Personal Month: A time of quiet with emotions in balance while awaiting developments related to home and family.
11 Personal Month: Increased awareness may add balance, harmony to domestic environment.

JUNE 3 PERSONAL MONTH
A time to entertain, socialize and enjoy spouse, children or close friends. Creative or artistic talents may be used to beautify home life.

JULY 13/4 PERSONAL MONTH
Matters involving home, family may be organized with hard work. Domestic duties, responsibilities are likely to feel limiting and oppressive.

AUGUST 14/5 PERSONAL MONTH
Restlessness and need for excessive physical stimulation may upset harmony at home. Fear of taking risks may impede needed changes or expansion in domestic matters.

SEPTEMBER 6 PERSONAL MONTH
Duties and responsibilities of home and family may bring satisfaction along with a sense of restriction. Deep pleasures of love and marriage may be especially enjoyable.

JANUARY 7 PERSONAL MONTH
Time may be spent alone reviewing past and present, contemplating future of home and family matters.
End of 5 Personal Year: Waning expansive desires may conflict with introspective needs.

OCTOBER 7 PERSONAL MONTH
Time may be spent alone analyzing domestic responsibilities. Home and family matters should be taken care of when necessary.
Start of 7 Personal Year: New awarenesses may be developed to aid in harmonizing home environment.

FEBRUARY 8 PERSONAL MONTH
Dynamic power used now may advance business interests, strongly affect domestic life.
End of 5 Personal Year: Unusual or exciting opportunities may conflict with family needs.

NOVEMBER 8 PERSONAL MONTH
Decisive actions may be taken to better balance domestic matters with business interests.
Start of 7 Personal Year: Long-range plans may be contemplated to reduce family/business conflicts.

MARCH 9 PERSONAL MONTH
Completion of friendly or loving relation may create strongly emotional situation. Tolerance and compassion are probably required.

DECEMBER 9 PERSONAL MONTH
Completion of phase of domestic activity may add to household harmony.
Start of 7 Personal Year: Experiences may be completed to allow for more contemplative time next year.

CHART **20** THE EPICYCLE	**7** ANALYSIS UNDERSTANDING

7 PERSONAL YEAR

A time to study past and present—plan for the future.
A time to reflect, analyze, meditate.
The subject should be receptive.

	MARCH 1 PERSONAL MONTH A time to start or expand meditative or study activities. Changes may be made to reflect inner growth.	**DECEMBER** 1 PERSONAL MONTH *Start of 8 Personal Year:* Old conditions may be changed to reflect this year's new awarenesses as well as the coming change from this introspective 7 Personal Year to the approaching materialistic 8 Personal Year.
	APRIL 11/2 PERSONAL MONTH *2 Personal Month:* Cooperation may be necessary with others on projects related to inner harmony. *11 Personal Month:* A time to reflect on ways to transmit awarenesses to others.	
	MAY 3 PERSONAL MONTH A break may be taken from studies, but activities should be kept muted. Some of the new awareness may be expressed in artistic creation or quiet joyfulness.	
	JUNE 13/4 PERSONAL MONTH Hard work may be necessary to take care of other duties while keeping contemplative studies on course. Time alone is likely to feel limiting.	
	JULY 14/5 PERSONAL MONTH Restlessness, need for stimulation from others may interfere with study or meditation. Expanded horizons may be related to inner growth.	
	AUGUST 6 PERSONAL MONTH Spiritual growth is likely to relate to home and family. Domestic responsibilities have to be taken care of even if they interfere with introspective ventures.	
	SEPTEMBER 16/7 PERSONAL MONTH Very introspective needs—possibly withdrawal or great shyness—may make for difficulties with others. Possibility of intense inner growth is present.	
JANUARY 8 PERSONAL MONTH Business affairs may be planned to relieve responsibilities for this year's introspective activities. *End of 6 Personal Year:* Domestic responsibilities must be planned for, too.	**OCTOBER** 8 PERSONAL MONTH Some of year's awarenesses may be put into practice using a practical, realistic approach. *Start of 8 Personal Year:* Business opportunities may conflict with new illumination.	
FEBRUARY 9 PERSONAL MONTH Activities may be completed which interfere with spending time alone or in study. *End of 6 Personal Year:* Emotional situations must be handled with tolerance and compassion.	**NOVEMBER** 9 PERSONAL MONTH Phase of inner growth may be completed. New awareness in humanistic, philanthropic endeavors may be expressed. *Start of 8 Personal Year:* Phase of business venture may be completed in preparation for next year's movement.	

CHART **20** THE EPICYCLE	**8** MATERIAL SATISFACTION

8 **PERSONAL** **YEAR**	A time to act dynamically. A time to accomplish, advance and achieve recognition. The subject should take action.

		FEBRUARY 1 PERSONAL MONTH Dynamic action may be taken aimed at achievement and recognition. *End of 7 Personal Year:* Old conditions impeding inner growth may be changed.	**NOVEMBER** 19/1 PERSONAL MONTH Self-centeredness, aggressiveness or fear may impede progress. *Start of 9 Personal Year:* A time to begin closing out an experience so that it can be completed next year.
		MARCH 11/2 PERSONAL MONTH *2 Personal Month:* Current power may be used, in cooperation with others, to move forward. *11 Personal Month:* Nervous tension may impede progress.	**DECEMBER** 11/2 PERSONAL MONTH *2 Personal Month:* Sensitivity and receptivity may be helpful in business activities. *11 Personal Year:* Inner growth of this Epicycle may be consolidated.
		APRIL 3 PERSONAL MONTH Friends may present opportunities for advancement and recognition. The feelings of power may be enjoyed—for contrast, a break from the dynamic activity may be taken.	
		MAY 13/4 PERSONAL MONTH A time to work hard for forward movement. Details and organization may have to be taken care of. Disturbing feelings of limitation about power may be felt.	
		JUNE 14/5 PERSONAL MONTH Restlessness or fear of risks may impede accomplishments. Strong action may be taken to expand horizons by initiating or taking advantage of change.	
		JULY 6 PERSONAL MONTH Current power may be used to deal with home and family responsibilities. Action may be taken to maintain and improve domestic harmony.	
		AUGUST 16/7 PERSONAL MONTH Power derived from "different" wavelength may be used but others may be confused with self-contained or inflexible approach.	
		SEPTEMBER 8 PERSONAL MONTH A time to move forward dramatically toward business expansion, financial improvement and recognition. A time to act for maximum impact.	
	JANUARY 9 PERSONAL MONTH Activities which delay accomplishment, advancement and recognition may be completed. *End of 7 Personal Year:* Last year's contemplative ventures may be phased out.	**OCTOBER** 9 PERSONAL MONTH Business activities which have run their course should be completed with compassion and understanding. *Start of 9 Personal Year:* A time to prepare for additional endings in coming year.	

CHART **20**
THE EPICYCLE

9 SELFLESSNESS
HUMANITARIANISM

9 PERSONAL YEAR
A time to complete experiences.
A time to contemplate future plans.
The subject should take action only in order to complete.
He should be receptive.
He should be prepared for an important change.

JANUARY 1 PERSONAL MONTH
A time to emphasize originality and individuality in revising old conditions.

End of 8 Personal Year: Waning power may be used to make dynamic changes.

OCTOBER 1 PERSONAL MONTH
Start of 1 Personal Year: Change of Epicycles may begin to be felt. Completions should be phased out and replaced by new activities, relations and plans for the future.

FEBRUARY 11/2 PERSONAL MONTH
2 Personal Month: Developments related to completions are likely to take time.

11 Personal Month: Spiritual illumination may clarify direction to endings.

End of 8 Personal Year: Waning power may be used to help others with their completions.

NOVEMBER 2 PERSONAL MONTH
A quiet pause as one Epicycle ends and another gets under way. Quiet harmony should be the objective in this interim period.

Start of 1 Personal Year: Plans for the coming year may be contemplated.

MARCH 3 PERSONAL MONTH
Activities or relations with friends may be completed. Social times and travel may be enjoyed as a break in an emotion-filled year.

DECEMBER 3 PERSONAL MONTH
The end of the Epicycle! A time to celebrate, relax and express the joy of living. Imagination should be used to have a good time.

Start of 1 Personal Year: A time to plan for changes and new beginnings in coming year.

APRIL 13/4 PERSONAL MONTH
Restrictive feelings are likely from completions in progress. Rigidity or laziness may interfere with the work to accomplish.

MAY 14/5 PERSONAL MONTH
Restlessness or fear of risks may stop movement toward completion. Conflict between desire to expand and desire to complete may prove confusing.

JUNE 6 PERSONAL MONTH
A time to complete experiences related to home and family to provide increased domestic balance. Endings related to love and romance are likely to be very emotional.

JULY 16/7 PERSONAL MONTH
Inflexibility or a timid manner may add difficulties in completing experiences. Time should be spent alone contemplating future plans as well as additional endings this year.

AUGUST 8 PERSONAL MONTH
Dynamic action may be taken to complete experiences with compassion and understanding. Advantage can be taken of endings for possible advancement or financial improvement.

SEPTEMBER 9 PERSONAL MONTH
The ending of the completion period of the Epicycle is at hand. Loose ends should be cleaned up. Much emotion is likely as last endings in the Epicycle take place.

| CHART**20**
THE EPICYCLE | **11** ILLUMINATION |

11
PERSONAL
YEAR

A time to be open for illumination.
A time for inner growth and heightened sensitivity.
    The subject should be receptive.
See 2 Personal Year also.

AUGUST 19/1 PERSONAL MONTH
Opportunities opened by inner growth may be started but may be slowed due to egotism or fear.

SEPTEMBER 2 PERSONAL MONTH
Developments based on illumination may require patience. Issues shouldn't be forced.

JANUARY 3 PERSONAL MONTH
Friends may open doors to new awarenesses. Nervous tension may get in the way.

OCTOBER 3 PERSONAL MONTH
A time to enjoy and express creatively. The expression may be based on inner development.

FEBRUARY 13/4 PERSONAL MONTH
Illumination may prove disturbing and heighten nervous tension. Feelings of restriction likely with problems due to heightened sensitivity.

NOVEMBER 22/4 PERSONAL MONTH
4 Personal Month: Work may be required to understand and use illumination.

22 Personal Month: The potential for significant forward movement is probably based on new awareness. High-level progress is likely to be accompanied by strong nervous tension.

MARCH 14/5 PERSONAL MONTH
Freedom and expansion may be due to exciting inner growth, but may be impeded by restlessness or nervous tension.

DECEMBER 14/5 PERSONAL MONTH
Freedom and expansion based on current year's awarenesses may begin now, extend through next year. Freedom and expansion may be slowed at this time by nervous tension.

APRIL 6 PERSONAL MONTH
Illumination may effect family relations or close personal relations. Nervous tension may disturb domestic harmony.

MAY 16/7 PERSONAL MONTH
"Different" approach and nervous tension due to new awarenesses may confuse or alienate others.

JUNE 8 PERSONAL MONTH
Illumination may help with material or business advancement. Nervous tension may impede business matters.

JULY 9 PERSONAL MONTH
The completion of an activity or experience related to inner growth may require sensitivity and understanding.

CHART **20** THE EPICYCLE	**22** MASTER BUILDER

11 PERSONAL YEAR
A time to progress on significant projects or on ventures with significant influence.
    The subject should take action.
See 4 Personal Year also.

	JUNE 1 PERSONAL MONTH A time to change old conditions and take actions to move ventures forward dramatically. Individuality should be expressed through the work.
	JULY 11/2 PERSONAL MONTH *2 Personal Month:* Issues shouldn't be forced. *11 Personal Month:* New awarenesses may have important bearing on ventures. Heightened nervous tension is likely to be present.
	AUGUST 3 PERSONAL MONTH Ventures may be expanded by using imagination, creativity and verbal capabilities. There should be some time out sometime this month for just having fun.
	SEPTEMBER 4 PERSONAL MONTH Hard work, organization and attention to detail may be required to move ventures forward. Nervous tension may be present.
JANUARY 5 PERSONAL MONTH Horizons may be dramatically expanded by dynamic potential or because of progress of projects with significant influence.	**OCTOBER** 5 PERSONAL MONTH A time to feel loose and free. A time to initiate or take advantage of changes to move ventures along. Responsibility should be minimized now. A break for fun and pleasure is desirable.
FEBRUARY 6 PERSONAL MONTH Conflicts between home, family and work on significant projects may provoke unbalanced emotions.	**NOVEMBER** 6 PERSONAL MONTH Nervous tension is likely to be high, may make it difficult to harmonize important work and family responsibilities.
MARCH 7 PERSONAL MONTH Time alone may be spent developing and analyzing plans for important ventures.	**DECEMBER** 7 PERSONAL MONTH A time to meditate and reflect. A time to examine this year's progress and make plans for the coming year with the understanding that this year's strong potential isn't likely to return.
APRIL 8 PERSONAL MONTH Strong forward strides are possible, particularly in business affairs related to promising ventures. Status and recognition may result.	
MAY 9 PERSONAL MONTH The conclusion of a phase of work or the planning for an important venture. There's likely to be much emotion or drama here.	

BIBLIOGRAPHY

Balliett, L. Dow. *The Philosophy of Numbers: Their Tone and Colors*. California: Health Research, 70 Lafayette Street, Mokelumne Hill, CA 95245. Originally published in 1908, republished 1969.

A volume by the founder of the modern study of numerology has much historical interest.

Buess, Lynn M. *Numerology for the New Age*. California: De Vorss and Company, P.O. Box 550, Marina del Rey, CA 90291, 1978.

Excellent insights with emphasis on spiritual and psychological interpretations. Development of new modifiers and a new twist to progressions should be of interest.

Campbell, Florence. *Your Days are Numbered*. Pennsylvania: The Gateway, Pleasant Valley, Bucks County, PA, 1931.

A must for any student of numerology. The author's fine perceptions and breadth of coverage have kept this book vital for fifty years.

Hitchcock, Helyn. *Helping Yourself with Numerology*. New York: Parker Publishing Company, Inc., West Nyack, NY, 1972.

A fine text with many different modifiers discussed.

Jordan, Juno. *Numerology, The Romance in Your Name*. California: J. F. Rowny Press, Santa Barbara, CA, 1965.

Another must for any student of numerology. Excellent discussions of the elements, many of the modifiers and the progressed chart (here called the Table of Events) from a sensitive, humanist viewpoint. The Life Path (here called the Birth Force) is discussed as secondary in importance to the Expression (here called the Destiny Number).

Taylor, Ariel Yvon. *Numerology Made Plain*. California: Newcastle Publishing Co., Inc., North Hollywood, CA, 1973.

Of particular interest is the listing of over 1500 common names with their Expression and Soul Urge.

Vaughan, Richard Blackmore. *Numbers as Symbols of Self-Discovery*. New York: Phantasy Press, 358 State Street, Brooklyn, NY 11217, 1973.

This book lists hundreds of birth dates and birthnames of celebrated personalities along with their core elements.